The Foghorn's Lament

The Foghorn's Lament

The Disappearing Music of the Coast

Jennifer Lucy Allan

WHITE RABBIT

First published in Great Britain in 2021 by White Rabbit,
an imprint of The Orion Publishing Group Ltd
Carmelite House, 50 Victoria Embankment
London EC4Y DZ

An Hachette UK Company

1 3 5 7 9 10 8 6 4 2

ISBN (Hardback) 978 1 4746 1503 7
ISBN (eBook) 978 1 4746 1505 1
ISBN (Audio) 978 1 4746 1606 8

Typeset by Goldust Design
Printed and bound in Great Britain
by Clays Ltd, Elcograf, S.p.A

www.whiterabbitbooks.co.uk
www.orionbooks.co.uk

If it
Was we who gave tongue to this cry
What does it bespeak in us, repeating
And repeating, insisting on something
That we never meant?

W.S. Merwin, 'Foghorn'

Contents

Prologue

22 June 2013

The foghorn sounds.

Its abrupt and terrific interjection comes from two rectangular black mouths, a colossal metallic holler that is stupefyingly loud. It floods my ears and shakes my guts. I am overwhelmed. I freeze. Tiny hairs rise on my covered arms. Its moaning blast ends in a gruff grunt that jolts me from my stupor. One eternal second of absolute and total silence follows, and the crowd around me erupts in the type of giddy laughter reserved for moments of awe. It is true aural obliteration.

In June of 2013 I drove from London to the north-east with friends to see *Foghorn Requiem*, a vast open-air performance that assembled three brass bands with a total of sixty-five players on the cliffs at Souter Point lighthouse in South Shields. They were joined by a motley flotilla of over fifty ships out in the North Sea that included a ferry and fishing boats, sailboats and lifeboats, ketches, yachts and tugs. At its centre was the almighty Souter Point foghorn, which sounded from the middle of the crowd over the heads of the brass players and out to the ships on the horizon, a voice of compressed air from hulking diesel engine lungs.

It was a bright and blustery day, chilly under a blue sky. The crowd had amassed around the whitewashed lighthouse and foghorn building – square like an electricity substation, with two outsized trumpets on top, gaping like black doorways tapering into two narrow necks. There were families with children on shoulders; people huddling in bright waterproofs around flasks of tea; couples with dogs; grandparents perched on camping chairs; kids lifted up to sit on the boundary wall of the lighthouse compound; and people like me, underdressed in jeans and light jacket for the brisk 11-degree Celsius summer day in South Shields. We waited, shivering and harried by the wind, for the performance to begin.

As the brass players filed in, a quiet descended. This reverent silence was broken by one high clear note, sounded by a single trumpet player from the top of the lighthouse. Then the brass began, and a sequence of sombre phrases was lifted by the breeze, the notes carried out to sea. The ships and boats replied in harmony – tuned to the notes of the brass – as if they were an echo from the vast landscape itself. Their answers came in staggered and idiosyncratic voices, the ferry loud and adenoidal, the small ships pinched and whinnying. Their conversation, between brass and boat, colliery and maritime, filled the blue-grey seascape from the cliffs we stood on all the way to the distant horizon, a mournful exchange on a scale much bigger than ourselves, as if these industries had been given voices with which to compare misfortunes.

And then, into this lament, the foghorn bellowed, a sound to call through fog and heavy weather, that could reach twenty miles across the sea. Over the heads of the audience, it bellowed again. It sand-blasted my ears with a force and power that diminished the brass and ships, those formerly huge sounds now mice to an elephant. Each time it sang, I felt more excited, more alive – it was shaped by the cliffs and water, from the first giddy interjection to a noise that gathered emotional power as it traversed the landscape.

The final note of the *Requiem* let the air drain from the foghorn's tanks, and as the pressure faded, the hardness of the sound was lost. It hummed, sang in broken-throated keening, and when it no longer had the strength for that, it stuttered and wheezed until its last breath hissed like air from a punctured balloon.

When silence settled, I stood frozen to the spot. A lump rose in my throat and my eyes watered. I looked around, and saw tears and glazed looks in the faces of the crowd. Something had departed, and we were alone. In that last gasp, the foghorn had articulated not just its own death, but the death of an industry and all that was left behind. This was industrial music, and it meant something – only not in the way I was used to.

A few years earlier I had been working for a music magazine covering underground and experimental music, and was commissioned to review an album that became the unexpected beginning of my obsession with foghorns. The record was called *Audience of One*, by an avant-garde Australian percussionist and composer called Oren Ambarchi, on which cymbal skitters and anxious strings sound like wind on rigging and the shifting of great hulls. Dropped into this mix without warning, is a huge vibrational blast of brass, a French horn reaching further and lower than its familiar range. When I heard it, I had imagined a harbour, and instinctively compared the brass to a foghorn in my review. But then I stopped, to fact-check my comparison: what is a foghorn, anyway, and what does it sound like?

In looking for the answer to that question, I stopped being a music journalist and became something else – a foghorn obsessive, a historian of sound, and the favourite anecdote of many friends ('a book about *foghorns* . . .?'). I also discovered something much bigger than the French horn on that album in a horn made to compete with the seas and the weather, that could parp, moan, holler and wail louder than anything else on the coast, that was big enough to shout down death.

Plenty of musicians over the years have proudly worn a badge of loudness, and many had suckered me in with chest-rattling sonics, from dub to doom metal, noise and hardcore punk, played on sound systems that looked like aeronautical engine parts in cavernous spaces co-opted specifically for their acoustics. I had always loved these vibrational ecstasies, where sound became physical, where I was silenced by noise. I was from a landlocked county in the north-west of England, but this was bigger and better than any band I'd seen or rave I'd danced through, a level up from even the greatest of speaker stacks: a sound system playing for the open sea at the almighty volume the endless oceans demanded. It had got me, hook, line and sinker.

Soon I was losing hours to foghorns on YouTube, scouring online images, digging for mothballed local history sites typed a decade ago in basic fonts with textured HTML backgrounds. I found images of the foghorn's machinery, housed in domed blocks of concrete architecture or squat brick buildings where their huge trumpet mouths poked surreally from holes in the wall, or sat proudly on top of the structure, as if crushing the low-slung buildings. I scrolled through pictures of square horns and elegant bell-shaped mouths, trumpets that curved gracefully in swan-like necks. I tracked down the only book on foghorns ever written, by a historian and film lecturer called Alan Renton, whose recordings of foghorns were held in the British Library. I even joined the Association of Lighthouse Keepers, a heritage organisation for ex-keepers and lighthouse enthusiasts.

Other people heard about my growing obsession and passed on their stories. I started talking to people – anyone – about foghorns. I heard stories and memories, and photos reached me from unknown ramblers; emails arrived from strangers in British Colombia, Belfast and Orkney. What emerged were myths, stories, modern folklore and unsubstantiated anecdotes. One emailer suggested I had been unconsciously collaborating with them in the psychic realm. A writer friend emailed to ask if foghorns were used in underwater tactical deception manoeuvres in the Second World War, and someone else related a brilliant story about how the foghorn sounded all day and all night when Jersey was liberated.[1] An urban myth reached me about a sound system in Sheffield that had acquired a decommissioned foghorn as rival crews competed to have the loudest dub. The sound system probably wouldn't have worked with the big old horns I was hunting, but the image of a gigantic siren next to bass bins and tweeters was irresistible: the story of a foghorn finding its rightful place in music, the control it had exerted over the coast at the hands of nineteenth-century maritime colonialists boldly reclaimed by a Jamaican diaspora. This latter tale was so compelling I contacted half of the sound system experts and crew members in the UK, trying to find a thread that would lead me to this profound fusion of sound, sea and music.

Along the way I picked up other stories of industrial machines co-opted for their power: a group of artists who had made steam whistle orchestras; of cacophonous harbour compositions; of Russian symphonies that had turned coastal cities into orchestras.

As someone interested in music and technology, the stories I heard meant something to me. This was not just about inventing instruments, or ways to play music, but about how industrial machines with pre-existing functions had been incorporated into unexpected zones of culture. Added to that, most of these stories were only half true, and I became fascinated by why they stuck. What was so compelling about an obsolete technology of a recent past made new again, resurrected and given a new function and folklore for the next generation?

What most of us think of when we hear a melancholy sound calling out from the coast is a foghorn, but a foghorn is just one type of fog signal. There is a whole arsenal of instruments used as navigational aids on the coast – bells, explosives, horns and sirens of various types – but there was one I became more interested in than the others. The sound that I heard from those gaping trumpets at Souter Point came from a particularly huge piece of technology, and was what had become a familiar motif in film, literature and music. While what someone calls a foghorn might be a ship's horn, an electric siren or a honking great diaphone – where high pressure air passed through a piston – like I'd heard in South Shields, properly speaking a foghorn is the latter, and it was the latter that I craved. It turned out to be difficult to get a fix, because when I came to look for them, most foghorns were silent, and those that could still be heard were often not used by mariners, but switched on weekly during the summer for tourists to be awed by their power.

The foghorn at Souter Point ran off diesel-powered air compressors – engines that filled tanks and fed pressurised air through pipes to a valve at the neck of the horns, which open and close to make that gigantic sound. Ships and boats also carry fog signals – these can be anything from horns that sound like their shore-based counterparts on big ships, to beeping electric horns, to small pleasure boats carrying the sorts of aerosol air horns you're more likely to see at a rave or carnival. The big ships can compete with smaller foghorns in moody tone and power, but the truly iconic horns are the big beasts installed around the coasts at lighthouses, ports and harbours.

We recognise the sound of the foghorn as a staple of the coastal soundscape, particularly in the UK and North America. But take a step back from any familiarity you have with this sound, and look again. It is an audacious and surreal technology, a huge 120-decibel instrument that is as loud as any up-to-11 rock group, only it is found on the most rugged and isolated edges of the land, calling loudly out to sea from absurdly huge trumpets. Their calls are deafening and their architecture is alien: conspicuous sentinels in the landscapes they serve. Other big horns exist, but nothing speaks to the sea like the foghorn does, nothing gives such comfort while it warns, and nothing else comes imbued with the colossal weight of life and death, memory and melancholy that I heard that day on the cliffs at South Shields.

This conjunction of sound and place and people had snagged me, because nothing I saw or heard or read could quite explain this scene. There is no other sound tied so deeply to a type of weather, and no machine sounds quite that massive. Its brass trumpet mouth is often big enough to crawl inside, and it is powered by hulking engines that guzzle fossil fuels. What had hooked me was the foghorn's scale and feeling in that instant of experience, but I wanted to understand this sound's story. Who had decided that this terrible horn was a good idea? Where did such an obscene machine come from? Where could I hear it again? Why had it moved so many people to tears? And did it actually work? I had to know, and to know, I had to go much, much deeper.

This is a book about the foghorn – a keynote in the chorus of coastlines, and a music we take for granted if we know it well, without ever considering how absurd it is. But this is also a book about how rethinking the sounds we know and the way we listen can tell us something of our place in the world, revealing stranger details and more complex histories than we might at first realise. Sound and music are as important as what we can see, and they can transport us through the past, present and to the future, in the invisible vibrations of the air around us. It wasn't just deafening music I heard in the foghorn, it was its potential to make connections between history, culture, industry, landscape and, most importantly, between people.

Part One

ATTACK

Origins – obsessions – encounters

I

First blast

The foghorn was invented, the story goes, by a man named
Robert Foulis, in Canada, in the 1850s. He had apprenticed
as an engineer in Scotland, and then worked as a painter
in Belfast, where he met his first wife, Elizabeth Leatham,
who died shortly after their daughter Euphemia was born
in 1817. Foulis crossed the ocean to start a new life. He was
headed for Ohio, but his ship hit stormy weather and had
to dock in Nova Scotia, where apparently some Scottish
friends convinced him to stay.[1] Euphemia, who had been
staying with an aunt in Edinburgh, was sent for, and they
eventually settled in Saint John, where Foulis remarried.
He worked on technical aspects of coaling and steam ships,
was variously employed as either a painter or an engineer,
and established both an art school and a foundry in New
Brunswick. A monument to him was erected in 1928, in a
cemetery in Saint John.

These are the facts of his life, but it does not tell me
how, or why, he invented something like the foghorn. That
is a different story, a tangle of folklore and fact that marks
an arbitrary origin. When commonly told this story is a
narrative that is easy to believe, but impossible to prove, and

which imbues the foghorn with its emotional power from its very first cry. It goes like this...

One foggy evening in Saint John, Foulis went walking along the shore. As he walked, he could hear the sound of his daughter's piano practice and, as he listened more closely, he noticed that the lower notes sounded louder than the higher, and that they were carrying better through the fog. Being led home by her piano playing while mired in fog inspired him to design a machine that would sound loudly, and with a low note, to warn ships away from the shore when the lighthouse was not visible. So he built a foghorn, which was installed at Partridge Island in 1859, but failed to patent his invention, and he died in poverty in 1866.[2]

This story of the foghorn's invention is told in books and on websites, on TV shows and in encyclopedias. For a long time I accepted it without question. But the more I looked at it, the thinner it became, and the more questions I had. It is really just a fragment, a romantic fable about an industrial sound. While Foulis the inventor existed, and did install a steam-powered horn on Partridge Island, who knows if he ever took that walk in the fog, or if his daughter ever learned piano? There is so little to flesh out the connection, to explain how he got from piano in the mist to the first steam-engine-powered foghorn. Because, really, why would a piano make you think of a foghorn? What sort of person does it take to hear the soothing sound of a child's music practice, and be inspired to revolutionise safety at sea with a bellowing machine?

I searched for the source of this story in cold grey archives and ornate reading rooms alike, in London and Scotland, on digital archives and genealogy sites. I found a record of someone with the same name travelling between Boston and Canada, took a detour around his relatives in the printing industry, considered whether he changed the spelling of his last name upon arrival in his new home to amplify his social status, as many did at that time. I expected to be able to find him at the end of a few keystrokes, but while I could patch together a biography, what I couldn't find was the thing I was looking for – a date or diary entry, anything that might be the root of the story. Instead of confirming the foghorn's origin, the harder I looked, the *foggier* the story became.

I found alternative versions, some sensible, some absurd. One source suggested that Foulis had been driven to apply his engineering knowledge to the improvement of fog signalling at Partridge Island lighthouse, where he was working, after reading news of the collision between the SS *Arctic* and the SS *Vesta* in heavy fog off the coast of Newfoundland in 1854, where over 300 lives were lost – including all the women and children. However, numerous sources claim Foulis's horn was invented in 1853, before this tragedy occurred. One engineer who had worked on a foghorn restoration told me Foulis had sat on the foggy beach with a piano, playing it himself, but this later turned out to have been confused with an episode of the BBC TV series *Coast*, where they'd retold the story and had a go at playing a piano on a beach to test how well the sound travelled. The foghorn had even popped up in a surrealist opening montage to Vic Reeves and Bob Mortimer's comedy show *The Smell of Reeves & Mortimer*, where its invention was attributed – for no apparent reason – to John Betjeman, in 1961.

The Foulis origin story is one I'd read with minor variations since the very beginning of my plunge into foghorns.

It wasn't until some years later that I went back and tried to unpick it. I thought when I'd found that story, I'd discovered the origin of the foghorn, but there's a tangle of connections between Foulis walking along a foggy shore and the moment the Souter Point foghorn was installed on that flat clifftop in South Shields.[3]

Our lives are lived in stories often more complicated than can be effectively contained. Foulis's is a neat story – man on Canadian coastline connects steam engine to massive horn, and thus a sound is born. This may have been the first time a steam engine had been used for the purposes of fog signalling; however, the facts of an invention are rarely as compelling its resonances. A closer listen to Foulis's story revealed a ballad, steeped in pathetic fallacy, and in fog.

In fog, time and the visible world are muted, and in the grey light of a world suspended, we are faced with ourselves and our memories, and perhaps Foulis was too. When he was led home, was he also being led out of fogbound feelings of loss? He was guided towards the sound of his new family, and in this the piano becomes the foghorn by calling him back to safety. The story of him walking in the mist is only partly about him inventing the foghorn. It also carries his grief, because of his biography.

Considered like this, the tale can turn from historical fact to industrial folklore. When he walked along the New Brunswick shore as the fog rolled in, thick and fast as they do on that coastline, what was he thinking about? Why was he alone? Mired in the mist, was he thinking of the wife he lost? Or of the new life that was signalling to him in halting piano chords through the fog? The story of how the foghorn was invented is about more than just an idea. That walk with Foulis on the beach is also about the emotional power of the foghorn, and these resonances are still audible in the melancholic wail of a foghorn real or recorded, whether from a soundtrack or a remembered soundscape.

I'd always been curious about where music comes from – who makes it and why. The foghorn was the first time I had thought about a specific sound, rather than a band or composition. When we talk about origins in musical histories, stories are simplified and romanticised, just like they were with Foulis. The known facts are parts of more complex narratives, many of which have been reduced to tidy chance discoveries. Sometimes errors creep in, details are transposed, sanitised or amplified, and we gobble up these creation myths – they become gospel. I started thinking about the ways in which other distinctive sounds had been born; about unreliable narrators and the fallibility of so many of our histories. If Foulis's foghorn was an isolated case – he did not patent his invention – where does the sound really get started? Where do you mark the establishment of a sound, historically speaking? By its technology? Its acoustic signature? The spread of the machinery? If his foghorn blew on a lonely coastline, did it really make a sound if there was nobody there to hear it?

Exotica, the tiki-torch lounge jazz that proliferated in 1950s America, is sometimes said to have started in a chance encounter between Martin Denny and his band and some frogs, when said amphibians started croaking along to the music, stopping and starting again in sync as they played in the Shell Bar in a hotel complex in Honolulu. Just like Foulis, it reduces to a single, simple, light-bulb moment, thanks to an ordinary event being punctured by an unusual sound. The reality, though, was that Denny had been collecting and augmenting his orchestra for years with instruments he had collected from around the world while on army postings.

That great American modernist compositional movement, minimalism, is claimed by some to be the work of a small handful of composers – Terry Riley and La Monte Young, Steve Reich and Philip Glass – but these men were all surrounded by a more wide-reaching group of composers and musicians, many of them following similar philosophies and principles, from Julius Eastman to Joan La Barbara. Denis Johnson, a one-time composer and friend of Riley and Young, wrote a minimalist piano composition called *November* in 1959, which only came to light in recent decades and predates the movement's more oft-cited 'big bang moment' – Terry Riley's 1964 composition *In C* – by years. Nobody heard or knew of Johnson's composition until many years after the fact. Where, in these cases, does a sound begin? With the anomalous first entry, or when people began to recognise someone else's innovation?

Acid House is sometimes belittled as being 'accidentally' discovered by Phuture's Earl Smith Jr (better known as the peerless DJ Spank-Spank), who one night stayed up till the small hours playing with a new Roland 303 drum machine he and DJ Pierre were trying to work out how to use, when the signature squelch 'came out of nowhere'. In fact, Phuture were actively building and developing the nascent sound of acid house in Chicago as part of that febrile local scene. In the same way that the steam engine was being utilised to expand the possibilities of what could be mechanised, drum

ATTACK

machines were being utilised to push what club music could
do. While it might seem arbitrary to connect acid house and
the foghorn, the development of both sounds relied on a
certain type of technological progress that craved forward
movement. Club music and the Industrial Revolution both
have, at their core, an exalted technological quest for newness and modernity even though they're centuries apart. The
parallel is in a sound discovered through experimentation.
In both cases, a new and distinctive sound is made because
of a new technology; however, the sound is not inevitably
defined by that technology, but in how the people listening
chose to control and use that sound. In other words, the
sound of the foghorn is not wholly defined by the material
components that make it, and it is not simply reducible
to its technological function. Cultural and social factors,
as well as arbitrary decisions, made the sound what we
recognise today.

Musical genres and world-changing inventions – whether
they're foghorns or acid house – are almost never the work
of one lone genius. Hero narratives often require caveats or
collapse under inspection. Foulis, it turns out, wasn't the
only one working on fog signalling, nor was his machine
the one that spread out along the coasts. The reality is that
a number of people were working on similar inventions
during the later decades of the nineteenth century, and it
is these that led to the broader adoption of foghorns. An
American named Celadon Leeds Daboll took out patents
on the use of compressed air horns in America in 1860, and
in Britain three years later.[4]

A chemistry professor called Frederick Hale Holmes
developed a reed trumpet around 1863, and a few years

C. L. DABOLL.
Fog Alarm.

No. 28,837.

Patented June 26, 1860.

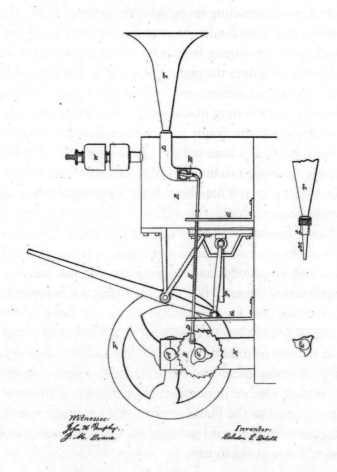

Witnesses:
John H. Dunphy.
J. M. Crane

Inventor:
Celadon L. Daboll

after that a pneumatic horn was patented, followed by a manual diaphone-like foghorn, a piston-driven foghorn, and others in the 1880s. Robert Hope-Jones – the inventor of the Wurlitzer organ – filed a patent for a diaphone mechanism for his organ in 1896, listing sound signalling as another application for the organ's machinery. He later filed a patent solely for a fog-signalling invention.

However, it is to Foulis that the foghorn's origins have stuck. Just as the singing frogs add an irresistible detail to Denny's story, so does the piano in the fog in Foulis's. Both are historical MacGuffins, and both lend themselves more to explaining the feeling of the sound more than anything else. What made the Foulis story so compelling – that he was an underdog, a lone outsider, who died poor despite inventing the huge machine I was in love with – had absolutely nothing to tell me about how his invention led to foghorns being so familiar to me, a music journalist from a landlocked county, born over a century later.

The Foulis story was elusive and romantic. I was seduced by its cinematic moods and setting, and the grief and loss that permeated the story like the fog in which it happened. I realised that this fog that drifted across the shore nearly 170 years ago was a key to unlocking deeper connections, as one of the few cold hard facts at the heart of Foulis's story. While in the fog there was mood, metaphor and menace, there was also, more importantly, cause and effect. It was not just crucial to the Foulis story, but was the sole reason the foghorn existed. So if I was ever going to understand the foghorn, I was going to have to understand the fog.

No. 702,557.

Patented June 17, 1902.

R. HOPE-JONES.

SOUND PRODUCING DEVICE SUITABLE FOR SIRENS, &c.

(Application filed Nov. 26, 1901.)

(No Model.)

2 Sheets—Sheet 1.

Fig.1.

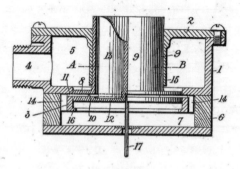

Fig.2.

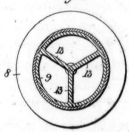

WITNESSES.

INVENTOR.

Robert Hope-Jones

by Foster & Freeman,

attorneys.

No. 702,557.   Patented June 17, 1902.

R. HOPE-JONES.

SOUND PRODUCING DEVICE SUITABLE FOR SIRENS, &c.

(Application filed Nov. 26, 1901.)

(No Model.)   2 Sheets—Sheet 2.

Fig.3.   *Fig.5.*

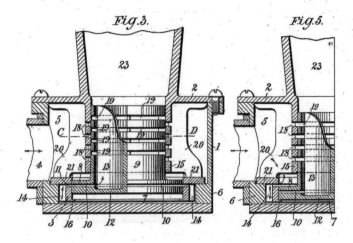

Fig.4.

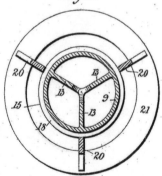

WITNESSES.   INVENTOR.

Robert Hope-Jones

by Foster and Freeman,
                                        attorney.

2

Heavy weather

One chilly November morning, I head out to my rented office along the Thames estuary, where from the window I can see the tidal edge of Leigh Marsh. Once there, I work to the rhythm of the tides – if it's out when I turn up, I don't leave till it's back in. If it's in, I stay until the water has retreated to reveal the wet sands of the marshes, which are bright green in summer and mud brown in winter. I get there by bike, cycling down the same estuarial landscape that opens Joseph Conrad's *Heart of Darkness*. Marlow sails out of London down to the sea reach of the Thames, where the sea and the sky are 'welded together without a joint', and a mist hangs on the Essex marshes 'like a gauzy and radiant fabric'. But on that coastline where I now stop to catch my breath, there is no horizon for me, no sky and sea and no marshes draped in mist, because I am suspended in the bright grey nothing of a heavy morning fog.

The air is thick with moisture that gathers in droplets on my clothes. My eyes strain to focus, and the air is clammy and close. The fog crawls around my cuffs, teasing wet tendrils from my tied-back hair, and the handlebars drip with condensation where the mist has hit cold metal. Lampposts and bollards loom as shadows. Just like in the dark, my breath, quickened from the cycle, seems louder. But while the fog obscures what I can see, I am not in the dark. I am in a bubble of depthless light. The world has shrunk to the size of what I can hear, and what I can hear stretches further than what I can see. The fog amplifies sound, relegates sight to second place and sharpens my sense of smell and touch. I can even taste the air if I take a deep breath, briny seaweed on my tongue and oily exhaust fumes in my throat.

I slow my pace and listen.

Glowing headlights pass like floating orbs with engines, revving and idling in the slowed traffic. The modern fog signal beeps at the end of the mile-long pier, although it is easy to miss over the sound of cars and the squawk of ghostly seagulls. It is meant for kayaks and small pleasure boats that might be passing and is much quieter than the horns of the container ships that glide down the dredged estuary to the London Gateway Port. When fog like this rolls in the huge ships often stop, or slow, out in the main shipping channel, and sound their horns to signal their position and movement. They are too big to even notice the tiny beep that marks the end of the pier, the captain and crew closeted away in sealed wheelhouses and cabins high above the water.

I luxuriate in this fog, safe on solid ground, enjoying the momentary muting of the world around me. Edmund in Eugene O'Neill's *Long Day's Journey into Night*, in which fog becomes pathetic fallacy of addiction, puts his escape into the fog beautifully:

'The fog was where I wanted to be. Halfway down the path you can't see this house. You'd never know it was here. Or any of the other places down the avenue. I couldn't see but a few feet ahead. I didn't meet a soul. Everything looked and sounded unreal. Nothing was what it is. That's what I wanted—to be alone with myself in another world where truth is untrue and life can hide from itself. Out beyond the harbor, where the road runs along the beach, I even lost the feeling of being on land. The fog and the sea seemed part of each other. It was like walking on the bottom of the sea. As if I had drowned long ago. As if I was the ghost belonging to the fog, and the fog was the ghost of the sea.'[1]

Fog is weather made material, at once tactile and ungraspable. A foghorn sounds *in* the fog and *for* the fog, sound and weather bound by the play upon our senses. Fog blocks out the visual, while the foghorn's holler shouts out in the gloom as a sonic anchor. Being in fog is not the same as being in darkness – night can be illuminated but little lifts fog. Can you think of another sound so contingent on the weather? An ice cream van? Tide sirens in Venice? Tornado sirens? All of these are different to the foghorn. An ice cream van tinkles its music whether it's sunny or not. Sirens come *before* the tornado, their warnings a call to action, to move. The foghorn is something different, not just technologically but also functionally. It is, formally speaking, an aid to navigation. It wasn't just designed to warn ships away from dangerous shores and sandbanks, but also to tell them where they were.[2]

Experiencing weather uses all our senses. It involves sight, sound, smell, often touch. A summer rain involves a shifting in light, a darkening of the skies, the appearance of leaden clouds. In cities, the smell of dust from hot concrete signals the first fat wet droplets of rain, which we feel on our skin, on open palms. In the countryside, the smell of soil and foliage is lifted to our noses.[3]

Distinctions between different types of fog are largely based on how and where it forms. Radiation fog occurs when the earth, which has absorbed heat during the day, cools by night; it hangs over marshes and lowlands in the early morning, dispersing as the sun rises and warming the ground. Advection fog moves horizontally, and rolls in, when moist air drifts over a colder surface like sea or snowy ground. Then there is valley fog, hill fog, upslope fog, evaporation fog and freezing fog. There is such a thing as a fogbow – a pale halo of glowing white mist.

Fog, mist and clouds are variations on the same principle: condensation. The definition of fog is one that is acutely anthropocentric, dependent on having an observer. The only difference between a fog and a mist, according to the Met Office, is the distance we can see. To reduce fog to its pure science is to remove the observer at the heart of the definition of fog.

Have you ever been to a concert or club where so much dry ice has been used it separates you from your friends? How did it feel? Did it make you feel disoriented, lost? Now imagine that feeling, of not being able to see what is right next to you, but you're in a ship, at sea, and you have no idea in which direction you're facing. It becomes very dangerous. The effect is of a marooning, a removing of orienting features that you might usually use to navigate – whether it's to the bar or back to harbour – but the implications are very different.

Musicians who pump their concerts full of dry ice know that fog is setting and scenery for the music the audience are about to hear. In the case of the cloaked and hooded ritualistic doom metal act Sunn O))), whose heavy guitar drones obliterate from monolithic amp stacks, it is a way to elevate the intensity of sound – they use it so prodigiously it has been known to set off smoke alarms in neighbouring buildings. In one context these instant special effects that a fog machine can produce are a thrill, because they change everything about the world in an instant. In another, being at sea with no solid ground, when nothing can be seen, there is terror.

Fog, once it comes down on sea and coast, is a mortal danger, because in fog death can crawl silently out of the sea and swallow ships whole. All mariners know how fast a thick fog can roll in, and what it means for your sense of direction. Chris Williams, who worked as a caretaker and part-time keeper at Nash Point lighthouse in South Wales and used to do boat trips around the Bristol Channel, remembers once getting completely turned around in the time it took him to put a glove on in a deep fog.

Fog is threshold, and fog is mood. When Ella Fitzgerald sings the Gershwin song 'A Foggy Day', it's not really about the weather, but about the fog being a mirror for a private misery. The figurative fog clears at the appearance of the singer's love interest. The fog is not just an external manifestation of Ella's feelings, but something that has the power to affect those feelings too. When Bob 'The Bear' Hite mutters, on Canned Heat's *Live at Topanga Corral*,[4] 'I'm already in a fog, I don't need the machine', he's in a very different type of figurative fog – a chemically induced one – that might be more properly called a fug.

Fog runs through Western culture like a wisp of smoke, from Aphrodite spiriting Paris away to safety in a thick mist in *The Iliad*, to John Carpenter's fog rolling into a sleepy town on the Californian coast carrying leprosy-riddled zombie pirate ghosts. Stephen King's *The Mist* carries monsters; James Herbert's *The Fog* carries madness. Gothic literature is particularly infested with fogs, where it is both pathetic fallacy and spectral threshold. Fog is a presence in Susan Hill's *The Woman in Black*, in Sherlock Holmes, in H.G. Wells. Robert Louis Stevenson's Dr Jekyll enters a foggy alleyway and emerges as Mr Hyde.[5] My favourite is the fog that brings Dracula to the shores of Whitby (where the lighthouse didn't get a foghorn until 1903, some years after Dracula's arrival). The ship lands in clamouring fog that is oppressively British: 'Then came another rush of sea-fog, greater than any hitherto – a mass of dank mist, which seemed to close on all things like a grey pall, and left available to men only the organ of hearing, for the roar of the tempest, and the crash of the thunder, and the booming of the mighty billows came through the damp oblivion even louder than before.'

In San Francisco, fog is the city, and the city is fog. With these fogs come the foghorns. Around San Francisco Bay they sound for an average of two and a half hours a day, and the region's breweries make beers called Lost in the Fog, Fog Breaker, Fog City. San Franciscans are said to refer to clouds as 'high fog', and when that high fog meets the city streets, residents describe being 'socked in'. These fogs are, as Edwin Rosskam put it in his 1930s book on the city, 'not weather, they are floating islands in the weather'. It is such a constant presence that it is personified with its own Twitter account – a sardonic character named Karl the Fog (named after a character in the film *Big Fish*). Karl brags about ruining Fourth of July fireworks, 'photobombs' tourists and takes selfies – squares of grey in varying shades – which is a good joke, because fog cannot really be photographed in any meaningful way, except in relation to things it has partially obscured. A man named Gareld M. Corman claimed in 1966 to have invented a lens that meant he could see through San Francisco fog, and called it the 'ohmichlescope'.[6]

Harold Gilliam's pocket book *Weather of the San Francisco Bay Region* – more correctly described as a book on San Francisco Bay fog – states that one million tons of water an hour can float through the Golden Gate as vapour and fog. In the late spring and summer, the fog can be anything from a hundred yards to more than hundred miles wide, and from a hundred feet to half a mile in height, which perhaps makes it seem more solid and material than it actually is. The writer George Sterling, who called San Francisco 'the cool grey city of love', believed that one day the fog would be harnessed as a power source, because the fogs can speed through the Golden Gate at forty miles per hour.

I inhale these stats, their enormous scale, but they mean both something and nothing when applied to what is essentially a mass of heavy air that moves. What does a ton of water look like anyway? I cannot hold or photograph the fog – its presence must always be measured in relation to other things.

The speed, density and prevalence of fog in the Bay Area is the result of geological movements that happened along the Pacific and North American plates 650,000 years ago. The Bay represents the sea-level breach of Californian mountain ranges by the Pacific Ocean, and this breach, with its narrow entrance, means hot and cold air is sucked in and out of the Bay with a power that moves the air fast enough for sun to turn to fog in ten minutes or less. If a San Francisco fog, with the power of its geographic particulars, was transplanted to where I am on the Thames estuary right now, I could race the fog on my bike and might not beat it.

The spring and summer fogs in San Francisco are advection fogs, caused by moist air on the waters of the Bay, or, if the water's warm, when that warm air is pushed up the hills to cooler zones. The winter fogs, or 'tule' fogs, are radiation fogs, created when the land is cold and warm air passes over. They are named for a Spanish-Aztec word for the bullrushes around which they gather. It is the winter tule fog that settles in the Bay which causes most shipwrecks.

Other geographically particular fogs and mists abound in dialect – ones that come on fast, or cold, or icy, or those that bring phantoms. In South America, *camanchaca* are dense fogs that do not produce rain; *garúa* are cold winter fogs in Chile and Peru; the Shoshone in the Western United States call a freezing fog in deep mountain valleys a *pogonip*. Dutch folklore talks of the *witte wieven*, white women in veils of mist who appear in autumn. A haar or a fret is a sea fog in Scotland and the north-east of England.

Fog is at the heart of much folklore and mythology. It brings things, reveals things, creates a bridge between the living world and other realms. In British coastal folklore one sixteenth-century story from Cornwall describes a great fog out of which a castle emerges, and then a fleet of ships, with

smaller boats in its wake. Legend says that the Isle of Man
was once sunk beneath the sea, and when it rose it remained
hidden under a magical mist. Avalon too is said in some
versions to be magically shrouded. These appearances are not
limited to the UK. In the *Popol Vuh* – the Mayan story of
creation – the speaking of the word 'earth' causes the land
to arise and form suddenly from the water, 'like a cloud,
like a mist' – thought to be a reference to the way clouds
and hill fogs move around the mountains of that region.

All the way through to the present day, fog's presence
is rarely benign. In the Second World War, foggy airfields
stopped Allied craft landing safely when returning from
bombing raids, and so a system called FIDO was developed.
The Fog Investigation and Dispersal Operation was two
large pipes full of petrol which were set alight in an attempt
to burn off the fog, at a rate of 450,000 litres per hour. A
burning airstrip seen through heavy fog was a hellish image
for pilots to return to, although prior to this, procedure in
fog when a pilot couldn't see the runway was to bail out
in a parachute over the sea, and plunge the aircraft into
the waves.

As I cycled further down the coast, I passed a bell ringing
from a buoy out in the water that was being rocked by the
tide. I could hear the shape of the landscape, knew the tide
was not yet in. For the sighted, fog distorts one's sense of
direction. And still it remains elusive – we cannot hold it in
our hands and yet it smothers us, isolates us, maroons us.

Artists such as Olafur Eliasson, Antony Gormley and
sculptor Fujiko Nakaya – who creates outdoor synthetic
fog sculptures like shifting clouds harnessed invisibly to

outside spaces – have all exploited these properties of fog and the way it can play with our perceptions of the world while being untouchable. All three have held shows that attracted record-breaking audiences, who clamoured for the experience of being mired in these synthetic mists and the immediate sensory escape they promised. Artworks like this need no pre-existing knowledge – they affect a sensory experience of the world simply and directly: with fog.

The reordering of perceptions happens for those with different sensory abilities too. The blind call snow 'blind man's fog' because it removes all the information about the world they usually gather from listening – where the sighted see edges and surfaces, paths, routes, obstructions, a blind person hears them in the form of echoes, and when it snows all this information is muted. In *Notes on Blindness*, the writer John M. Hull describes how opening his front door to a heavy rain is like a sighted person drawing open the curtains – the rain paints in an image of the world in sound.[7]

Back in Essex, as I cycled further down the coast, I heard the geese gobbling and the clang of metal rigging on masts at the sailing club. These sounds all told me where I was, put edges on my hobbled sense of space. Listening to my surroundings in fog gave me a context for the history I hadn't yet understood, about the foghorn's place in the coastal soundscape.

Foghorns became the soundtrack to fog and all its associations, a means to overcome this state of not seeing when all depth and detail had been shrouded in a white-grey veil; when your sense of direction is in doubt and when you may not be where you think you are. There on the estuary, submerged in this depthless light, I was completely isolated from a place I knew like the back of my hand. The fog had not just rearranged all my senses, but distorted this place, bringing with it all its associations, with gothic literature and magical thresholds. I was under fog's spell, mired in the weather, its meanings and the ways its damp fingers had folded around writers and sailors alike.

Submerged, I understood the force of the sound sent to break the spell. I could not turn off the fog, nor could I escape it. The only thing that told me where I was, which could reinstate the world I had lost, was sound. When fog obscures and overcomes the lighthouse's beam, a foghorn is not just warning you off the rocks, it is illuminating an entire landscape.

However, while foghorns were the biggest sound, they weren't the first and they didn't arrive all of a sudden upon silent coastlines. So what did call out from the edges of the land before the foghorn's engine-driven holler, and what happened for something so monstrous and melancholy to be developed?

3

Underwater bells

Foghorns did not arrive on mute coasts, but in places already chattering with explosive retorts and the ringing of bells, in sounds powered by clockwork, firepower and, in one instance, by a horse.

The earliest surviving notice of a sound being used for ships in fog is from 1771, now held in the National Library of Scotland's collection of nineteenth-century papers from the Stevenson dynasty of lighthouse engineers, who worked for the Northern Lighthouse Board. In the library's cool, silent reading room I pick the loose notice gingerly from its folder and lay it out on the desk. The reason it is preserved is only because someone in a previous century also had an interest, or maybe an obsession, with ephemera like this.

The notice was already a century old by the time one of the Stevensons collected it. Printed in heavy black ink with a bold woodcut of Bamburgh Castle off the coast of Northumberland, it states that 'a bell on the south turret will be rung out in thick fog, as a signal to fishing boats'. A nine-pound cannon is also fired, and – in a vision like in 'All Along the Watchtower' – two men on horseback are directed to ride out in stormy weather to patrol the coast, with a reward promised for whoever first spots any ship in distress. The money was doubled if it was after midnight, presumably as leverage to encourage sleepy riders to stay alert.

Perhaps this notice was collected with an eye to building a history of navigation on the coasts, perhaps it is forgotten ephemera, but for me it is a crucial part of the puzzle – confirmation in bold black ink on fine paper that the coasts were given a voice a century before the foghorns we now know arrived, and the voice that rang out was a peal of bells and retort of guns. I transcribe it word for word, place the notice back in the file, tie the cotton cords and hand it back to the archivist, my silent research ritual completed.

For some people, obsessions with old technology are rooted in machines and their movement – in pistons, valves, brass and steel – but for me and others gripped by a fascination with foghorns there is also an impossible striving to grasp something transient and immaterial about sound, through ingestion of papers and documents, mechanisms and engines. My quest is about soundings, whether they're documented second hand on bits of paper, or heard first hand as I cower under a trumpet. The process is often one of ritual and chance encounter, reverence paid to woodcuts of castles and municipal pronouncements. The question is not what a foghorn sounds like, but what it sounded like then, and there, for the people who heard it.

My obsession with foghorns is not an obsession with a machine, but with a sound and its contexts, and in this, the woodcut notice gave me a bookend, a bell to ring in my search, as it were. After this discovery the coasts began to sing to me, in a haphazard medley that included bells, explosives and animal-powered sirens. That I can know of these sounds is down to people like the Stevensons preserving the things they found along the way. So, after some investigation, I headed to Wales, to a rock on the outermost shoulder of the country, to an island off an island off an island, where a condensed history of sound signals had clustered, from bells, to guns, to foghorns.

South Stack lighthouse is on a rocky stack off the western tip of Holy Island in Anglesey, North Wales (Ynys Môn in Welsh). The island is scattered with prehistoric standing stones and burial mounds, which give it its name, and some of the rocks here are 570 million years old, the geology more varied than in most parts of the UK.

On a bright day in August a light wind has scattered commas and apostrophes on the surface of the sea, which is settled in a low hush, bustling against the rocks. The lighthouse, painted in bright whitewash, is reached by over 400 steps that zigzag down through mossy greens, stone greys, canary-yellow gorse and the purple heather of the coastal heathland. At the bottom of the steps there is a chasm, bridged by a narrow suspension walkway, which was once just a hemp cable, strung 21 metres above the sea. Anything that needed to reach the lighthouse, from supplies to human beings, had to climb in a large basket and be winched along the rope, with the roar and churn of the waves in the crevasse below.

Over the walkway, I take the official lighthouse tour, where we gather in the engine room that now houses information boards telling of keepers and their life on this rock. We follow a guide up the spiral staircase to the lamp room, where we look out at the distant horizon through the salt-stained glass, peer through the rainbow distortions of the prism array that makes up the lens. We listen to a story of a hurricane two years ago, when the waves hit with such force that they took out all the lower windows, and crested over the top of the tower, over 60 metres above sea level. When the fog rolls in here, the guide says, you can't see the sea from the lamp room and seem to be floating in mid-air.

In 1864, South Stack lighthouse was fitted with a 43-hundredweight bell, a large two-tonner, the same size as that of a town hall or small cathedral bell. However, the bell and its clockwork mechanism that powered it rarely worked properly. Soaked in seawater, it often failed.

In operation now is a modern fog signal, an array of electric sirens that look like an elaborate sound system, as if a load of bass bins have been strapped together and painted white. I stand on tiptoes to get a glimpse, leaning over the fence that gates off the very edge, but get told off. I am not allowed to inspect the fog signal because it is on unstable and restricted land, and the tour guide claims to have no key for the gate (which I find implausible). I spend the rest of the tour daydreaming of shifting the pitch of these new high-voiced sirens down to the growl of the old beastly horns, and to stand in front of the speakers as they blast out to sea. For now, though, these speakers are a distraction.

There is a route round the headland from South Stack's modern fog signal which takes you to North Stack, where there is a fog warning station. It's this site I'm really interested in, because it's the home to a largely forgotten history of science and sound, some of it underwater, where esoteric new navigational aids were trialled, and may still lie, clad in barnacles on the seabed.

North Stack Fog Warning Station can be seen from the lighthouse, perched on rocks that poke out into the sea as if leaning out to wave in greeting. It looks close, and the guide selling tickets tells me it is a half-hour walk. I trot off around the headland, but as soon as I round the corner I lose sight of my destination. The path is a narrow slice of rocky ground gouged out of the knee-high heather and gorse that carpets the land in ridges that rise and fall, echoing the waves that are so close at hand. Other ramblers have driven their own paths through, probably in better shoes than me, and the foliage is criss-crossed with stony paths of pale sandy stone and turquoise schist – metamorphic rock worn soft and chalky. There are no trees, so the landscape is deceptive – things seem high, or close, or near, or far.

I traverse ridge after ridge, expecting the fog signal station to be laid out under me on an outcrop, but as I crest each one it just reveals another hollow, more gorse and more heather. I follow a path around the base of Holyhead Mountain, which looks less like a mountain than a glacier erupting from the undergrowth, an angular shard of reflective grey quartzite. Jets fly overhead above the cloud cover, the sound of their engines diffused and filling the sky as if the cumulus have become speaker cones.

An hour after leaving the safety of South Stack I finally spot the fog station, crouched in a shadow of the landscape at the bottom of deep steps and a precipitous driveway that is filled out with materials from a demolition of some sort – plaster and concrete that was once red and green walls. I skid and stumble down to the outer wall of the compound, gasping, and pause to catch my breath. As my breathing calms, and the blood stops pounding in my ears, all becomes still. I take in my surroundings and I feel the land rear up behind me, looming silently as if looking over my shoulder. I realise I am completely obscured from the mainland here. Nobody can see me, and I am alone. I have no phone signal, an empty water bottle, and a steep climb back over the endless ridges is the only way back to civilisation.

From the 1850s right up until 1958 this fog station housed two gunners and their families. It was the gunners' job to sound two huge eighteen-pound cannon with three pounds of charge every fifteen minutes when ships were due in at Holyhead port. Otherwise, if there were no ships but the fog blanketed their view, they would fire every half an hour, just in case, pummelling the weather with explosive retorts as if at war with nature itself.[1]

The station is a low lying, one-storey black and white building, inhabited by an artist now, although it doesn't look like anyone is home. A little further down, inside the white walled compound, is the arched roof of the gunpowder magazine, now used as a storage cupboard – its retrofitted plywood door is wedged open. The signs are worn and barely legible from exposure to the damp salty air, but the faded Helvetica conveys its threats clearly enough: 'NO TRESPASSING'. I clamber around the outside of the wall to get a better look at the building teetering on the edge of the cliff, but the closer I get to it the less I can see, and the ground becomes unstable and drops off into a salty maw. I imagine a gust taking me off the cliff, the long fall, a plunge into the snarling Irish Sea, with no way to get out, no chance of swimming to anywhere. I step back to solid ground. I want to peer down into the rocks and water below, at the outermost point of the stack, but I can't even get close, and I suspect I wouldn't see what I was looking for even if I did manage it.

In 1909, 150 metres offshore, an underwater bell was fitted here. This was a device that would ring from below the waterline, out into the murky surrounding sea. Sound travelled further and faster underwater, and it was much easier to pinpoint where it was coming from. North Stack's underwater bell could pierce the water like an arrow for fifteen miles, but few made use of it, because while underwater bells were accurate, the technology was cumbersome, requiring all vessels to fit a special receiver in their hull. It was, in effect, the Betamax of fog bells – very effective, but it just didn't catch on.

The order for the submarine bell likely came from Trinity House, the lighthouse board responsible for lighthouses in England, Wales, the Channel Islands and Gibraltar. The Scottish and Irish lighthouses are run separately, by the Northern Lighthouse Board (who also look after the Isle of Man) and the Commissioners for Irish Lights, both set up in the last years of the eighteenth century. The US Lighthouse Board was created in 1851, reforming a government agency called the Lighthouse Establishment that had run navigational aids for a century. India's lighthouse board was inaugurated in 1929 by colonial powers, when it was still British India. Russian lighthouses are owned and looked after by the Russian Navy. In some countries, such as Japan, navigational aids come under the umbrella of the coastguard, and in others, including Iran, Namibia and South Africa, they're in divisions of port and maritime operations. Trinity House is therefore an unusual institution in this respect, being both more regal and more independent than other organisations with similar responsibilities. It is the oldest of the lighthouse boards by hundreds of years, incorporated by Henry VIII in 1514.

Trinity House began as a loose group of ship's masters, concerned for the safety of ships and those that sailed them. The early iterations of the organisation can be traced in part to a church along the Thames estuary, just up the road from my office, at St Clement's in Leigh-on-Sea, where the sloped, slanted and eroded stones stand higgledy-piggledy. One has a rectangular stone top, worn into ridges and soft hollows, and is known as the cutlass stone, said to be the where pirates would sharpen their swords when coming into town from the coast, the loud shink of the deathly whetstone acting like a macabre burglar alarm. Inside the church, in the chancel, there are brasses marking the burials of some of the earliest members of Trinity House, from so long ago that some of their names denoted professions. The Salmons are recorded in the Domesday Book, making a living through fishing, and Robert Salmon was an early master of Trinity House. From people like these, Trinity House gained power and profile, not only lighting the British coastline but also giving it a voice.

Trinity House was, and still is, run by an executive board called the Elder Brethren, made up of decorated figures from the admiralty, accomplished seafarers and explorers. A list of these people is like a colonial who's who of famous white men from history, from Samuel Pepys to Ernest Shackleton. The master (the top spot) is always a member of the royal family. From 1969 it was Prince Philip, and in 2011 the role passed to his daughter, lighthouse bagger Princess Anne.[2]

Some of Trinity House's wealth comes from dredging the Thames; it made a fortune through having a monopoly on ballast, which is the material loaded into hulls to make the ship sit at the right depth in the water when the ship is without cargo. Dredging below London Bridge clears the river and stops it silting up, and from 1594 Trinity House was one the few organisations that had the means – and the licence – to dredge. The dredged material was then sold back to the ships that sailed the river.

The mud raked from a riverbed might sound like a particularly tedious topic, but this grey-brown muck and gravel hides a history of the ecology and trade of the colonial and capitalist world. In it are stowaways, seeds that can lie dormant for months, seasons, years, even decades. Plants have been travelling like this for centuries, and some are now well established enough to be counted as domestic. Reposaari, an island in Finland, has 'domestic' exotic plants that arrived from South America and the Mediterranean over a century ago. Container ships now carry ballast water – a hull full of water carried from one sea to another and belched out, complete with any surviving species that were unwittingly swallowed at port.[3] The North American warty comb jelly has a diaspora in the Azov Sea; the Black Sea jellyfish can be found in the San Francisco Bay; the ruffe fish from Europe has made it to the Great Lakes. Colonisers brought with them colonising species: the flora and fauna that travel are often invasive and overwhelm native plants and animals, hogging habitat and decimating indigenous species.

The vessels that carried this ballast needed navigational

aids to get them around the world, and where colonisers went, lighthouses were built to light the way, with bells and guns to sound their location.

Bells installed around the British coast were sometimes big enough for cathedrals, and the cannon that fired were powerful enough to sink a warship. But they were still feeble compared to the sea, which sometimes swept away not just bells but the lighthouses in which they were suspended.

Bishop Rock's entire bell was carried out to sea during a storm where the waves reached up higher than the lantern and stole a quarter-ton of cast and tuned metal.[4] An even bigger bell was fitted on the legendary Eddystone lighthouse, a triumph of engineering off the coast of Devon that was martyred more than once. The one that stands now is the fourth iteration. The first, by engraver and inventor Henry Winstanley, was swept away in 1703 with Winstanley on it. The second caught fire and burned from the lamp room downwards – the keeper Henry Hall accidentally swallowed molten lead as he looked up and a shower of liquid metal fell from the lamp room. Nobody believed his story of lead ingestion, as he appeared to be on the mend. He died on the tenth day, after which an autopsy removed a 200-gram puck of solid lead from his stomach.[5]

The third Eddystone started to wobble as the rock reef underneath it eroded, and was moved to the safety of the mainland and memorialised. The fourth was lit in 1882 and still stands. Its huge bell, struck by clockwork, was the pride of its makers, Gillet, Bland & Co of Croydon, who boasted of it in full-page magazine adverts. But bell clockwork and salty coastal air did not mix, and many mechanisms would seize up.

Juliet Fish Nichols (real name) was one of the few female lighthouse keepers ever officially appointed, and was keeper of the Point Knox Fog Signal Station on Angel Island on the West Coast of the US. The area gets thousands of hours of fog every year, and the *Chicago Tribune* reported that one summer in 1906, when the automatic bell mechanism broke at her station, she heroically sounded the bell by hand for twenty hours straight.

On headlands and reefs, firing guns and sounding bells, keepers would have been exposed to the worst of the weather. Standing at North Stack, even on a pleasant day, I can feel salt and sun on my skin as the wind tangles my hair. In coastal places like this, weather has complete power; it smothers and controls. I can escape before the sun sets, get in a car with heating or air conditioning, drive somewhere the weather does not have such a firm grip on life and death, comfort and hardship. Keepers on duty rarely had such luxury.

When guns like that at North Stack were used as fog signals, cannon were loaded with gunpowder and no charge, and fired into the mist. At the entrance to the Bay on the opposite side of the Golden Gate Bridge in Marin County, sticking out on a rocky outcrop and now only accessible through a tunnel blasted into the rock, is Point Bonita lighthouse. In 1855 a siege gun was installed here, an army-surplus, eight-foot long, 24-pounder from the Benicia Arsenal, which was to be fired every half-hour in the fog, and 'by the help of it alone, vessels came into the harbour during the fog at night as well as in the day, during foggy and thick weather in the first year, except for a time when powder was lacking'.[6]

43

The first gunner was an ex-army sergeant named Edward Maloney, who apparently thought a retirement job firing a gun every now and then on a beautiful bit of coast sounded like a sweet set-up. But a posting as a fog gunner in San Francisco Bay is a Sisyphean task – a San Francisco lightship once recorded 2,221 hours of fog in a single year. Nobody had calculated how much he'd have to fire the gun, and he would often run out of powder.

Soon enough Maloney was complaining that he'd been up three days and nights firing the gun, with nobody on that remote peninsula to relieve him (and no easy access back to the city – this was decades before the bridge was opened). Maloney and his gun used up more supplies than the authorities had anticipated, and the signal was deemed too expensive to run, added to which, as soon as Maloney was relieved from duty, he went AWOL in the city, escaping into the fog he had been charged with resisting.

Other sounds were also used in fog, some more esoteric than others. At the Longships Rock a 'roaring cavern' acted as a natural sound warning – only one you couldn't switch off. Before the lighthouse was built at Wolf Rock, the rocks were said to howl like a wolf through a cavern hollowed out by the tide. Wreckers would stop up the hole and send ships onto the rocks – along with their cargo and the precious building materials their hulls were constructed from.[7] The muzzling of the wolf was a sign that the wreckers were at work.

In the 1850s, on the Farallon Islands forty miles off San Francisco, a thousand bricks, four barrels of cement and a whistle were fitted into a particularly turbulent crevice. When the waves rushed into the rock formation, the air was pushed out through the opening and whistled in warning. On the island of Heligoland in the North Sea a rocket was 'hurled into the air to explode at a height of nearly 700 feet' according to a 1913 book called *Lightships and Lighthouses* by F.A. Talbot.

The sound of seabirds would also be used as navigational aids in fog: another lighthouse book from 1880 describes how on the Welsh coast, 'many thousands of seabirds, whose home is among the towering cliffs, perch on the rocky ledges and continually utter loud and piercing cries', which mariners used to navigate. Illustrated plans for a horse-driven siren foghorn, now in the National Archives, show a horse standing nervously inside the doorway of a circular building, harnessed to a mechanism which will make a siren sound as the horse walks, or trots, in circles. How well this worked, given the poor animal's proximity to the sounding mechanism, is unclear.

There was a time when people like Maloney and Juliet Nichols, damp and exhausted, might have saved your life, if you'd heard them soon enough. However, the short report of a gun could be easily missed; the sound of bells only reached short distances, leaving mariners little time to change course, and underwater fog bells like North Stack's never caught on. The port it served at Holyhead is still there of course, where now ferries and cruise ships carry people across to Ireland and beyond. The port is not visible from the fog station, and only appears when I clamber back out of the smothering landscape to higher ground. I feel the sun on my face again and realise I had been in the chilly shadow of this gloomy sibling to its flashy lighthouse sister. While the lighthouse is still in use, ships coming in and out of

Holyhead stopped needing the guns that fired from North Stack a long time ago. Few of them will even notice the small fog station now, a piece of sonic history on a remote corner of the coast, silent and hidden by gorse, rock and white water. I turn my back on this lost history, haul myself across the next ridge, and when I turn back to look it has already been swallowed by the landscape.

4

Shipwrecked

Cape Race is on the Avalon Peninsula, on the fog-prone
south-western tip of Newfoundland, where the cold south-
ward Labrador Current flows down from the Arctic, curling
around the coast to meet the warm waters of the Gulf
Stream. The meeting of the warm and cold currents causes
sea fogs, with the open land of Cape Race experiencing an
average of fifty-one foggy days in the months between May
and July. Sailing directions for the area describe psychedelic
swirls of colour in the water, as the olive-green waters of the
Labrador Current meet the ultramarine of the Gulf Stream
in a place called the cold wall, where temperature changes
from forty to zero degrees Celsius have been observed in
less than a ship's length.

In 1863, the steamship the SS *Anglo Saxon* was en route
from Liverpool to Quebec and was scheduled to collect a
mail packet as it passed Cape Race.[1] Captained by William
Burgess, it had 445 passengers and crew. Many were young-
sters from Ireland, men and women aged twenty-one and
under, looking for better prospects in North America. On
25 April the ship hit a bank of fog and ice, and slowed its
engines. The weather held fast and thick, lifting a little on

the 26th, but quickly resettling around the ship. After two days of zero visibility, navigation had become guesswork, and at ten minutes past eleven on 27 April, the shout went out that breakers could be seen on the starboard beam of the ship. Breakers are extremely bad news, because breakers are breaking on something.

The engines were put in reverse too late and the heavy sea drove the ship full onto the rocks, which tore off the rudder, stern post and propeller. The ship started filling with water, and an evacuation began. First-class passengers were allowed the first spots in the lifeboats, most of which were launched. A boom was rigged up so people could climb onto the sea-washed rocks, women going first. But by noon, the stern swung off solid ground and the ship sank fast in deep water. The chief engineer said the scene was 'dreadful', describing a vision of horror. There was panic and terror: accounts said many jumped into the water when the ship slid off the rocks and were swept away by the surf. The deck was still full of passengers trying to escape when it swung back into the sea, but all were dragged into the water and most drowned.

The third officer, a Robert Allen, tried to climb into the rigging with Captain Burgess, but the ship went over and they were thrown into the water together. Allen, at the inquiry, accidentally added a morbid moment of humour to the grim proceedings: 'While under the water I got hold of the captain's coat, thinking it was one of the sails, and commenced hauling myself up by it, and presently I got hold of his whiskers.'

The captain though, became trapped in wreckage, sur-rounded in such a way that he had nothing to hang on to, and Allen watched him drown. Allen then reached a raft with the cook and a few passengers who made a failed attempt to save someone they spotted, and drifted until evening, when the fog finally cleared and they were able to make land. The survivors on the rocks sent four people off to find the lighthouse, and in the meantime made a fire. Those sent off came back with the captain of the Associated Press news boat, who took them back to the telegraph station for shelter.

In total, 237 people died.

Shipwrecks like this feel like a thing of the past for those lucky enough to have never travelled in poorly-maintained and overcrowded vessels.[2] As reports of the disaster went out on both sides of the Atlantic, a tragedy turned into a scandal as it emerged that a foghorn had been rejected for the area because it had presented a conflict of interest to have the Associated Press – a private company – buying and controlling navigational aids for 'public' use.

In protracted sea journeys, a century before GPS, fog obscured the stars by which you navigated, the land sightings by which you might get your bearings, and removed all anchor points to the land. The formal inquiry of the wreck said that Captain William Burgess was an experienced and cautious seaman, but that he did not use the lead line enough, which would have told him the depth of the water and what material was on the seabed.[3] It also commented that a sound signal could have saved lives. This latter point was the one sprung on by the media, and prompted a public outcry. News wires went out, carried along telegraph lines laid on the ocean floor that passed the place the ship had gone down.

People on both sides of the Atlantic endured agonised waits for news of loved ones – newspapers published partial lists of who had been saved, sometimes with their names spelled incorrectly. The story reached the *Cork Examiner* via New York on 30 April; news articles were printed in early May across Britain, Ireland and North America. On 1 May, the *New York Herald* set the tone for the way it would be reported, in an article titled 'Who is to blame for the loss of the Anglo-Saxon?' It placed the blame squarely on the lack of a foghorn, and pressed the British government to allow for one to be installed, although the inquiry into the sinking had reached a more complex conclusion. Despite this, it took until 1873 for Cape Race to get a puny steam whistle for sounding in fog. It wasn't until 1907 that a foghorn powerful enough to pierce through the fog and out into the sea was installed, despite the fact that shipwrecks continued.

The loss of life on the SS *Anglo Saxon* was high, but such sinkings were not uncommon. One source states that in the fifty years between 1866 and 1904, ninety-four ships were lost at or near Cape Race. Just a couple of months earlier a ship called the *Orpheus* had sunk off the coast of New Zealand, with the loss of 190 lives. These numbers pale in comparison to the millions that had died at sea on the middle passage as a result of the slave trade but in the case of the *Anglo Saxon*, it was the loss of white Europeans that sparked grief in the newspaper-reading public.

At the time, Europe was experiencing a mass migration, and many people were travelling by boat. Between 1871 and 1891, 27.6 million Europeans emigrated from their country of origin, compared to 1.5 million between 1800 and 1845.[4] This meant that for people on either side of the Atlantic in particular, travelling by sea was familiar, as many knew friends or family who were making journeys over oceans. The historian Gillian Beer wrote that people in nineteenth-century Britain were 'far more conscious of the manifest waves of the sea than we are. They experienced their action. They, or their kin and acquaintance, were obliged to take sea voyages, often long ones. Emigration, imperialism and trade depended on protracted sea journeys.'[5]

In the decades around the Cape Race disaster, ships ran aground or went down in fog all the time, particularly around Newfoundland. Today, one wreck-diving site lists as many as 318 wrecks in a single area on that coastline. The SS *Acis*, SS *Acton*, SS *Rhiwderin*, SS *Mariposa* and SS *Rhodora*, all went down in fog. It wasn't just Newfoundland where fog caused ships to run aground either. Fog was a danger before foghorns and it was a danger after.

In the late 1960s a librarian called Charles Hocking published a huge two-volume set, bound like a PhD thesis, which catalogues every shipwreck recorded between 1824 and 1962. After wartime U-boat losses, fog features heavily in the litany of sinkings. His date range looks arbitrary, but it's chosen around the beginning of available statistics at one end, and the advent of containerisation at the other. The period before Hocking's study may have been worse – bad seamanship and poorly maintained vessels were rife, and uncounted numbers of people were killed as slaves. The waters of the Atlantic are particularly dense with death, which makes the image of sunset on a flat sea not an idyll, but a tomb.

Music has always reclaimed the lives of those lost at sea, from traditional folk songs like 'Sweet William', where a sweetheart laments her sailor who never came home,[6] to the subaquatic black futurist society that formed the origin myth of 1990s Detroit dance music duo Drexciya. Their music claimed redemption for those thrown overboard, imagining that the babies born from the pregnant slaves had survived and thrived underwater. It simultaneously confronted the murderous pits to which humanity descended, re-sounding these depths with a vision of the sea as a restorer of life.

Systems for counting wrecks didn't get moving until the middle of the nineteenth century, although there are some statistics from the decades before. Lloyd's of London reported in their records that 362 ships were wrecked or missing for the year 1816 (from various causes), but these only listed ships over a certain tonnage, leaving out smaller fishing vessels and pleasure craft, and by no means covered the globe. Hocking's catalogue also does not include fishing boats or sailing boats, and only includes 'foreign boats' if they were bigger than a thousand tons. Despite the caveats and uncounted losses that mean his research is incomplete, after I waded through and stuck a Post-it on every entry that mentioned fog, the two volumes looked as if they had been through a morbid ticker-tape parade, where each tab contained a tragedy.

The British steamship *Sobraon* was wrecked on Tung Ying Island off Fuzhou after leaving Shanghai in a dense fog in 1901; the *Stella*, full of Easter holidaymakers, heard the Casquets foghorn too late and struck the Black Rock off the Channel Islands in 1899, foundering in eight minutes (the year before the *Channel Queen* had gone down in fog on the same rock). Forty people died when the *Sirius* – the first steamship to cross the Atlantic, sunk after ricocheting from rocks in Ballycotton Bay and Smith's Rocks off the coast of County Cork. The *Afghanistan*, a four-masted sailing ship, was stampeded by the Channel Fleet and eighteen lives were lost in a night of fog and shipwreck off Dungeness; Costa Rican steamship the *Adelfotis*, loaded with ammonium sulphate, went ashore in fog the day before New Year's Eve in 1956 and broke in two; the British Steamship *Alecto* collided with the *Plavnik* in 1937; the Greek ship the SS *Aliakmon* was part of a wartime convoy, sailing from Loch Ewe for Nova Scotia, but was never seen again after the convoy dispersed in thick fog; the supposedly unsinkable *Andrea Doria* collided with the *Stockholm* in dense fog and listed so heavily 52 people died; the *Sirenia* sank in 1888 on the Atherfield Ledge off the Isle of Wight after running onto the rocks in dense fog – in the heavy seas of the rescue operation one of the lifeboat's crew was drowned, and when the *Spirit of the Dawn* ran aground in fog off Antipodes Island in sub Antarctic waters south of New Zealand in 1893, the eleven survivors lived off birds and mussels and roots for eighty-seven days, and were rescued when a passing ship saw the sailcloth flag they had erected on the island's peak.

Navigating safely in fog was not just about being able to hear a horn or bell, it was about good seamanship, well-maintained vessels and luck. There are so many variables it's impossible to know whether foghorns actually did make a significant difference – a bell might be less audible, but how would you calculate which boats had been saved because of a foghorn, and which hadn't? A lighthouse keeper cannot see ships passing when the foghorn is sounding, so has no idea who might be listening. It may be nobody at all. The foghorn alerts a boat in trouble that it is in the wrong place, but to get out of difficulty requires smart and responsive seamanship, well-drilled crews, the cooperation of the sea. On the other hand, there are very few cases where fog can be isolated as the sole cause of death at sea.

  If death came for you at sea in the nineteenth century, there was little safety net. Lifeboat crews and rescue operations back then were just fearless people in rowing boats, and ships could go down in minutes. Those that have dived wrecks like the *Bismarck* and the *Titanic* have found boots placed close together as if the invisible man is napping on the seabed, the corpse dissolved and consumed by the creatures of the deep. A powerful sound in fog offers a last-ditch warning, not salvation, but news reports from the *Anglo Saxon* disaster suggest people felt better if it was there, even if it boasted of a safety it could not guarantee.

The same year as the Cape Race disaster, letters began to be exchanged between Trinity House and the entrepreneurial merchant Celadon Leeds Daboll, who wrote to their scientific advisor Michael Faraday – the scientist whose work on electricity had electrified lighthouses – to pitch a foghorn he had invented.[7] It was his horn that had been rejected for Cape Race, and their letters are punctuated by mentions of the tragedy. But Faraday was seventy years old by this point, and appears to have been struggling to keep up with his workload. When Trinity House (with the involvement of Irish astronomer Thomas Romney Robinson) asked Faraday to test Daboll's horn, Faraday appeared to misunderstand them. He thought they asked for a new scientific body to be set up, and resisted a few basic tests. Eventually, though, the confusion was cleared, and Faraday agreed to take the Daboll invention to Dungeness.

Much has been written about the landscape at Dungeness. It is often reported to be Britain's only desert, but this is not true. It is a shingle spit, on which there is a nuclear power station, a miniature railway, a lighthouse that has been moved as the rocks underneath it shift, and the house and garden of the late writer and film-maker Derek Jarman. Nearby, there are also sound mirrors, developed in the First World War to detect incoming enemy aircraft by long-distance listening, but which were obsolete by the time they were installed. It is a strange place, where the weather sweeps across the flats as the waves tear at its edges. It's here that, on 17 November 1863, an experimental Daboll foghorn was installed, alongside one – variously described as a foghorn and a steam-whistle – that had been developed by a Frederick Holmes (who would later install a reed horn at Souter Point), and the lighthouse's existing bell.[8]

Faraday travelled out on a boat to test how well the sound carried, but his afternoon of listening didn't last long as he was struck down by such a violent bout of seasickness that the session was cut short. They were done and dusted by 4 p.m. It was little more than a soundcheck, but Faraday thought these few hours were enough to prove its efficacy, and Dungeness became the first place in the UK to get a foghorn, and one of the first in the world, after Foulis's steam-driven horn at Partridge Island in New Brunswick, Canada.

In September 1864 a notice to mariners was issued, a sonic revolution hidden in plain sight, that stated: 'Notice is hereby given that from and after this date, the Bell heretofore sounded at the Dungeness lighthouse in foggy weather will be discontinued, and that in lieu thereof, a powerful fog horn will be sounded.'

However, the arrival of the Dungeness foghorn in the mid-nineteenth century was no accident. In the years around the Cape Race disaster, London – where Trinity House had its HQ – was also frequently sunk in smog. The city had expanded at pace with houses and factories, and there were no regulations on how high industrial chimneys should be; these belched heavy smoke and particle-filled soot low into the atmosphere, where it mixed with the fog that came naturally to the Thames basin into a miasma of toxic air. This air literally killed people and animals, sometimes terrifyingly quickly – in Christine Corton's biography of London fog she recounts a gory incident where a whole herd of cattle asphyxiated in Smithfield market where they had been taken to be sold, in a scene where the sound of a dying herd of cattle would have been heard but not seen through the soupy yellow air.[9] Regulation was hobbled by disagreements over who was the cause of the deadly airs – the factory owners blamed those burning domestic fires, and vice versa. It wasn't until the 1950s, after a four-day-long bout known as the Great Smog in 1952, that clean air regulations came into force. But this was nothing compared to some bouts a century before – one deadly smog in 1879 lasted four whole months. When the Dungeness foghorn was installed, London was beset by these foul airs. It was a problem that demanded a solution.

Artists on trips to London at this time documented what they saw, or rather what they didn't see. Oscar Wilde said in 1889 that there may have been London fogs for centuries, but that 'they did not exist until Art had invented them'. French artist Gustave Doré, when he stayed in London in 1870, made engravings that show day to be indistinguishable from night. The fog permeated both high art and low culture. It also made its way into nineteenth-century pulp fiction, where London was destroyed in various disaster stories under cover of, or because of, fogs and smogs. In William Delisle Hay's *The Doom of the Great City; Being the Narrative of a Survivor, Written AD 1942*, published in 1880, a grandfather recounts the degenerate state London had found itself in, before a killer fog comes along and wipes everyone out in minutes. J. Drew Gay's *The Mystery of the Shroud* starts from the premise of coal and iron ore being discovered in the south of England, which leads to green spaces being all but obliterated around London (in a pulpy echo of John Evelyn's seventeenth-century ecological text *Fumifugium*).[10] The fog caused by the removal of the trees is then used as cover by an anarchist-socialist cult (who, confusingly, have a king) who start kidnapping and murdering people in power in an attempt to force socialist policy into government. The message: fog is a harbinger of communism!

The presence of these pea-soupers was very real, immediate and extreme. These smogs – which became known as the 'London particular' – were common in the capital. Is it possible that their toxic presence might have made the danger of fog at sea more immediate? As those making decisions about navigational aids often did it from London, inside buildings smothered in smog.

By 1901 light vessels with powerful sound signals were scattered all over the Thames and its approaches. They were often named for the channels they were anchored on, and their names are like poetry when read together, more magical than cartographic. A year into the new century, Sunk, Kentish Knock and Swin Middle all had fog sirens, and there were fog trumpets on Tongue, Black Deep, Girdler, Galloper, Nore, Long Sand and Mouse, along with the Princes and Edinburgh Channels. Bells sounded at the sea reach and on piers all the way to Southend.

The steam engine, as pride of the Industrial Revolution, was the obvious means to combat fog – it had revolutionised life in Britain, turned rural places into urban places. It was also a prime cause of the smog. Industries were locked in a fatal cycle around which fog and smog swirled in deathly veils – at sea, fog sank ships speeding towards a destination and carrying cargo or migrants; in the cities, the factories producing goods to be taken out to sea were smothering their workers. The smog was inhaled by those making decisions in the city, and exhaled as a commitment to improving sound signals around the coast.

When the Dungeness horn was installed, little was known about how sound travelled in fog, and nobody had really tested how effective foghorns were in comparison to bells, whistles and guns. However, following Faraday's bilious soundcheck, Trinity House nonetheless slowly started installing foghorns at other larger stations.

Faraday didn't last much longer at Trinity House, and it's said that he never fully recovered from his violent bout of seasickness. It was his successor, friend and protégé John Tyndall – a scientist more interested in sound than light – who expanded on the tests, becoming a figurehead for foghorns and acoustics in the UK along the way. His tests were, in contrast to Faraday's, a durational theatre of miserable music.

5

Testing, testing

The South Foreland lighthouse is three miles along the coast from Dover off the Kent coast, a whitewashed octagonal tower with crenellated gallery, built in the 1840s to warn ships away from the Goodwin Sands. Offshore, under the surface, the sandbank is an invisible trap in the shape of a huge comma, on which ships pause, stick and often sink. For the history of foghorns it is the most important place in the UK, because it is where Trinity House conducted its first large-scale foghorn testing sessions. It was here that foghorns were absorbed into official institutions, where their huge surreal sound became part of the infrastructure of the coast in the nineteenth century. This was thanks to a set of testing sessions where a cluster of foghorns were installed, and put through their paces, sounded daily for months (but rarely in fog). Unlike the richly emotional siren I heard in South Shields, these horns irritated the locals and made them quite miserable.

The lighthouse is still open, but there is no foghorn now, and no remains of one. On the clifftop at the Foreland, the stubbly grass drops off on a raw edge, where fresh earth and rock crumble into the sea. Portions of the path periodically disintegrate from coastal erosion; fences and stiles to nowhere hang over the vertiginous drop.

Documents relating to the tests that happened here are elusive, and nothing marks the site now. This absurd and dramatic theatre has been almost forgotten, relegated to a footnote in sonic history, but the tests are the centre of a wheel whose spokes tell us about the state of science in the UK when the foghorn arrived, about the way sound has been stored in the archives, and about how the foghorn, right from the very beginning, was not the reliable safety measure that was needed.

I guessed that evidence of the tests would be found in Trinity House's archive, but it has been decimated, firstly by bombs, and latterly by bad management.[1] Trinity House is a 500-year-old institution and its historic headquarters are at Tower Hill in London.[2] It houses, among other things, two-foot-high pewter lighthouses, ceremonial plates, chandeliers and the second biggest single-loom carpet in the British Isles.

This building was bombed during the worst night of the Blitz, obliterating huge amounts of Trinity House's records. In a photo showing the damage, the building has been gutted, history swallowed into a fiery gullet. Sometimes when I took a volume out it had charred edges, a blackened spine and smoke-damaged pages. It's still not really known what was lost – there are known absences, and unknown absences. What remains are often traces, fragments.

As evidence of the tests in the archives is fragmentary, I had to go further afield to find them, eventually unearthing them in the parliamentary record. In doing so, I discovered that foghorns really only exist as machines in the archives, not sounds. My specific interest in foghorns – in their sound, meaning and resonances – is not shared by the archive. Anything I found was accidental, anecdotal, acknowledged only as marginalia in the endless dull volumes of valve and gasket pricing that constituted the day-to-day maintenance of this awesome sound.

The historian Jules Michelet described an archive as being 'the great, brown, slow-moving strandless river of Everything, and then there is its tiny flotsam that has ended up in the record office'. Another researcher, Maria Tamboukou, compared archival research to a lighthouse beam sweeping across a landscape. Despite such appropriate metaphors, looking for the foghorns in the lighthouse archives was a combination of strategy and chance that developed into almost superstitious practices. The nature of the sound is not as important, in terms of official records, as the fact of that technology sounding reliably.

Many archive devotees get a fetishistic attachment to the sensory in their research: the ritualistic shedding of one's coat and bag in order to be granted access to the quiet inner sanctum of the reading rooms; the scent of antique bound volumes; fingertips blackened by the dirt of centuries past. For me, the sound of the reading rooms induced a spiritual calm. They often have a particular sort of not-quite-silence – a studious bustle of minds as bodies shift on chairs; the swish and hush of pages turning; the low voices of archivists responding to queries; an accidental laptop start-up sound; and without fail, someone who has left the shutter sound on their digital camera while photographing each page of a tome the size of a torso. Archivists are the priests of these spaces, for they offer guidance and direction, sometimes translations or explanations of the mysterious, and more frequently, facilitate the enlightenment of the archive's lowly subjects, the researchers, into a higher plane of understanding.[3]

Archives are not omniscient, but collections put together by a sequence of people through the years, who may have all had slightly different directives concerning what goes in and what stays out. Things move unpredictably, are discarded or ignored, or are unindexed within vast volumes. Added to this, archives so rarely contain the sensory that going to look for accounts of a sound in a repository like Trinity House's, even if it is the defining sound of its operations, is futile. I found revelations in the wrong boxes when having a browse; picked up loose threads that led to chambers of valuable information; read things for fun that turned out to contain voices that redrew what I knew. Archives do not hold truths; they are always incomplete, in one way or another. Within this, all events retain the potential to be told endlessly like *Tristram Shandy*. How many words you add to the telling is just about the number of details, thoughts and witnesses you choose to include, and where you decide to stop.

Eventually, I found two documents – two rare records, as exciting to me as if they were private press LPs gleaned in dusty junk shop corners. These were scientific reports, and what they recorded was primary information concerning the history of the foghorn, the way it had been tested, sounded and chosen as the sound to mark the coasts. More than the story of Foulis and his daughter's piano playing, this was the root I was looking for.

These documents contain a detailed account of vast and bizarre experiments that dwarfed Faraday's lousy morning at Dungeness, painting a scene far more dramatic than the performance I had witnessed at Souter Point. One was a 1960s photocopy, on experiments done by Lord Rayleigh in 1901. The other was the one that really sang, an older, rarer thing that told, in the lyrical language of Victorian science, of how the iconic white chalk cliffs at the Foreland had been transformed into a stage for colossal and durational sound performance. This report, published in 1874, documented sound tests in 1873 conducted by Trinity House's scientific advisor at the time, John Tyndall.

It is through Tyndall that the foghorn – particularly in the UK – becomes anchored in a particular time and place. The foghorn belongs to him in a way it did not to his contemporaries such as Lord Rayleigh, as it was Tyndall who published scientific articles on it, and who communicated with his counterpart at the US Lighthouse Board, Professor Henry,[4] and who made great leaps in acoustic science, partly through his own experiments with foghorns.

Tyndall did not test just one foghorn at the South Foreland, but a chorus line of various horns, bells and guns, that sang for an audience of a few privileged men in a boat, and the surrounding seascape. The entire clifftop was transformed into a stage for these audacious experiments, a steampunk fantasy in sound and machines.

John Tyndall took over from Michael Faraday as scientific advisor to Trinity House in 1865. He was primarily a physicist, credited with discovering the greenhouse effect (the principle that underpins climate change) and explaining why the sky was blue. In the nineteenth century he was quite the celebrity, pulling in huge crowds to his Friday night lectures at the Royal Institution, where he did some of the flashiest demonstrations.[5] He used contraptions such as a 'blue sky tube' to show how light scattered, and once donned a sou'wester and waterproofs to demonstrate fogbows in the steam of a gas boiler. His scientific works were widely read, including by a young Virginia Woolf.[6]

Tyndall was also an underdog. He had climbed up the social ladder from the Irish working classes, borrowing money from a friend to go to university and taking on a raft of paid and unpaid responsibilities. He was also literally a climber, or rather, mountaineer, and was the first to climb the Weisshorn in the Alps (with his two guides). He married late, to Louisa Charlotte Hamilton, who was more than two decades his junior and would often help with his work (despite his refusal to believe that women were capable of intellectual pursuit).

In reading biographies of him, as well as his correspondence and the scientific reports he produced, I found that he seemed to suffer from what we would now recognise as stress and anxiety. He was, as we would say now, often nearing burnout. He often had a stomach ache or vague pains that would return as soon as he got back from any brief holiday. He complained of being under pressure, and that there was just no let-up in his work, despite writing successful books, being granted exalted positions in various institutions, writing tens of letters a day, along with amateur poetry, and publishing important scientific papers.

The first biography of Tyndall writes that he hated to dance and did not like music, but raw sound was a different matter. Tyndall wrote exquisitely about sound, with a talent for metaphor and description. He was economical and evocative with language and used comparisons that were sometimes domestic, but always familiar, that operated in the sweet spot between the clichéd and the obtuse, bringing to life that which was invisible in the air around us. In his book on sound, he described how the waves' movement of pebbles on a shingle beach ran 'from a scream to a noise resembling that of frying bacon'. In the reports of the Foreland foghorn trials, gunshots are said to sound like 'the shock of a soft body against sheet iron'. In *The Glaciers of the Alps*, a document of glacial movement and mountaineering that is part nature writing, part physics, he describes being trapped in a storm in the Grands Mulets on Mont Blanc in 1858:

> And as the pulses of a vibrating body, when their succession is quick enough, blend to a continuous note, so these fitful gusts linked themselves finally to a storm which made its own wild music among the crags. Grandly it swelled, carrying the imagination out of doors, to the clouds and darkness, to the loosened avalanches and whirling snow upon the mountain heads.

His life ended in unexpected and gruesome death aged seventy-three, when Louisa accidentally administered a lethally large dose of chloral that was supposed to be given in tiny amounts to cure his insomnia. She realised immediately, and Tyndall's biographer Roland Jackson recounts a comically understated exchange. She is said to have remarked: 'Oh John, I've given you chloral', to which he calmly replied, 'My poor darling, you have killed your John.' He hung around for ten hours, writhing in agony, before dying.

While Tyndall was a crucial scientific figure when he was alive, memories of his popularity quickly faded after his death. His legacy is in his work on sound and light, including the testing sessions at the South Foreland, which contributed to changes that were happening in the way European scientists understood the contents of the air. The foghorn was central to his body of work and a major part of the legacy he left behind. The writer and academic Steven Connor puts it beautifully, crediting Tyndall with fundamental changes in the way we think about the air, from it being an 'empty space to one populated and full, teeming with waveforms and energies we cannot perceive', through which it became a 'vehicle of universal communication'.

Tyndall arrived at the South Foreland in the May of 1873, and his objective was to find a sound signal that was reliable at a distance of four miles (a distance calculated based on the turning circle of a ship). His eighty-plus page report of his experiments at the Foreland describes the noise each horn makes, how far it travels, and mysterious effects, with technical drawings of the devices and a sound map of the South Foreland that showed how the sound travelled across the landscape.

On the day he arrived, laid out on clifftops were two 11-foot brass trumpets, a railway whistle and a steam whistle. At the bottom of the sheer cliffs, seventy metres down and accessed by a system of twelve ladders jerry-rigged together, were two more trumpets and a whistle. During the next nine months, other small horns, big horns and whistles were tested. On some days a howitzer, mortar and 18-pound cannon – all fired by gunners from Dover Castle – were tested. A bell was briefly added for comparison. It was found to be feeble when compared with the horns.

I stand in the spot I estimate would have been covered by all these machines, and there is no trace of them left. I wonder how far the cliffs have crumbled since then, where the ladders led down the vertiginous drop. There are no fences and the grass stops abruptly in a great expanse of air.

Those listening to the din on an elegant Trinity House yacht steamer were a committee comprising Elder Brethren, many from the Royal Navy and Admiralty, along with Tyndall (and the steamer's crew). They spent days steaming out from the Foreland to listen to the horns, whistles and guns. The prose that describes these sessions is rhythmic in its repetitions, and often contains vivid descriptions. The weather and sea state are frequently described in what to modern readers are writerly poetics: 'an exceedingly heavy rain shower approached us at a galloping speed', on one day; a few days later the sea is 'rough and noisy' where the sound waves are reflecting from 'the undulating sea'.

Tyndall tested the signals doggedly. He compared and contrasted; changed the horns' directions; experimented with creating 'beats' by sounding two horns at once, effectively jamming with pulsating, industrial blasts of sound. It sounds like a hyper-specific music festival, although one I've missed by almost 150 years. On 11 June 'two small horns sounded together yielded a fine sound. Their beats were very characteristic, but at times irregular. Three small horns sounded together yield a jarring, unsatisfactory sound.'

Those in the surrounding villages and towns, which included the busy port town of Dover, were also experiencing Tyndall's sound experiment, whether they wanted to or not.

One of his men walked around the local area, noting where the sounds had penetrated, and the voices of the people he met crept into the report, as they complained of being hassled by the horns. Five miles away at Walmer a landlady said that she could even hear the foghorns inside the house, and they were making her 'quite miserable'. One chap recounted a story of a horse bolting while tethered outside a mill when the foghorns started up without warning. In other places the cacophony from the testing sessions smothered towns and villages, 'rising over the moaning of the wind and all other noises', according to the assistant sent to listen. A newspaper article about the tests called them 'Tyndall's demoralised and brutalised sirens, those pretty foghorns that make one on land doubt whether hearing is a blessing, but at sea doubt whether there is a more useful faculty'. These are not the gleeful voices of those moved and thrilled by horns like I was at Souter Point. These are people whose lives and sleep were disrupted in the name of science and maritime safety.

However, there was one crucial element missing at the South Foreland: fog. So, when a dense fog descended on London in December 1873 Tyndall headed down to the Serpentine with an assistant, taking three organ pipes, a whistle, a small bell and some percussion caps to stage an impromptu concert of his own. The clanging, ringing and tooting he made travelled easily, and he could chat with his assistant across the water – the fog apparently no barrier to the transmission of sound.

Two curious policemen also approached to see what this man in mutton chops was doing making noises in the mist. He explained his experiment, and they recalled with some enthusiasm how clearly they had heard Big Ben in the fog, and that it had been even louder the previous night when the fog was denser, whereas on some clear days they didn't hear it at all. As a vignette, I recognised it – strangers excitedly remembering a sound they know, accidentally becoming a part of your research by knowing what you don't: how weather affects their familiar surroundings. Tyndall's policemen know the sound of Big Ben, walking a beat that means they notice the day-to-day changes in its pealing. Most importantly, chatting in the Serpentine fog was evidence that fog did not muffle sound. It was a breakthrough, a finding that ran counter to the established scientific knowledge.[7]

Tyndall published his discovery, but there still remains –

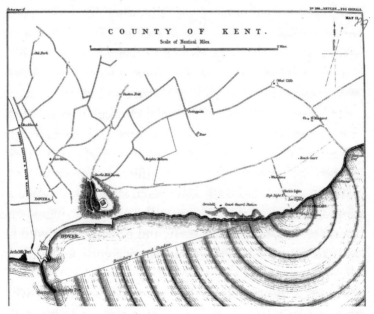

The sound map of the South Foreland Tyndall included in his 1874 report, which shows the acoustic shadow and dispersal of the sound.

perhaps appropriately – a fuzziness around the relationship between fog and sound. A number of the living ex-lighthouse keepers I spoke to told me that fog dampened the sound of the foghorn. It's understandable – it seems to make sense that a weather front that presented a visual barrier would also be an aural one – there are more, heavier particles in the air after all. However, this is not correct. Contemporary acoustics holds that fogs and mists alone have little effect on sound propagation in air. It is the conditions under which fogs form, and the way in which they are often accompanied by other atmospheric conditions, such as temperature inversions, which affect how the sound travels.[8] Fog is made of water molecules, but these molecules are not close enough to affect sound transmission as they would do if the sound moved through water. It does remain a suitably blurry and relative set of conditions, though, because fog is never just fog, it is coupled with and caused by other meteorological factors. It remains elusive, distorting and mysterious.

Back at the Foreland, Tyndall also described what could be called psychedelic sonic encounters while testing foghorns. In these moments, whether in a boat on the flat water under hot sun, or in the shadow of the cliffs, his report includes accounts of the foghorns' calls being bounced around by invisible forces, or muted completely. The phenomenon sounds almost mystical: great swathes of water where sound is turned on its head, silenced, or reflected back.

I had read about these illusory effects, been wowed by their descriptions. They seemed so extreme as to be unreal, and I had presumed them to be exaggerated by florid Victorian descriptions, but as I stand in the same spot on a chilly March afternoon, I can see how the landscape conspired to entertain. The hard white cliffs, blustery winds and reflective water are perfect tools for sound to be silenced, distorted, reflected or swallowed whole. Tyndall described encountering 'acoustic clouds' – where the sound of a foghorn would be muted for a period, with no perceptible cause, only to reappear again as they steamed further out into the sea. Echoes came back to the boat from open water and ricocheted into the distance, described in prose that reads like verse. One witness said that the echoes seemed to come from 'the expanse of the ocean', and described how 'the echoes reached us, as if by magic, from absolutely invisible walls'. Another account states that: 'From the perfectly transparent air the echoes came, at first with a strength apparently, but little less than that of the direct sound, and then dying gradually and continuously away.'

I try to imagine what it would be like to be working at one of these tests, to be the keeper on duty when trunks and crates arrived at the lighthouse bearing strange machines and colossal trumpets, and to watch a crew of assistants setting up this scaffolding day by day, until the broad natural seascape of grey sky on grey sea was confused by a boisterous collection of foghorns, like a temporary installation of Bauhaus sculptures.

From here, I tower above the port and the glittering surface of the sea, and everything below is miniaturised. I imagine tripping out on this carnival of sound as echoes came from nowhere and the rhythmic pulse of horns sounding together spread out across the seascape. I am snapped from my reverie as the sound from a trio of ferries making the trip over to Calais from Dover carries up to me curiously – initially I look in the wrong direction. The modern concrete port looks petite from up here, its angular concrete extrusions dwarfed by 300-feet of prehuman history condensed into a cliff face. Discerning the ferries on the horizon induces a sort of optical illusion, because the sound and the image are not commensurate – this vantage point distorts size and distance, and the acoustic environment seems to amplify the engine sounds. They rumble up to me loud and clear, making the ships seem small, rather than far away.

Tyndall put the mystical sound phenomenon around here down to the 'caprices of the atmosphere', which makes it sound charmingly like a mischievous child. But as well as the cliffs and sea, the hot and cold air courses in invisible temperature inversions and humidity changes, as the sun and the sea warm and cool. Seabirds wheel around me like they did around Tyndall, on air jets I cannot see and he did not understand, these currents as powerful as those beneath the sea's surface. In these moments, the brute force of the foghorns is easily overpowered, toyed with by invisible hands and rendered feeble. To think of such a deafening noise being so easily muted is to acknowledge the immense power and unpredictability of the elements of earth, water and wind.

Unpredictable echoes that come from invisible walls pose an immediate problem to the operation of a foghorn. While reliable echoes have long been used by those sailing regular routes in thick fogs – with stories recorded of mariners shouting from wheelhouses into the mist and navigating using the echoes that come back, often to detect icebergs – how would a mariner be able to locate a danger if echoes are distorted and redirected?

Tyndall doesn't seem overly bothered by this seemingly

fundamental flaw, just curious. I was confused. The nine months of tests were a huge undertaking, and the subsequent installation of foghorns was going to cost a fortune – the equipment they required was costly and cumbersome, and they needed maintenance, fuel and a lot of looking after. What were they thinking, when sound could get spun around and scattered in the wind? If sound could be reflected, swallowed and silenced, was the foghorn the biggest folly of the Industrial Revolution? It was supposed to be a sound as reliable as a lighthouse, one that could act when the light could not be used, but it seemed about as reliable as sending a drunk to do your weekly shop – you'll get something back, but it might not be quite what you needed.

Tyndall had been tasked by Trinity House to find a sound signal that was reliable at four miles, but what he found was a signal that might carry twenty miles or one mile, depending on the weather. He stumped for the next best thing to the most *reliable* sound signal, and that was the *loudest* one. He also added a caveat to his report, advising caution to those mariners who would navigate with nothing but a foghorn, and the same caveat is still present. The UK Hydrographic Office's List of Lights still includes the following in bold on its page on fog signals:

Sound is often conveyed in an unpredictable way through the atmosphere and the following points should be remembered:

Fog signals are heard at greatly varying distances.

Under certain atmospheric conditions, if a fog signal is a combination of high and low tones, one of the tones may be inaudible.

There are occasionally areas around a station in which the fog signal is wholly inaudible.

Fog may exist a short distance from a station and not be observable from it, so that the signal may not be sounded.

Some fog signal emitters cannot be started immediately signs of fog are observed.

Mariners told me that orienting yourself with a foghorn was almost impossible. It was a useful warning sound, usually, but was not a gauge of location or distance in the same way as a lighthouse. Looking at a lighthouse gives an instant lock – there is no doubt about where the light is coming from – but between the horn and hearing it, there is a world of doubt.

Despite this, at the close of nine months of testing, Tyndall declares that 'the syren horn is the most powerful fog signal available to man',[9] and with this single sentence, buried in a report that is itself now buried, he locked the sound of the foghorn to British coastlines for the next 120 years. It is with this sentence that Tyndall tips a domino – not Foulis or Daboll – that has a knock-on effect leading directly to this page.

His expansive and surreal tests represent what might be the biggest and longest foghorn symphony ever performed, but they also represent the moment the British coast gained

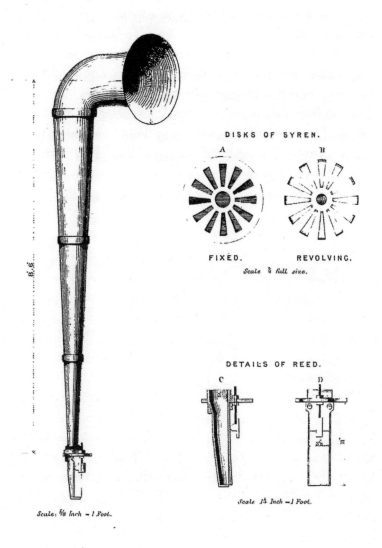

A sketch of the brass trumpets Tyndall tested, with a cross section of the reeds used, and the siren mechanism.

a new sound, albeit an unreliable one. For my part, I still hadn't seen the inner workings of a living foghorn. There were still a few beasts left of the type Tyndall endorsed, and through him their sound had spread through time to reach me. I had been staring at these documents and diagrams in silent archives, trying to understand the beginnings of a sound, but that sound still lived, just about. I needed to get my head out of these books and bound volumes to find them, to swap the smell of old paper and clean desks for salty air. I was leaving the ghosts of the archives to head out of the city and out to the coast. I was going north.

6

Sound of sirens

In February 2018 I stay for a month in the lighthouse on the southern tip of Shetland at Sumburgh Head. I want to experience a place, to get as close as possible to what it would be like to live with this sound, to understand the rhythms of the weather and the movements of the tides. To understand the foghorn I need to know the people it came from but also the place, and the natural theatre it plays to. Following this logic I have chosen to isolate myself on a brutal headland alone in winter and it is fifty–fifty what will come first: finding the sound, or losing my mind.

Because nobody is here in the off-season, I am allowed to use the café as an office. Its curved panoramic window looks north-west towards the white sand of West Voe beach, Jarlshof and Sumburgh airport. I can make out Fair Isle to the south-west on a clear day, and see its blinking lighthouse at night. In the other direction I can see the Bressay light east of Lerwick, but for the most part this view is sky, sea and headland.

This view changes with the light and the weather, sky reflecting sea reflecting sky. Standing alone at the curved glass I want to record it all, but it changes too fast. The camera only captures a static view, and it is the movement that I want to record. Sheets of rain come down with no warning, clattering against the big windows on their way over the headland, as cumulus race across the sky. The sun breaks through in shards of thin pale light, and low-lying squalls make the horizon a blurred band of charcoal. The light shifts from blue and grey, to violets and toxic yellows at sunset.

Off the coast here between me and Fair Isle, there is a patch of water called the Sumburgh Roost, its old Nordic name – *rost* – referring to a 'thunderous noise', caused by two currents jostling together. The *British Islands Pilot*, which gives sailing directions and routes in coastal waters, describes the Roost as 'confused, tumbling, and bursting' where 'the sea rises to a great height and breaks with violence' even in calm weather, meaning vessels 'often become entirely unmanageable and sometimes founder, while others have been tossed about for days together'.

The day I arrive, the sun goes down in an *ombré* of blue and peach, and the first night stretches ahead of me as a great lonely desert. I heat up my coffee for the third time and take two of the soft striped pillows from my bunk bed into the empty café with the panoramic windows. As the last dim glow backlights the low clouds on the horizon, they become scenery for a play in which a black cumulus bull drags a matador by its tail, speeding across the foreground in a tragicomic scene as the darkness lurks deep and blue and depthless in the east, and the sea turns horribly black against the sky.

My seclusion becomes acute as gloom falls over the landscape. Ravens fly past the window in the eerie late afternoon, wings tucked and fighting across to the radar station on the next hill. Night is drawn like a curtain, the first time I have understood this cliché. The huge expanse of window means I can be seen but cannot see out, and my mind conjures images of zombies crowded at the window: men with wild eyes crushed against the glass and rattling the door handles.

At home I can hear the neighbours above me, hear cars and the sound of people nearby, living and arguing and cooking and watching TV. But on Sumburgh there is no one else, and as the wind comes up, it knows. It taunts me. It whistles and rattles forcefully through every crack in every door and window frame like a trick-or-treater, jeering and whooping at the door. It scrapes along the curved sides of the café where the sea spray has literally torn the paint away. During the day, Sumburgh Head had been a place made of things I could see, but at night, it is made of things I can hear.

When all light has gone, the lighthouse beam sweeps across the silent hills and stewing seas, and the clouds faintly glow against a starless sky. I have no memory of being scared of the dark, but I find it in me now. Time spent in cities and towns under the yellow glow of streetlights and hum of traffic has made the depth of night-time foreign. My heart is in my throat and I can barely move for fear of being noticed by whatever my imagination has brought to life, lurking on the cliffs. I do not go outside.

In the morning the light banishes my fear. I discover that there are people staying at the holiday let in the old keeper's accommodation across the way, someone walks a border collie, and a few hours later a whole coach unloads at the car park, a crowd in bright waterproofs traipsing up the hill to look at the view and wave to me through the window. I mock myself for being such a scaredy-cat.

I have lived alone in Essex for four years, and know that in secluded houses you can be the architect of your own reality. Alone, you remember less of what you have done, experiences become less real, fear or anxiety can spread freely. So I send messages on group chats, to family and friends, tweet photos of my view, as a way of solidifying my experience. If only you are the witness to your days, the imagination embellishes in the telling, can correct bad behaviour, and can censor sadness and frustration. A friend comments that keepers must have been lonely, but while I was alone, lighthouse keepers were not so solitary.

A keeper had a routine, and two other people (at least) on station with them, with some bigger shore stations housing spouses and children too, making the lighthouse station a bustling little hamlet. There would be a rota, and tasks to do – making the tea and cooking, or watching the light, or cleaning, painting, polishing the brass. At their first training session, keepers were taught how to bake bread from scratch, how to read the weather, how to run the foghorn engines. In the earlier days of the lighthouse service, supplies did not come so readily, and here at Sumburgh there is a door in the lowest part of the building which was, I'm told, for the lighthouse cow, so that keepers could have fresh milk. Any loneliness – and there was loneliness – was not from actually being alone, but from separation from friends and family, towns and cities. At a lighthouse, you were always with two others, because of a tragedy 200 years in the past.

The Smalls lighthouse is twenty-two miles off the

Pembrokeshire coast on wave-washed rocks. In 1801 it was the site for a much-repeated ghost story, one that actually happened. I will tell it the way it was told to me.

There were two keepers on the Smalls, a tall one and a fat one. It was known in the town on shore that they did not get along, as they had been seen arguing in the pub on the occasion they came ashore. One winter the weather got heavy, and the relief boat could not land supplies. Little did they know that one of the keepers had become ill, and died. The other keeper, without relief and not wanting to give the man a burial at sea for fear he would be given the blame for his death, wrapped the dead man in a tarpaulin and hung him from the side of the lighthouse.

The weather did not ease. The townspeople on shore looked out to the lighthouse and worried for the keepers' supplies, but saw that there was often a man waving from the balcony, and the lamp was lit each night, so it was assumed all was well.

And then the light went out.

When the weather finally cleared, the boat set off to relieve the keepers. As the lighthouse came into view, the man began to look strange – he would not stop waving.

The boat drew closer, and horror descended upon the relief crew, for what they had seen was not a man waving in greeting but the decomposing hand of a dead man, hanging from the tarpaulin in which he was trussed and jostled by the wind. They landed the boat and, with trepidation, entered the lighthouse. The other keeper was found insensible, having driven himself to madness with the fear he would be accused of the other keeper's murder.

This story is largely true, a perfect ghost story if ever there was one. From then on, there were always three keepers on duty to work a light.[1]

Three keepers per station meant it could be difficult to get time for yourself. In a film called *Keeping Light*, made for the Association of Lighthouse Keepers to document the stories from the ex-keepers among their members, one of the keepers recalls going out onto the doorstep, to sit in the sun and have a quiet cigarette. Within two minutes another keeper appeared asking what he was doing, and sat down to join him in the patch of sun. Two minutes later, the third joined, having come down to see where they'd both got to.[2]

While the stereotypical lighthouse keeper is a reclusive soul stranded on a rock far from shore, in reality only some postings were like this, often rock or island stations. A rock station is one built straight out of a reef, with little space to go outside except perhaps at low tide. It was, effectively, being stuck in a stone cylinder for weeks being bombarded by the sea and wind, with only UHT milk for your tea.[3] As well as this, there was also the wildlife.

An ex-keeper called Charlie Riding, in a long interview conducted by a researcher some years ago, recalled a grim story from the Scottish island of Ailsa Craig.[4] Its lighthouse, keepers' cottages and dalek-shaped concrete foghorn were all a short walk away from each other, but there were no outside lights, so the keepers took torches when moving between buildings at night. 'You'd shine the torch across and there's millions of eyes staring back at you,' said Charlie. 'The place was alive wi' rats . . . thousands of rats looking at you.'[5]

Charlie was also posted on the Bell Rock. He told of one day when, feeling trapped inside the lighthouse as one particularly big storm refused to let up, he kitted himself up in a helicopter suit and wetsuit, and strapped himself to the outer railings, for an experience of the sea that sounds like near-death benediction at a temporary altar to the almighty oceans: 'I could hear this wave coming, could just see it, in front of me,' he said. 'Suddenly, the rocks were all exposed, from the suction of the water . . . you could see all the metal grating, all the rocks glistening underneath me. And it was a sound like an express train, and this wave hit the back of the tower and just went whoosh, right the way up, a hundred and twenty foot, and then it curved round and the two halves of the water met above my head and just went smash! . . . And it was like being inside the nave of a cathedral, but it was green, it was solid green, I was inside this space of just solid noise and green water.'

In Charlie's watery green nave is the highest terror of the absolute sublime, a cacophony of roaring water and tempestuous forces dwarfing the man-made lighthouse and one madcap keeper who has decided to try and stare down the gods.

Lighthouse keepers lived and worked in structures that had often withstood more than a century of storms and high seas, isolated from civilisation and yet charged with protecting people. The keeper's job has a sacred duty at its core: to keep death from those at sea. Framed like this they sound like priests, and one keeper did once describe to me feeling like a monk in his job. With forces like this at play, the size of the machinery applied to fog warning becomes somewhat understandable.

On rock stations, you also made your own entertainment, in the days before TV. There are stories of keepers fishing with explosives, of having to kick seals out of the way to get to have a walk on the rocks at low tide. One lighthouse keeper in-joke says that those on rock stations had one leg stronger than the other or walked with a limp, as the only exercise they got was on a spiral staircase. One keeper recounted a summer day at Bell Rock, where he hauled a previous attempt at a makeshift shower (a children's paddling pool with holes in) and warm water up to the balcony in order to wash in the sun and open air, thinking he was twelve miles offshore and there would be nobody around. Stripped naked and splashing in the dribble of water, he heard the tooting horn of a boat on a tour around the lighthouse, and turned around to see all the passengers waving at him.

Rock lighthouses had no space for the cumbersome engine rooms and trumpets of a foghorn, so instead they had explosive signals, right up to the 1970s (when they were removed from all stations, sharpish, after IRA bombings led to an audit of all explosives in the UK). Beachy Head's explosive fog signal sounded once every ten minutes, upped to once every five minutes in 1903. These were called Tonite charges; made of guncotton and barium nitrate, they came in two parts that slotted together to make them live. They were then put in a jib and swung away from the lighthouse to go off, where the explosions were known to be enough to shake soot from the lighthouse chimney. The rules said keepers had to make one at a time live, but there are stories of keepers stacking up live charges in great pyramids that would have taken the top clean off the lighthouse had a loose spark danced in their direction.

***

A few days after I arrive on Sumburgh a gale blows in. The sea grows muscles, the churning water in the bay flashes to white, and breakers crest the hundred-foot-high cliffs across the coastal path to the bus stop. The weather has turned hostile, but all I have is half a loaf of bread and a jar of Marmite, and no milk. While the landscape has grown a new topography in the violent weather, I have resolved to write here, to be isolated and independent, so I have chosen stubbornly not to hire a car, partly because I can barely afford to. So now, gale or no gale, I can no longer put off the three-hour round trip to the shop. I take the new tarmac road down from the lighthouse to the main road, because the waves have swept over the winding coastal path that runs along the steep edge of the land in raw crumbling soil and soggy skidding grasses. Down the hairpin of the driveway, past the fibreglass orca, spray lifts over the drystone wall and covers my face. As I scrape the wet hair from my eyes I hit a wind tunnel and slide, or am pushed, perfectly upright, five feet diagonally across the road into the muddy ditch, rugby-tackled by the wind. I dig my heels into the grass and lean in, but the wind feels stronger than the gravity that roots me. It seems possible that I might give up on planted feet and swim three feet above the ground through the wind as if it were an incoming tide, or tuck my arms in a V like the birds around me and take off.

Once I've regained my balance, I realise that nobody knows about my shopping trip. The coastal footpath is now partially dissolved by water, and new waterfalls coarse down the rocks into the sea, the land surrendering soil to the water in ugly wet chunks. I could have been washed away if I'd taken that route, disappearing with my empty rucksack into the frothing sea. Morbidly, I wonder how long it would have taken to solve the mystery of my disappearance, the speculation and investigations into my recent communications, extrapolation and contradictions between personal messages about feeling lonely and public posts about an apparently idyllic stay on a remote headland. It would be like a modern version of the Flannan Isles mystery, only with one thirty-something woman in waterproofs who had spent the morning WhatsApping their family and friends, instead of the strange disappearance of three experienced lighthouse keepers in a time before radio communication.[6]

If I had checked the shipping forecast this morning I would have seen the gale warning: force 10 falling to 9. A force 10 is measured out of a possible 12 on the Beaufort scale. Written by Admiral Beaufort in his notebook in 1805, the Beaufort scale describes weather in sensory descriptions. The scale is still in use, and describes a 10 more poetically than I can: 'Very high waves with long overhanging crests; resulting foam in great patches is blown in dense white streaks along the direction of the wind; on the whole the surface of the sea takes on a white appearance; rolling of the sea becomes heavy; visibility affected.'

I too am now visibly affected, and make it to the shop a windswept mess. I nearly lose a loaf of bread as I leave, as the wind practically whips it from the bag I am carrying. I resort to a taxi home, one of the few on this part of the island. My northern English accent is unusual here, so much so that I don't need to say my name or where I'm going when I call. The driver knows me from when I arrived. 'Lighthouse, is it?' he says. 'Be there shortly.'

Once outside the lighthouse, the driver comes around

to let me out, and not from courtesy – there's a knack, apparently, as wind like this can take off car doors.

In the visitor centre there are displays about the keepers who had been stationed here, and many of their quotes reference the wind on Shetland. They describe it moving parked cars, and one keeper recounts how he saw sea spray inside the lighthouse tower, roughly ninety metres above sea level. Someone tells me that the keepers here used to crawl between buildings in gales to prevent the wind blowing them off their feet.

When the Stevenson lighthouse engineering dynasty built lighthouses on Shetland, it was thought to be impossible, due to the weather, the inaccessible sites and the violent seas. At Muckle Flugga on the exposed northern tip of Shetland the waves would break constantly over the lighthouse site, sweeping away all building materials, soaking the workers and their temporary quarters.

Ian Duff, one of the last keepers to work for the Northern Lighthouse Board, remembers a gale at Duncansby Head, where he and his wife tried to wedge a faulty garage door shut so that the structure and the cars were not lifted away by the wind: 'The wind was so strong, it kept blowing us away from the door,' he said. Eventually they gave up, but as they turned to go back to the house, the wind picked them both up and threw them 25 yards from the garage to the engine room wall: 'We both got a mighty fright, but we both just burst out laughing and ran the ten yards in our front door again. It was incredible.'

Once back inside the lighthouse I watch the waves scaling the cliffs as spume flies past the window like heavy snow, only passing horizontally, not falling vertically. I had stayed in the town, Lerwick, when I arrived on Shetland, with a couple called Liz and Alan. I had asked Twitter if anyone knew a place to stay, and the son of a Scottish punk I had released a record by had a musician friend who had an older cousin, Alan, who was – among other things – a musician in local folk and brass bands. I knew nobody in this chain, but was received like a friend, and as an introduction to the island I couldn't have been luckier – their hospitality was overwhelming. Liz had said that the wind was such a constant presence that on the rare days it dropped she would wake with the feeling that something was wrong – the silence was deafening and uncanny.

I thought then that she might be exaggerating, or describing something only Shetlanders feel, until I wake up after the gale to an eerie feeling I cannot pinpoint. In the soft grey light, I realise the wind has gone. I cannot hear it whistling through the sash windows, or screaming under the green front door, or slapping the flaps of the bathroom extractor fan by clambering clumsily into the pipes. The wind on Shetland is a sound bed that is backdrop and identity, but it has disappeared, checking out like a guest leaving a hotel incognito. There is a stillness in its place and the building is quiet. The surface of the sea is softly crinkled and with no wind I can hear the water around the black rocks below.

Into this silence, my day stretches out in front of me in shapeless hours, until I pull myself together and impose some self-discipline. I formulate plans out loud while making breakfast. I place false markers, invent tasks, but by the end of the day I have gone off plan. This becomes a routine, until on the Monday of my second week, I receive a visitor.

***

Brian Johnson is the retained keeper at Sumburgh, and it is his job to look after the lighthouse, to make basic repairs, polish brass, and do anything else that needs doing, including keeping the foghorn's engines maintained for when the tourists come to hear it in summer. I am extremely excited about his arrival, not least because I have barely spoken to anyone in over a week, but also because he has agreed to switch on the foghorn for me.

In the decades after Foulis, different types of foghorns were installed at lighthouses on both sides of the Atlantic, driven by engine or steam boiler. A few types came to dominate the coasts, and different technology meant different sounds. There are sirens and diaphones, which is what most people alive today will have experienced, and there are also reed horns, more like saxophones than brass, although none of these now survive. It doesn't take a trained ear to spot the difference between a siren and a diaphone: a siren tends towards a clear full monotone, where a diaphone ends its honk on a meaty grunt. The muscular sound of Souter Point that opened this book is a diaphone. Sumburgh Head, on the other hand, has a siren, which was restored in 2015 as part of the renovations here.[7]

Foghorns require a lot of equipment. The siren mechanism of the foghorn, its trumpet and the clockwork timer that stops and starts the honk, are housed in a squat circular whitewashed tower, perched about as close to the edge of the land as it is possible to be without actually being in the sea. The lighthouse station's perimeter wall protects against the sheer drop, and on the cliffs below seabirds huddle, chattering in pairs on tiny ledges. The long, tomato-red trumpet reaches over the drop, a gaping mouth pointing out to sea braced on matching red supports. The air comes to this building, into the siren mechanism and out through the trumpet, in pipes that run across the lighthouse compound and down into the engine room.

In the engine room there are three diesel engines that take ten minutes to warm up and then send air into two huge ceiling-height cream receivers in the corner. It only takes one of these to sound a foghorn. It smells like diesel, grease and Brasso. It's heavenly. The floor is tiled in an ochre and terracotta pattern, and there is an ivy frieze painted around the wall in green paint. Brian starts the engines on a dinky capful of petrol that gets them moving in a spluttering rattle before they start turning over with a chug-chug-chug. When this happens he opens the valves and turns a lever. He switches to diesel power, and from here the engines pick up to a clunking canter, a steady post-punk four-four, loud enough to have to shout over and still not be able to make out the words coming back. After about ten minutes an engine valve is opened, which opens pipes into the braced and bolted receiver tanks. From the tanks, the air passes through underground pipes up to the siren and trumpet in the building on the cliff edge. When the air reaches the right pressure the horn is ready to sound, controlled by a valve that lets air out in a controlled pattern. It uses roughly seventy cubic feet of air per second of blast.

I run out of the engine room and across the grass, and climb the stairs into the foghorn building, where Brian unlocks the door and lets me into the small space dominated by the narrow opening at the neck of the trumpet, which pokes through the wall and out to sea. Inside this narrow neck is a siren valve that's getting ready to scream.

A clockwork mechanism is on the wall, the same type of thing as is inside a grandfather clock, in green paint with brass cogs, which clicks through a ninety-second sequence, a flat raised section of cog indicating the length of the blast. I watch it with a surge of excitement as it clunks into place and a whizzing sound rises as the siren reaches 1200rpm; then we step outside, fingers in ears.

The foghorn blasts.

I don't hear it only with my ears. I hear it with my whole body – stomach, skin, bone and skull all rattle when the foghorn sounds. The seven full seconds of its sounding feels like much longer, my guts buzz and ears hum – a flood of terrific sound ripples outwards. It is like standing next to a bass bin at a drum and bass night, only with no tops, and no rhythm. I feel the vibrational bliss and rush of physical sound.

I trot down the steps in between blasts to get a better view. From outside the horn building, even just a little distance away, the Sumburgh siren softens to a truly beautiful sound. It has no gruffness or grunt like the Souter Point diaphone, but is a velvety monotone that pours around the buildings on the headland.

Sumburgh has a seven-second blast, but other foghorns are different, with longer blasts, shorter gaps or with two notes. They were each given their own voice – a pattern of timed blasts and silences, known as their 'character'. Lighthouses already had characters, meaning their lights were made to flash in a unique sequence, in order to make navigational aids distinctive, so you could reorient yourself along the coast if fog or darkness had you temporarily lost.[8] When a foghorn was installed, a notice to mariners went out, informing them of the sound and its character, and it was added to the Admiralty's List of Lights and Fog Signals, which lists, in codes, the timings of the flashes, beeps and blasts of all coastal navigational aids. So, for example, when a foghorn was installed at Toward Point on the Clyde in April 1908, a notice went out stating that a reed fog signal had been installed, that would give one blast of three seconds duration, every twenty seconds.

A Notice To Mariners posted by the Clyde Lighthouses Trust in 1908, which informs of a new reed horn at Toward Point Lighthouse.

It's often said that every foghorn was unique in this regard, each one completely individual, but this is a myth. Brian can remember the exact pattern of Cape Wrath because it is exactly the same as Sumburgh, but as he points out, if you didn't know you were hearing Cape Wrath or Sumburgh Head, 'you really were lost' – they are roughly 157 miles apart as the crow flies. Months later, I find an interview with an ex-keeper called Alistair MacDonald, who had related an anecdote that suggests people *could* get that lost, when a sailor who thought he was off the Isle of Man put in a request to hear the foghorn, only to find he had drifted into Scottish waters:

> At Lang Ness I got a phone call from the Manx coastguard, and they were telling us that there was a yacht, and the person on board the yacht was stuck – they didn't know where they were, but they could see a lighthouse. And would we mind if we started up our fog signal? Because if we started up our fog signal, and the boat heard it, they could say that they were just off Lang Ness. Well, they asked Lang Ness, Maughold Head, Point of Ayre, and eventually it was the Mull o' Galloway lighthouse . . . !

The Yorkshireman thought he was off the south Manx coast, but had drifted well north of the island, and was in Scottish waters – the foghorns had been sounded all along the coast until he heard them. It was a bit like thinking you were in the Cotswolds, but finding out you were on the edge of the Brecon Beacons.

If a mariner in fog could not hear a nearby foghorn, they were obliged to send a report to the lighthouse board, and the lighthouse keepers would have to show that they had switched the foghorn on, or face dismissal. But since the sound could be swallowed or muted by wind and weather, the lighthouse board installed devices that recorded when the foghorn was on. They looked like wall clocks, but instead of a clock face, contained a circular disc onto which a bright felt-tip line was marked when the foghorn was sounding. At the end of the month the paper discs with their jittering seismographs were sent to the lighthouse board, and checked against any foggy moments when the horn was reported to have been silent. There is one of these recording devices at Sumburgh, and Brian loads it with paper before he starts the engine. When he sends air up to the tanks and lets the foghorn sound, a bright pink line records the foghorn, like a polygraph for the deceptions of the landscape.

Brian leaves the foghorn running as I sprint around the site in the spaces between soundings, across muddy squares of turf and into the ruined radar hut, trying to find a spot to record that is sheltered from the wind. People emerge from offices I didn't know were here. Some engineers in from the Northern Lighthouse Board are here fixing something to do with the radio masts, and they gather under the horn. One calls his boss in Edinburgh, and then his girlfriend, to let the sound play down the phone. He says his boss, working for the lighthouse board but stationed in an office, has never heard this foghorn. It becomes a party to our conversations: we pause in excited mid sentence as the siren sounds, then continue.

I have not seen this many people for over a week, and I feel awkward and observed. I don't want anyone to ask me why I've chosen to spend a month in a lighthouse alone, because I will have to expose myself as a foghorn obsessive, and ironically, the foghorn will interrupt my explanation. I climb the steps to stand underneath the red trumpet, out of view and nestled in the protective shadow of a great beast. From this spot, directly underneath the horn, I can hear the sound echoing into this open landscape like a skipping stone, bouncing off invisible air currents and the surface of the water, just like Tyndall described from the South Foreland.

It doesn't take much open sea to make me feel insignificant. It is a huge stage upon which the teeming, roaring chatter of my mind can roam freely, a cacophony only I can hear, that spreads itself across a blue canvas all the way to the dark band of the horizon. Three hundred feet above the puckered indigo surface, the horizon is a very long way away, but this view is not empty, nor is it relaxing. If I really stare, force my gaze to take in the blue-grey panorama from the edge of the land, an animal panic sets in and I have to turn, fix on people or buildings: some scenery with human scale. As I stand at the edge I realise that with each sounding of the horn, my fear of this open seascape lifts. In the ninety-second gap between blasts, a feeling of exposure and insignificance rises like blood to the head, the smallness of my human body against the enormity of the sea a deeper, more sublime terror than anything I have experienced inland. But when the foghorn sounds once more, there is no space for me to think of anything else, and I feel calm.

Out in a boat, the foghorn calls over the sound of the sea, overcomes fear, danger, calls to let you know of safety and security, of the community you left tucked up in bed to go out fishing, or trawling or transporting. I had thought of the foghorn as a lonely sound, a big melancholic beast echoing into the vastness of the open sea, often to nobody at all. But it isn't. This heaving machine is the sound of someone else, the sound of civilisation, of safety, regularity and rhythm. It is comedic up close and comforting from a distance, and after a week alone, the sound is a booming comfort. It is the sound of a warm bed, and it is the sound of someone watching. If the lighthouse represented the eyes of the coast, the foghorn was its familiar voice. As the siren whirrs its warning warm-up again, I shut my eyes against the view and wait for its soothing music to start up again.

Part Two

DECAY

Nuisance – complaints – comparisons

7

Revelations in music

Sound perceived as music or noise happens in the ear of the beholder. Music is not made in a vacuum and neither is it listened to in one. What we call music says more about us socially and culturally than it does about the actual sound of that music. While the differences between what is sound and what qualifies as 'music' or 'noise' might be useful for us to communicate with – as signposts for us to talk to each other and navigate all these vibrations – what's more interesting than how they're defined is the way we use these nouns, and what it tells us about the status and perception of a sound.

Music is heard as music in part because of the context. What I call music might be what you call noise. Radical music is also relative, to the who/what/where/when and how of its sounding. *The Rites of Spring* caused riots, but to the average contemporary ear, not attuned to its particular characteristics, it floats on by like anything else on Classic FM. What it means to make radical music is as much to do with when and where you make it as what the music itself sounds like.

Sound is not purely for pleasure, although we often treat it as such. It is also a way of knowing things, of understanding things, of navigating not just a coast but any environment – this can be as much vibrational as it is aural, more so for those with hearing impairments. To restrict our listening diets is to miss out on crucial nourishment.

Our ears, physiologically speaking, are open all the time – we do not have 'ear lids' like we have eyelids. I love music – it accompanies me everywhere, and is the passion around which I have built my life – but it was only when I encountered the foghorn that I realised I was also interested in that which was not typically counted as music. We turn to different types of music to guide us through emotional turmoil, through teenage lust and grown-up heartbreak; it expresses desperation and exaltation whether secular or sacred. We become attuned to what will lead us to light from darkness, but we can also turn to sounds around us to understand the world. I want to know and understand what I encounter, and the dividing line between these things is blurry in a way I see no benefit in untangling. Building a wall between encounters with sound and ones with music is the aural equivalent of trying to define what is art and what is not, or define what is beautiful. These exercises do not reveal truths, only justified opinions.

Revelations in listening worm their way into our biographies and memories. I have had a long affair with 'weird' sounds and music, and have built my career around these revelations, searching out music, sound, noise, recordings – whatever. I want to hear something I haven't heard before, and I want experiences that change me. In this, I am always chasing a feeling; one where the world around me drops away and I find myself momentarily, euphorically, in a new and wondrous place. It happens less now than it did ten years ago, as my ears and mind become increasingly calcified, but it still comes many times a year, still makes me feel briefly, and literally, high.

It happened when I heard the foghorn, and it had happened before. It had been happening since I was a teenager, since hearing Bowie's *Ziggy Stardust* aged sixteen, when something clicked into place (or maybe out of place). It happened when I heard the intimate and imperfect voices lifted together on bluesman Mississippi Fred McDowell's *Amazing Grace*, an album of spirituals recorded with his family. As a teenager in the north-west on a lonesome Delta blues trail, I had listened more often to 'Whispering' Bob Harris than to John Peel, but hearing McDowell and his family was the moment I really began to think about what it meant to record outside a studio, to hear the shuffling and scrapes of people in a space, at the same time as a musical history of the American South opened up to me through these traditional songs. It happened a few years later, hearing the full-frequency no-melody noise jams of Detroit band Wolf Eyes aged eighteen, turning round to my friend behind me in the scrum, mouthing expletives as the emancipatory possibilities of such an onslaught hit me like a slap across the face. It also happened when I made an open-voiced drone in the remains of a church, egged on by a musician friend called Laura Cannell to try a remarkable echo she had found. The monotone of my voice, soft and nervous, gathered in a cumulus above my head, a dense cloud of sound I felt I could almost touch.

These revelations continued through everything from New York minimalism to Chilean psych rock; early electronic music to NASA's recordings of the stars; Japanese punk to

Ethiopian pianists; field recordings of icebergs melting to amateur choirs singing. In these hungry searches I devoured magazines, mixes, books and radio shows, and the golden threads by which one can chase music around the internet, from P2P networks to forums, YouTube playlists and dead blogspots still haunted by MediaFire links. Somewhere along these paths, I ended up at my biggest revelation: the foghorn.

Despite music's power and prevalence in human societies, I have often been surprised to find people otherwise interested in mind-expanding ideas are resistant to thinking about songs or music, or sound, in less rigid ways.[1] There can be a resistance to so-called 'difficult' music – to that which is considered 'weird' or unconventional. There is perhaps comfort in the familiar, in verse-bridge-chorus, but too much comfort brings stagnation. Having a chorus is great, but have you ever heard Buddhist monks chanting for exorcisms? Ever heard brass stretched out into hour-long multiphonic drones? Ever heard the rhythmic clunk of vintage cable cars in Switzerland? Ever heard a foghorn up close?

When chasing a sonic dragon like this, at some point the distinction between noise and music becomes immaterial and redundant, because what I am looking for is a feeling, not a type of music, so it doesn't matter whether that feeling comes from a sound like the foghorn, a free jazz record or church organs. Is the only legitimate sound an instrument makes the one that it's supposed to make? Are the only legitimate instruments those designed specifically to play music? I don't think so. A foghorn is functionally similar to a brass instrument, so what's stopping us hearing it as music? In the tests that followed Tyndall's, the language and descriptions used were a hair's breadth away from just that.

In 1901, Tyndall's successor at Trinity House, Lord Rayleigh, conducted his own tests on the Isle of Wight. They were both more and less interesting than those at the South Foreland, because while they were not so scientifically rigorous, the foghorn was treated like a musical instrument, or at least, something with musical attributes.

Rayleigh was a scientist who discovered argon (and won the Nobel Prize for it), and was good at getting his name fixed to things: there are also Rayleigh waves, the Rayleigh number (associated with natural convection), Rayleigh flow, Rayleigh scattering, Rayleigh's equation, and the Rayleigh–Taylor instability. During his tests at St Catherine's on the Isle of Wight, the newspapers reported a 'stupendous noise' that could be heard continuously through the trials, and the 'hideous growl' of one of the trumpets. His test report, unlike Tyndall's, includes illustrations of the monstrous array of horns *in situ*, each one morphologically different and jostling for space on the edge of the cliff: the elongated horizontal cones of the two Rayleigh horns with oval mouths on wooden frames; the right angles of the Scottish horn; a tall, almost comical trumpet that shoots straight upwards and bends at the tip to form a gaping mouth like a giant tuba; the short bent trumpet of the French pattern horn, far smaller than the rest. Rayleigh also tested reed horns, which sounded via a tongue of metal vibrating in a tube, making them less like a trumpet than a giant coastal saxophone. All these were mounted in front of the double trumpet of St Catherine's existing horn. Most importantly, though, he included a musical scale within the report.

A plate from the report on Rayleigh's 1901 tests at St Catherine's on the Isle of Wight.

The pitch of the note each horn sounds is recorded and referred to with this musical scale.

The note is also sometimes raised or lowered to see if this changes the distance it travels, and also how it changed the quality of the sound. St Catherine's horn is found to be most effective, playing 'the musical notes of the lower D in the treble clef and the upper F sharp in the bass clef'. At one point, a horn sounds so deep and full that men emerge from the depths of the yacht steamer's engine room especially to listen to it, presumably in grubby workwear, black with coal dust and oil.[2]

It was while reading Rayleigh's less scientific, more playful experiments with the musical aspects of the foghorn that

I finally realised that sound and music had ceased to have any meaningful boundaries. I was listening to the sounds of foghorns while commuting; I was searching out music composed with foghorn sounds; I was reading about Rayleigh's tests and imagining them as colossal durational theatres of sound, not scientific experiments. The ordinary ways of identifying music through qualities like rhythm or melody had fallen away. But listening like this, I stopped being concerned with whether the sound of the foghorn was music or just sound. It could be musical and has been used as such by various composers, or it could be a nuisance. Neither of these is a fixed quality, only the opinion of a person listening. It was these listeners I became most interested in.

It wasn't that there wasn't music in it from the start – right at the birth of the foghorn, Robert Foulis was inspired by a piano playing music, and I was staring at a musical scale from 1901 that had been used to test them. The foghorn is born from music and into music, and I had heard it die as an instrument at the *Foghorn Requiem*. In between there had been compositions, performances and soundings for days in dense fog. Everything I could see, hear, feel and read pointed me to this one core revelation: that foghorns were the true music of industry – a sonic hallucination of the Industrial Revolution conjured by the chug and rattle of steam and pistons, heat and grease, and machine lungs.

But I didn't want to categorise the foghorn, I wanted to know how others had heard it, used it, and what feelings had become connected to it. I was excited by this massive howl, but interested in whether other people thought it beautiful or a nuisance, and when and where those people lived. I wanted to know how it was talked about, how it was received, to understand something about how we had got to a place where foghorns were nearly entirely lost from the coastal soundscape but were still present in composition and performance. Had everyone welcomed the foghorn into their lives? If not, when did they fall in love with it?

Distance had imbued it with the romance I felt so sharply – mine was both a temporal and geographic distance. Being at these vantage points meant I could see the magic in its sound in a way that a nineteenth-century neighbour or a twentieth-century lighthouse keeper might not. I found music in its roaring sound, but up close, day to day, would I still have heard it as such? If the foghorn is the most perfect coastal music ever made, do you have to be some distance away to hear any music in it at all?

It struck me that my delight at this revelatory sound might not be shared by those who experienced the arrival and fresh interjections of a foghorn. I had the benefit of being far enough away to choose when I heard the foghorn. It had rarity, and when I heard it, it was an event. I began to wonder whether when a huge sound arrived on a coastline previously decorated with the chimes of resonant bells or the infrequent retort of a gun, it would have been less a revelation than a rude and deafening imposition.

8

The greatest nuisance

Ian Smith is a life-long Shetlander, a gentle character who is into vintage bus tours. He once took a coach trip all the way from Shetland to the Isle of Wight, where he was amazed by the tree-lined streets – there are no native trees on Shetland, and so the trees rising straight out of the pavement were incredible to him. Nor is there a railway on Shetland, and so anyone who has never left the island – it can be fairly expensive to get on and off – may never have taken a journey aboard a train. Ian was the last person to sound the horn at Sumburgh Head before it was decommissioned, and so I want to talk to him before I leave. I ring Jane from the Shetland Amenity Trust, who are looking after me while I'm in the lighthouse, to ask if she could pass on an email address or phone number for him. 'Oh, I'll just go and find him,' she says.

Half an hour later, she rings to say Ian is at home and she and I can pop round any time. He lives in an old farmhouse in a dip in the land, and like all Shetland homes, it is not so much open to the weather as closed off from the biting wind. Buildings here often seem as if they are crouching in a sheltered dip in the landscape – low stone buildings with small windows and narrow hallways. Ian sits us down in the living room and goes off to make some tea. He comes back with his arms full of cakes. Five types of cake. This is a Shetland thing, Jane tells me. People always have cake in the house. In this case, there are more types of cake than there are inhabitants.

Ian has a strong Shetland accent, which is to say, not an obviously Scottish accent, and it is teeming with dialect, where the vowel sounds are often different to what I'm used to. Most things are easy to understand – when you know something, or remember it, you 'mind' it. The one I hear most – 'peerie' – means little and is applied to everything. Birds and animals all have their own Shetland names – a puffin is a 'tammy norrie', a fulmar is a 'mallie'. Ian is the person who tells me about the lighthouse keeping a cow before milk deliveries were possible, and he wonders out loud 'whan tha last coo was an tha hoos', saying it with a breezy rhythm. Earlier that week in town, I'd been talking to two older ladies about the Shetland accent, and they had chuckled and said, 'We're talking Queen's English to you, if we talked like we talk to each other, you wouldn't understand a word.' 'Southerners' here are from anywhere south of Shetland.

Ian was a part-time keeper, which meant he worked weekend shifts or when other keepers were off or on holiday. He never wanted the job he said, but they hired him before he had a chance to say no. The principal keeper knew he didn't drink, and they needed someone who could be relied upon not to be under the influence at short notice.

His first weekend he spent in a caravan next to the keeper's accommodation, which Sumburgh's high winds make a perilous prospect. He describes how deafening winds clawed at the caravan and threatened to lift him away. Then, to add to his misfortune, the keepers switched the foghorn on, which he says started the teapot rattling on the stove. He did not get a wink of sleep that night, and it stayed that way if the foghorn was going. He hated it, right to the day it was switched off. 'I never got used to it,' he tells me, scowling at the memory. 'Some keepers could sleep through it, but I never could, it was a horrible sound.'

The Sumburgh horn sounded for the final time on its regular Monday morning test sounding, and I asked eagerly if there was any fanfare. Did anyone else come to hear it?

'No,' says Ian. 'It was just like any other Monday morning foghorn test.'

This was a smack in the face. I had been forging on with my romantic quest, finding rare foghorns and getting as close as I could to that sacred gut-shaking rattle. What Ian said snapped me out of it, sharpish. Ian reminded me that the foghorn was disturbing, persistent, noisy – it often sounded for days. My adoration of the horn had come, in part, from the luxury of not having to sleep through it, work through it, talk through it.

Ian was the last person to sound that horn, and was glad to see the back of it. The sound that had become the call of a lonely mariner was actually – when you were the one operating it, working underneath it, sleeping next to it – a deafening addition to a life lived in close quarters with a rotating cast of colleagues and strangers amid the bother and bluster of wind and bad weather.

I had heard the Sumburgh horn's call, it was beautiful to me, but what Ian said made an impression because it was counter to what I had expected, and challenged my thinking up to that point. This story did not fit with my rose-tinted coastal scene.

There are plenty of people who loved the horns, and many feel a romantic nostalgia for them now, but really, why would anyone enjoy a 100-decibel horn being inserted into their daily lives? Sounded alone it's not overly tuneful or melodic, and when you're up close it has not yet picked up those contours of the landscape that soften and shape its resonances. Ian could not be the only person who found foghorns unpleasant. So I went searching for voices that had left traces and records, voices complaining about the foghorns. Pretty soon I was involved in a dogged search for what can only be described as nineteenth-century noise complaints.

I found complaints about a broken foghorn in Hull; about the 'Firth of Forth torment' near Edinburgh, where a new foghorn sounded for three days and nights, and was bemoaned as a breach of the peace. In the *Aberdeen Free Press* a letter from 1884 begged that the tone of a horn be altered, that its dreary and monotonous 'wailing moan' was 'surely too suggestive of shipwreck and misery'. In 1900, a local paper called the horn at Pomham Rocks lighthouse on Rhode Island 'The Greatest Nuisance in the history of the state', describing it as 'a sound to make the flesh creep, indescribably lonesome and cheerless, creepy, and dreary'. When the first foghorn was installed at Green Point light-house in Cape Town, residents complained about its noise, and nicknamed it 'Moaning Minnie'.

It was a cacophony, of people complaining about fog-horns in the years after they were first installed, along with nuisances caused by malfunctions or replacements.

When foghorns were rolled out in Britain and North America, it was a new sound for many coastal communities, in places that had little of comparable size or power. In the nineteenth century people did not love their new foghorns. The sound did not make them weep for its deep and heart-warming emotion, it made them wail with despair. The foghorn started as an unwelcome sound, an intrusion into the domestic life of not just lighthouse keepers and their families, but the towns and houses of anyone near enough to be within earshot. From far away the guttural bark of a diaphone is reduced to a comfortable moo, but sometimes the weather gods conspired to carry the guttural sound over water, through streets and houses to make it sound like the horn was right outside your window. Sometimes foghorns were installed at the end of people's gardens, ruining the idyll of shore-side living.

When the foghorn at the Lizard lighthouse in Cornwall was switched on in the late nineteenth century the newspapers described its sound as 'very weird and melancholy', and that it caused prolonged echoes to reverberate through the surrounding precipices and caves. It sounds beautifully gothic, but for one local resident, it was ruinous.

In 1868, watercolourist Thomas Hart built a house in a dip in the land just in front of the Lizard lighthouse and called it Polbrean. If you stay in the YHA hostel on the Lizard Point, you're staying in Hart's old house. It is the most southerly point in the UK, half a mile out of the village of Lizard. On this coast the feral sea churns around the sharp black rocks that are like teeth in a rabid mouth. When I walk from Lizard out here to stay in the converted lighthouse cottages, the tower is hidden by a slight incline in the land until I'm almost upon it. The long, two-storey lighthouse buildings are flanked by two towers – this was one of the biggest lighthouse stations in the UK.

Along the paths around the lighthouse the bracken and trees have grown up and over in an arch, and the wind carries the sound of the waves through this natural tunnel, amplifying their roar. Their noise has no rhythmic crash and hush of breakers on a beach, just the endless churn of furious water. Towards the cliff edge, there are a cluster of small cabins that include a café, the most southerly gift shop in the UK and a wildlife watching cabin. A broad spiral pathway leads down towards the RNLI station where there is a concrete boat shed and jetty, hidden under the cliff, visible from the edge. The sea washes onto a stony beach. The water snarls, a seal pokes its head above water, bobbing in the small inlet.

From this position I can see the lighthouse from the seaward side, bright white with chartreuse-green gloss detailing, which stands out against the landscape. The foghorn is mounted proudly in front like a stocky security guard, the two black horns pointing away from one another, two tall narrow pipes which curve sharply and open into enormous tuba mouths supported on narrow struts.

Thomas Hart had moved here by 1871 from Falmouth with his large family, when there was just a lighthouse at Lizard Point, into the house he had built in front of it. He intended to paint in peace (although given his family numbered twelve children, how much peace he would achieve anywhere is debatable).

A couple of years after he moved, he got wind of Trinity House's plans to erect a fog signal in front of the lighthouse, just a few hundred metres from his house. He wrote to the lighthouse board and complained, but Trinity House politely, apologetically, dismissed his concerns. Hart was not discouraged and passed the matter to his lawyers, who pleaded that a foghorn in front of the lighthouse would be 'as great a nuisance as it is possible to conceive'. Trinity House countered his objections again, arguing that maritime safety was the priority – more important than his painting, perhaps – and switched the foghorn on, much to Hart's dismay.

He wrote again in desperation, begging Trinity House to come and hear its awful noise for themselves. He said nobody could sleep in his house, and that the horn had been sounding regularly in the day and night. His frayed nerves are detectable even through the veneer of Victorian politeness. 'It has ruined my property commercially, and curtailed my time as an artist,' he wrote. But Trinity House didn't want to set a precedent whereby painters could demand the silencing of a fog signal, and the clamour for improvements to maritime safety was louder than Hart and his family's complaint. I imagined Hart at the Lizard, dropping his paintbrush as the horn started up again, a clan of tired and agitated children squealing and squabbling, knocking over paint pots, while his canvases clattered to the floor.

This coastline appears remote, but it's really nothing of the sort. The village has not one but two pubs. The lighthouse station usually housed three families and a procession of engineers and labourers. I thought about all the forgotten conversations, all the letters that didn't make it into the archives, that were never transcribed. I thought of people in cafés and pubs moaning. I thought of the lighthouse keepers on the receiving end of complaints about a foghorn that they had no control over, and which they had to live with in closer proximity than anyone else. I thought of the keepers themselves, their wives and children, not only having to work in days of din, but having to put up with disgruntled members of their local community. They had no recourse to complain like Hart, because their job was to ensure the safety of mariners, and for that they had to switch the foghorn on.

On a still and golden day in late summer the breath of autumn is in the air. I am aboard the restored nine-teenth-century steamer the *Waverley*, steaming down the Clyde from the centre of Glasgow, through Greenock and along the firth. When I booked this trip, I had expected the ship to sound like a clamorous machine, to be deafened by a rough engine and the flatulent slapping of paddles, but on deck, the sound of the engines is barely noticeable. The ship makes almost no sound as it slices through the glossy black waters of the Clyde like freshly sharpened shears through black satin. All I can hear is a low turning over of the engine, a rhythm that modulates gently as the speed of the ship increases or decreases. The engineer below deck assures me this was what the ship would have sounded like when it was originally in service.

As we hit a sharp bend in the Clyde near Dunoon where the firth narrows, I see what I am here for – the Cloch lighthouse. The squat black and white lighthouse sits low on the bank, close to the waterline. It is unremarkable, as lighthouses go, but 125 years ago mail packets would steam around the bend here trying to make good time, and in fog they often collided.

In early 1897, to make this bend safer, a new foghorn was

installed in front of the lighthouse, which replaced a much less powerful boiler-powered whistle.

The new horn was a diaphone that sounded four blasts – high-low, high-low – of two seconds each in quick succession, every half a minute. Compare this character to other horns – it's a lot. Sumburgh for example, sounds seven seconds in every ninety, a single long, low blast. In comparison to the Om-like monotone of that horn, the Cloch was practically cackling.

I had traced a lead to the Mitchell Library in Glasgow, which has a classical exterior and faded 1970s glamour inside, mid-century modern glass and warm wood, and bold carpets that are different for each reading room – orange spiralling designs, blooming red roses, yellow and brown cuboids like ties from working men's clubs. In this space are the city archives, mostly used for genealogy and local history projects, but which also include the largely neglected archives of the Clyde Lighthouses Trust, who looked after a small portion of the Clyde and managed to use it as a testing site for various new technologies before being absorbed into the Clyde Port Authority. When I tell the archivist I'm researching foghorns, she lifts an eyebrow and says sarcastically, 'Aye, well I suppose somebody's got to' before going off to collect my files.

She brings a once-blue archive box that contains a bundle of greying papers tied with white cotton tape and scrawled with looping handwriting that reads 'Cloch Fog Horn, 1897'. I untie this greying bundle, lay out its contents and they turn my fingertips black with dust. I peel the pages apart and wonder if anyone has looked at them since 1897. They are alive with civic fury.

Complaints about the new Cloch foghorn started soon after its installation, and by November the council petitioned the Clyde Lighthouses Trust on behalf of all those whose complaints it was fielding. The sound of the horn, they said, travelled in such a way that it seemed like it was right outside people's windows.

From its place low on the water, on this bend on the Clyde, the sound of the foghorn was sweeping across the water into Dunoon, marauding around the streets and rattling people's windows like a poltergeist. Some people said, as Thomas Hart did at the Lizard, that the sound had depreciated the value of their houses – because who would want to live in a place haunted by a beast that howled like the Cloch foghorn? Others are reported to have upped and left their homes, just to escape its sound.

As the *Waverley* rounded the bend alone on the water, I imagined the mail ships steaming through, all pomp and clatter and puffing their pipes. I spot what I am here for – the Cloch lighthouse, and its foghorn. Looking at these structures from the water, it's clear why the sound would travel so freely over to Dunoon. The foghorn is shorter than the squat lighthouse, and it is much lower on the riverbank; like a penguin and its chick, it cowers in front of the tower as if shielded from the land. Its call, this regular 'high-low – high-low' would have coursed straight over the water, its passage perhaps greased by a narrow layer of air over the water. I imagine it like a malevolent spirit searching for a host, wailing like a ghost in the ears of sleeping townspeople across the Clyde.

In the letters about the Cloch is one typewritten on thin leaves of paper, from the doctors at a convalescent home who complain desperately that their patients cannot recover, because the horn resembles the sound of someone 'in sore distress'. They are begging for respite, conjuring an image of nervous and hysterical Victorians trussed up in dark suits, deep layers of crinoline and societal repression, relaxing on cane chairs in cottage gardens, only for the Cloch horn to gatecrash the calm with its rough tones. Another person writes a letter with a trace of wry humour, saying that the horn has 'at least as much melody in it as a Wagnerian opera'. The opus of this bundle is a sixteen-verse poem from the *Dunoon Herald*, which includes the verses:

> *The Doctors in Dunoon declare*
> *Their patients nightly mourn;*
> *They cannot get a wink of sleep,*
> *And blame the Cloch fog-horn.*

> *And cows upon the Cowal hills*
> *Are fast becoming yeld,*
> *Because they hear the dreadful wail*
> *Of dying monster bull.* [1]

The further I went back, the more dissenting voices there were. This perhaps shouldn't have been a surprise – new sounds so often generate contempt, not just in our surroundings, but in music too. When John Coltrane started playing his free spiritual jazz, on albums like *Om* and *Ascension*, the sound was derided by critics as 'just noise'. Scott Walker's shift from pop idol to avant-garde composer got him dropped by his label, but set him on a trajectory to make albums frequently listed as the greatest he ever made.

When Bob Dylan went electric half the audience tried to boo him off stage. Could the foghorn be thought of like this? A new sound – a new music – of the coast?

I had started out looking for complaints to step outside of my own perceptions, which too often cast this sound in a blessed golden light. The dissenting voices told me about how people reacted to drastic changes in the sounds of their environment, and became a way to trace the way people's feelings on a sound had changed over time. The noise complaints were more than just a collection of anecdotes, they also posed the question of how we become accustomed to a sound. In all of them, particular comparisons kept coming up which offered some clues. It lingered in the periphery of my thinking as I ploughed through books, records and newspaper cuttings, and found metaphors about bovine monsters, cows or bulls from Aberdeen to Cornwall, sometimes almost a century apart. The foghorn was compared to a bull because it sounded like a bull, that much was easy, but there was something else here, and the more I picked at this seemingly obvious fact, the more examples I found.

Comparisons like this are not isolated, but are imbued with the effervescent associations of language and meanings. Bulls and beasts are symbols of enormous power and meaning stretching back to the beginnings of human history, through classical mythology, antiquity and the beginning of writing. Some of the complaints resembled moments from one of the earliest surviving epic poems from the beginning of human civilisation. The foghorn is a beast with its head in the nineteenth century and its tail in the present, and a bull is a creature that brings a history of its own.

9

Bulls, reoccurring

It is early May 1994. In Prospect Cottage on Dungeness, a one-storey wooden house surrounded by an unfenced shingle garden, the film-maker Derek Jarman dreams he is mounted on a dappled grey horse with an American tourist, crossing a ruined market square in front of Salisbury Cathedral. As they make their way across the square, a black bull materialises 'like an incubus' heaving and pawing at the ground and circling a matador. The menacing bull is dark and growing 'like a thundercloud', and Jarman's horse begins to buck, which wakes him from sleep. As he wakes, the bull transforms from a nightmarish vision of sweating beast to the abstracted bellowing of the Dungeness foghorn.

Jarman did not know it, but the foghorn manifesting as a bovine apparition was the culmination of a century of comparisons both real and imaginary, ones I had first noticed in the case of the Cloch, and which were echoed and reflected in the subsequent centuries of real and imagined foghorns. In the bundle of papers about the Cloch horn, one letter writer described the sound of the horn vividly as being like 'a gigantic bull and his gigantic mate, which had stolen noiselessly up to my chamber window, suddenly opened their mouths and emitted their characteristic notes – the male a hoarse roar, and two seconds afterwards the female a shrill skreigh'. The sixteen-verse poem included comparisons to bulls and cows, and another letter writer called it a 'howling fiend'.

It wasn't just Jarman's dreams and nineteenth-century Dunoon that heard foghorns as bovine. In Ray Bradbury's short story 'The Foghorn' the lighthouse and the foghorn wake a prehistoric creature from epochal slumber. It is the last of its kind, and mistakes the foghorn for the call of a mate, and the lighthouse beam for an eye. Thinking itself saved from aeons of loneliness, it raises itself from the seabed only to find that what it thought was companionship is the lighthouse and foghorn, and in its grief and rage, it destroys the tower. The salty old keeper delivers perhaps the most evocative and florid description of the foghorn ever written, describing it as:

> a voice that is like an empty bed beside you all night long, and like an empty house when you open the door, and like trees in autumn with no leaves. A sound like the birds flying south, crying, and a sound like November wind and the sea on the hard, cold shore . . . a sound that's so alone that no one can miss it, that whoever hears it will weep in their souls, and hearths will seem warmer, and being inside will seem better to all who hear it in the distant towns.[1]

On the other side of the Atlantic, *Quatermass* author Nigel Kneale wrote a short story called 'The Tarroo-Ushtey', a fable starring the foghorn, about how industry eventually arrived in remote island communities.[2] In this story a foghorn is heard by island residents, but nobody knows where the sound is coming from. It is described as being like 'a coughing cow far away on a calm night', and the locals look to local mystic Charlsie for an explanation of this strange new sound coming across the water. It is identified by Charlsie as what he calls a 'Taroo-Ushtey' – a mythological water bull, 'a tremendous big black bull, but their feet is webbed'. A sailor from the mainland knows the source of the sound and explains that it is a foghorn, but as an alien on the island, he is shunned and ignored. Charlsie discredits the sailor publicly, but cheekily absorbs his knowledge: 'Ye know, the sound of a Taroo-Ushtey's voice would be a good thing to imitate; as a warnin' to the ships; it has a frightenin' sort of a noise. I've a mind to suggest that to th' English government.' The Taroo-Ushtey doesn't bellow again for another week, and when it does, Charlsie takes the credit as inventor of the foghorn.

Kneale's Taroo-Ushtey is a creature borrowed from Manx folklore, a water bull that, when it mates with the herd, is said to produce lumps of 'flesh and skin without bones'. An analogue exists in Scottish folklore, the *tarbh uisge*, a malevolent bull that leaves the sea by moonlight to terrorise the countryside. Eighteenth-century Manx folklorist George Waldron recounts a story of a farmer who spots one in his herd, and gathers a troop of men armed with pitchforks, who attempt to chase down the amphibious beast. It eludes them by escaping into a river and swimming downstream, periodically poking its head above water in mockery of the braying crowd.

Kneale's water bull, Bradbury's prehistoric beast and Jarman's bovine dream visions are not exceptional. In the first foggy moments after installation, when theatres of sound were testing horns and new sounds were hollering out across the sea, horns were often represented as monsters, bulls and beasts in real and imagined scenarios. Often, the source of the sound could not be seen – so the imagination crowded in to give this new animal a body.

A bull is about muscle and force, but also about man's dominion over nature, about divine and earthly power. The epic of Gilgamesh tells of the destruction wreaked by the bull of heaven, sent down by the sky god Anu at the request of his daughter Ishtar, whose advances have been rebuffed by Gilgamesh.[3] When the bull descends from heaven, it is snorting and bellowing, and the earth breaks open under the bull's great noise. Each time it bellows, a crack opens in the earth, and a hundred men fall in and die. At the third, Enkidu slays the beast.

In ancient Egypt, the Apis bull of Memphis was considered an earthly manifestation of the creator god Ptah. The Minotaur was half-human, half-bull, the progeny of a goddess and a great white bull.[4] In ancient Mediterranean folklore, tremors of the earth were said to be the bull god roaring beneath the ground. In Chinese mythology, oxen were not always in service of humans.

One myth tells that humans would have to work hard for feeble harvests, only eating every few days. The Emperor of Heaven saw this and sent down the ox star from the sky to tell them that if they worked hard, they would be promised a meal every third day. But the ox star mistakenly tells the people that they will eat three times a day if they work hard. For its error, the ox is sent down from its heavenly realm and must pull the plough to make enough food for the people to eat three meals a day. Like the foghorn, the ox has a power that is put in service of human comfort.[5]

Many foghorns were given nicknames, and many of these nicknames invoked the bovine. Whitby's foghorn was referred to as the 'Hawsker Mad Bull', honking four mooing blasts every ninety seconds, and at the Platte Fougère off Guernsey the foghorn is known as the 'Lowing Cow'. St Catherine's foghorn on the Isle of Wight was said to sound like the 'sick bull's iterated bellow'. Girdleness foghorn in Aberdeen was known as the Torry Coo (cow) and Jersey's foghorn at La Corbière was said to sound 'like a dying Jersey cow'. One journalist, who tried and failed to identify all the foghorns around the Bay in San Francisco by ear, said the diaphones sounded like 'the snort of some monster from the cold depths of the deepest ocean, a basso profundo from another world'.

There is humour in these comparisons, as the machinery, particularly up close, bellows, grunts and moos. One modern-day lighthouse keeper in Canada, Caroline Woodward, recalls an instance in her memoir *Light Years*, where a B & B owner told her that when guests complained of the noise of the Lennard foghorn, she would tell them it was the sound of the whales mating.

The foghorn might sound like a bull, but language hides truths and connections, can make the strange familiar. Language like this is not accidental.

The sound of the foghorn is a sound made by engines – the raw machine power at the centre of the Industrial Revolution. These urban machines migrated to rural coastlines, and something deeper can be pulled from this repeated comparison. Bulls and beasts, foghorns and folklore: engine-powered sound signals on British coastlines represent the imposition of industrialisation at the limits of the land. Within these zoological analogies is embedded meaning and connection, whether it was intended or not.

Language like this contains change, it contains the history that made it, to the conflicts in transformations from the pastoral to the industrial; an echo of coasts experiencing the long decay of the Industrial Revolution, where agrarian lives were transformed by machines. Economist David Landes famously compared this shift – along with wider changes in Europe and the rest of the world – to Eve eating the apple in the garden of Eden, saying ominously that things would never be the same again.

The comparisons, literary fictions and nicknames connect and amplify the shifts and clash they embody, of rural life and urban technology, and the tension in remote communities coming into contact with the liminal manifestations of the industrialisation of work and production in urban centres. One of the ways they do this is through the language used by those complaining about the noise of the foghorn. Similes and metaphors are, after all, as the philosopher Donald Davidson said, the 'dreamwork of language'. The dreams in this case are of capital and control for some, which meant nightmares of dark satanic mills for others.

Industrialisation and urbanisation across towns and cities in Europe at this time was not just about an increase of volume and the number of engine sounds, but in the perception of this perceived noisiness. Noise was a class issue, where in the late nineteenth and into the twentieth century sensitivity to noise was, at least in the case of an intellectual elite, seen as evidence for having a refined, delicate and cultivated mind.[6]

Language describing machines as animals represents part of a bigger tension between the sacred and the secular, between the divine and the evolutionary, in a way that touched John Tyndall. Darwin's *Origin of Species* was published in 1859, but by August 1874, evolution was still up for debate and Tyndall was publicly shamed for what became known as 'the Belfast Address' – forgotten now, but a scandal at the time. In it he accused religion of slowing the progress of science, and argued that biblical explanations had held back human knowledge for generations. To a modern reader, it reads uncontroversially, but around the time it was delivered, another group of British scientists signed a collective declaration saying that science could not contradict scripture. Tyndall's speech caused outrage and some members of the press even called for his arrest for blasphemy.[7]

Tyndall was also part of a group called the X Club, a dinner club of nine distinguished scientists (who also sported distinguished facial hair) who wanted scientific discussion free from theological invocations. Also a member of that club was Thomas Henry Huxley, whose ferocious defence of the theory of evolution led to him being nicknamed 'Darwin's bulldog' – his mutton chops and jowly features may have lent themselves to the comparison. He pointedly used animal/machine comparisons in his ground-breaking zoological study of the humble crayfish in 1861, by repeatedly referring to its functioning as a 'living engine'. The comparison had meaning and baggage – animals are not divine designs but evolved machines.

While machines were making working life noisy and dangerous for many, for others they came to represent the

forward march of progress. Luigi Russolo's 1913 futurist man-
ifesto, *The Art of Noises*, imagined a future music made from
the noises of machines and technology. It was composed as a
letter to the composer Francesco Balilla Pratella, noting that
'noise was really not born before the nineteenth century, with
the advent of machinery. Today noise reigns supreme over
human sensibility.' He described a walk through a modern
capital, where 'the rumblings and rattlings of engines [are]
breathing with obvious animal spirits'.

Russolo demanded a revolution in music where machines
and cities become sonatas and symphonies. In some corners
of experimental music, along with the great symphony I
witnessed at Souter Point, his vision has now arrived. 'Our
ears, far from being satisfied, keep asking for bigger acoustic
sensations', he wrote. Much of the music that had changed
my life subscribed to this ambition for bigger acoustic
sensations – electronic music of overwhelming density; free
jazz saxophonists who could blow the roof off; the iron
girder rhythms of industrial groups like Throbbing Gristle.

While I can easily hear Russolo's embrace of industrial
sounds in music now, it is impossible for me to conceive of
what it was like to experience the emergence of these sounds
in the cities and towns that were subject to these changes.
Russolo wanted music to reflect industrialisation, by filling
our lives with bigger, louder sounds.

As part of his project to embrace the engine-like, the
mechanistic, the clangs and rattles, Russolo designed instruments to play his new music, which he called '*intonarumori*'
– noise machines.

An image of him with his radical noise-making instruments resembles a miniature version of the plate from

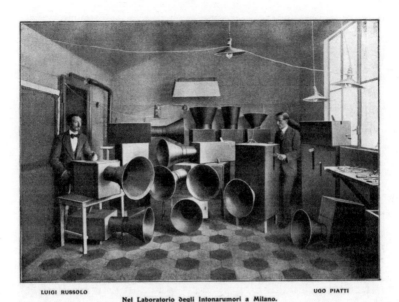

LUIGI RUSSOLO   UGO PIATTI

Nel Laboratorio degli Intonarumori a Milano.

Russolo, 1913, with his intonarumori.

the foghorn-testing sessions, with him and his assistant standing behind an array of variously sized wooden boxes with trumpets pointing every which way. In comparison to the foghorn-testing sessions, though, his inventions remain petite and domestic, almost quaint in scale.

Russolo wanted musical paeans to progress that reflected the city he was living in – at that time, Milan – but within this ambition he also asked that people change the way they listened. Why hear the city as noisy, when you could hear it as symphonic?

The October Revolution of 1917, where the Bolshevik government seized power in Russia, meant there was also a push to revolutionise music, resulting in some bombastic and monumental concerts which dwarfed anything I have ever seen or heard in my lifetime, and make Russolo's bulky *intonarumori* sound like mere toys. The Bolsheviks began designing new instruments and writing new symphonies to reflect their changed nation, using new technology to convey the everyday life of the proletariat. One composer, Arseny Avraamov, embraced this in bold proclamations, ambitious performances and outlandish instruments.

Avraamov began as a political revolutionary, and then in his twenties became a radical composer, music writer and theorist. The story of his life is a wild one: he took part in a number of violent protests in various parts of Russia and Ukraine, was gifted a Mauser rifle by an Armenian terrorist who sympathised with the communist cause. He fled Kiev after bomb-making equipment was found in his laundry basket, but by 1906, at the age of twenty, he'd abandoned these efforts to focus on music, taking his radical leanings with him. He railed against the Western twelve-tone tuning system, instead developing his own theory of microtonal 'ultrachromatic' music. As early as 1916 he proposed methods of making music that resembled sampling, processing and synthesis, and after the revolution he put forward a serious proposal that all pianos in Russia ought to be burned.

According to writer and researcher Andrei Smirnov, he designed a 'steam organ' – a steam train loaded with a rack of locomotive whistles which could be sounded via a large keyboard; composed a piece called *Shumrhithmuzika* ('Noiserhythmusic') that involved the sounds of axes, sledge hammers, saws and wood files. He proposed a sound system built into aeroplanes that would blanket the land in sound in a method he called 'topographical acoustics'.

Smirnov quotes him, in 1927, as imagining the sounds of

the theremin and harmonium (two early Russian electronic instruments built by Leon Theremin and Sergeĭ Nikolaevich Rzhevkin) coming from the sky: 'And if the sound of sirens is not powerful and qualitative enough, what could we dream about? Clearly: about the devices of Theremin or Rzhevkin, installed on aeroplanes, flying above Moscow! An Aerosymphony!'

I had come to Avraamov's work through a 2CD set, which documented and was named after a re-recording of a 1922 concert by Avraamov called *Symphony of Sirens*, which was staged using the industrial and military sounds of the whole city of Baku in Azerbaijan.[8] It realised Russolo's vision of machine music in bombastic style, a symphony for Soviet progress and industrial might, a paean to the Soviet future. The sleeve notes credit the Baku performance as including 'choirs thousands strong, foghorns from the entire Caspian flotilla, two artillery batteries, several full infantry regiments, hydroplanes, twenty-five steam locomotives and whistles and all the factory sirens in the city'. The 'players' were given scores, and were conducted by Avraamov from a telegraph pole. There is a scuffed black and white photo of him on the day, face taut and grubby under cloth cap, arms flung upwards waving flags to direct his orchestra of people and machines.

The ship's foghorns in Baku had become one instrument in a city-wide musical performance, where the sounds of modernity had become music. This monumental symphony was about power, control, as well as the unity and togetherness of the Bolshevik project.

In the bulls, in Russolo, and in Avraamov, there was the language of change and the cultural adoption of it. The folklore like that imitated by Nigel Kneale did not just invent, but also represented. Stories tell us something about the way things were and the way things are, and about the way things have changed. When we say, 'it sounds like . . .', we are not reaching into emptiness, but into webs of connections and associations that have built up in our own minds.

What I heard in the bellowing of bulls in the nineteenth century was a cultural echo of a transformation from the pastoral to the industrial, of coasts that were experiencing the long decay of the Industrial Revolution, and the power of the urban in working communities. Foghorns were not to be found in cities, but instead were industrial outliers on the edges of the land, and in these places, like the Manx island Nigel Kneale parodies, myth and legend remained, clashed with modernisation and new technologies.

When I first compared that French horn to a foghorn as a door opened onto my new obsession, I reached for a comparison to something big, something bold and unexpected, and came out with a foghorn. For many others, as foghorns were first fired up around the coasts, that picture was a bull with steaming nostrils. Whether they were embracing or rejecting these sounds, the comparisons speak of animalistic machines in a way that is embedded with notions of strength and control. The comparisons to bulls and beasts showed me the almost mythological power of these new machines over the people that heard them, reflecting the way their working lives were changing, and also the ways in which these powers were extending their reach.

John Best, a member of the Association of Lighthouse Keepers, pings my inbox with a leaflet printed in comic sans. John is always chipper, and seems always to be legging it around the world, belly laughing and being practical. He has seen a lot of lighthouses, and is one of the core members of the madcap enthusiasts at Hurst Castle on the south coast, where the Association of Lighthouse Keepers Museum is housed. The leaflet John sends is a scan of one he picked up in Tasmania. It describes a G-type diaphone at Low Head, on the northern coast of Tasmania, appropriately sited in Bass Strait. Low Head is the only G-type diaphone in the world. The uniqueness in its engineering is invisible to me – but underground knowledge networks and secrets outside the archive like this provide more than just engineering histories. It looks, frankly, completely pathetic, housed in what looks like a garden shed, a small horn poking out of the gables, but I am not interested in its architecture. I am interested in its sound, in its gut-shaking, eyeball-vibrating holler, which is said to sound not like a raging bull, but like 'the roar of ten thousand elephants'.

I start planning how to get to Low Head to hear the horn, but the flights take a whole day, there is no ship, and the amount of CO_2 the trip would put into the atmosphere amounts to more than twice the average yearly emissions for many of the world's residents. It is out of reach, so I instead plan a fantasy route around the world that hops between foghorns. To reach it, I could trace an itinerary along the trade routes. These marine highways have evocative names: the Horse Latitudes, the roaring forties of the westerlies south of the equator, the doldrums – otherwise known as the Intertropical Convergence Zone, where in days of sail ships languished, trapped and stilled. A pilgrimage to Low Head by ship would take me past coaling stations on the colonial routes to India and the Antipodes, breadcrumbs of imperialism left by colonial nations spreading themselves across the world. I would hear foghorns sounding from the coast of Namibia and China, the tip of South Africa, from corrugated steel huts on the coast of Japan, before making it to Tasmania.

Bull-like and bull-elephant-like foghorns are scattered around European, North American and Russian coasts, but they also trace a partial route of colonial expansion. Wherever ships went, lighthouses and foghorns went. There are fog signals in South Korea, Gibraltar, Morocco, Bulgaria, Taiwan, Chile. Reef lights in Ghana, and Sudan still have fog signals. From the machinations of power that made the foghorn such an iconic part of the coasts, we can trace the expansion of Europe across the world. There are foghorns that trace the route from Europe down the west coast of Africa and round the Horn. There are foghorns on the coast of Namibia at Dias Point near Lüderitz, where the Shark Island concentration camp was located.[9]

Lighthouses were built by colonial powers to aid their movement around the globe, but the nature of them means everyone used them, from the smallest boats to the biggest ships: enemy, ally, rich or poor. There remains a duality in these navigational lights and sounds – they are part of an infrastructure of violence, but offer salvation to anyone at sea, not just those out to conquer.

I was finding that in the foghorn there was a knot of profound themes: music, sound, culture and politics could come together when it sounded, and the way people talked about it and told stories with it was a way of unpicking that knot, whether they were complaining to a newspaper or constructing a new society – their comparisons come with associations, implications and meaning. While for the keepers working them it was a part of the everyday, there remains a dance between the mythical and the mundane on a coastline sunk in fog with a horn bellowing like a dying bull. It is this play, between the imaginary and the everyday, between urban power and rural territory, which the foghorn can articulate, and which lends it to coastal myths, bovine comparisons, and a folklore that is always closer at hand than you think.

10

New myths, old power

At the summer solstice I head down to Thorpe Bay from Leigh-On-Sea as the sun is setting. As I race along the coast, trying to beat the sunset, teenagers are splashing and squealing by the groynes, and a gaggle of kite surfers is out by the plastic changing huts at Chalkwell. The light of the longest sun is still golden, but night gallops in from the west.

I sprint from the pavement, leap the sea wall, stumble down the sand and shingle to meet the nearly-high tide at 22:22. Here, not so many miles from where the Thames flows into the North Sea, the sea is turning dark and agitates the shore. I peel off my sandals and unbutton the loose dress I have thrown over my costume, but by the time I reach the water's edge, the gold has shifted to black, and shadows are growing on the surface of the water, the sound of lapping waves transformed by the darkness into a hungry chomping. The streetlights from the road do not reach the water's edge, and I am alone on an unlit beach, where shiny ice-cream wrappers and bright plastic bottle tops stand out in the shingle.

When the tide comes in to its highest point here, the currents flow in fast from the deep central channel, over and around the slower waters that have streamed across the mud heated by the afternoon sun, warmed like a bath. To swim at high tide in an afternoon or evening tide is to move through water in discrete channels, warm water on legs and belly then the sudden shock of a chilly slipstream scraping calves; hot and cold currents swirling around limbs. I step into the dark water, which holds the warmth of the day as the mud releases the afternoon sunshine, and submerge.

It feels alive, feels like slippery fingers curling around my legs, coming with presence and intent. The breeze has picked up and the light from the street catches the ruffled surface. I shiver, and not for cold. The day before, I had sprinted into the clear green water and the same fronds of seaweed had embraced me, but now they paw at my legs like slimy tentacles. My eyes are wide like an animal's, and I jump at every tendril's caress. My arms no longer shimmer with refracted sunlight, but look like the pale arms of a corpse floating beneath the greasy surface of the water. I swim a few strokes, and the feeling does not pass. There is nobody here watching me, so nobody cares how long I'm in. I stop trying to impress myself, and get out.

Wrapped in a towel and sitting on the slope of the shingle, sound carries along the shoreline. I come here often enough to know it is changeable, depending on the level of the tide, the reflections of the water and the way hot and cool air sits upon these surfaces. On some days I hear the creaky little diesel trains grumbling down the pier a few miles away, distorted or amplified so they sound much closer than they are, funnelled across to me in a rumble. On other days I can hear the fluffy white sanderlings from down the sloping shoreline, cheeping noisily on black twig legs as they crowd up to the wash, chasing waves.

I am usually alone on these visits, without my phone, so things go unrecorded. Sometimes, they scarcely seem to have happened at all. The coast is a liminal zone, an edgeland, but my headspace becomes a boundary in these spaces too, a lost transition between work and leisure, a clash between inner thoughts and social performance, where hours disappear in evenings spent alone.

The estuary here goes out over a mile to the deep channel where the container ships pass in and out of the London Gateway Port; at low tide they can look as if they are gliding directly over the mud. Even the apparently easy flats of this shallow shoreline can mean stranding, or drowning, if you read the tides incorrectly. Five miles away the coast at Foulness Island hides quicksands and rushing currents that move faster than you can run, which have swallowed people, horses and carts loaded with bricks. Even with its easy weather, amusement arcades and pier, its swimmers and wind surfers, this coast possesses tides that can take a life in just a few minutes of missteps.

While the estuary is open wide and seems safe, others are morphologically and moodily different. On all of them there rages an eternal conflict between water and earth, life and death, where water tears at sand and rock, even around this small island nation. In Dornoch on the east coast of Scotland the deep grey breakers roll slowly on a small inlet of yellow sand and dunes with waist-high grass. From the broad sweeping beach at South Shields I see big ships on the horizon glowing gold in the winter sunshine. At the Lizard in Cornwall pale-blue water breaks white and frothing over sharp black rocks; in Llandudno the water is always brown and agitated; at Bradwell-on-Sea in Essex the sea and the land are blurred by a shingle spit that is ankle deep in pink-white shells that crunch under foot. In all these places the sound of the sea, the acoustic space, the way sound travels, is different.

In tandem with this, people move, goods move. On the estuary there are huge container ships, tankers and bulk carriers. In Cornwall fishing boats and small yachts bob in St Ives harbour. Along the edges of the Firth of Clyde huge ships lurk in hangars, and in Barrow-in-Furness Trident submarines are docked in concrete bays. These places are all hybrids, where water and land, the physical and the political, social and cultural come together. Even the coast as a line on a map is a fiction, or rather, a function. It is a multiplicity of imposed cartographic boundaries, the lines decided by the purpose of the map rather than an accurate reflection of reality. There is no objective coast*line* that we can draw, point to, or identify. The boundaries we see on our phones are never really where they appear to be. Coastlines are cartographic paradoxes: the more accurately we try to measure one, the longer it gets.[1]

The high waterline is what frames road maps. Navigation charts include the low waterline. Lines may also be drawn for predicted levels of severe coastal storms and sea level rise. Mean high water defines the national cartographic shoreline, and in America is what is referred to when, for example, the limits of private and public land are being established. Nautical charts show the line of the coast as the seaward edge of the intertidal zone, an area that is above water at low tide and underwater at high tide, also known as the littoral zone.

The coast pans out in distinctive zones. The pelagic sea

is the open water beyond tidal shifts. Pelagic is a word that contains the rhythm of the waves in its form – vowel-consonant-vowel-consonant; peak-trough-peak-trough. The modern fog signals that beep scarcely make it beyond the littoral zone if they're mounted on the coast. The big old horns like Souter Point, Sumburgh and Nash Point can stretch their soundings right out into the pelagic sea, twenty miles out or more if conditions are right. The deepest part of the ocean, the trenches 10 kilometres down, are called the Hadal zone, named for Hades, the underworld.

On the coasts, myths, folklore and storytelling swirl around lighthouses like the mists and storms that envelop them, and true stories and ghost stories can be indistinguishable. These places are thresholds, between a rural past and an industrial future, between sound and vision when the fog comes down and the foghorn begins its warnings, and are an elemental meeting point between land and sea. They are also, as folklorist Jennifer Westwood writes, places where legends flourish: 'All things supernatural favour the territory linking one state with another.'[2]

Myths still circulate that ocean waves can store sound. Deep-sea forums discuss whether the sounds of Second World War battles are still bouncing around in deep-sea trenches, trapped in the same seabed channels that whales use to communicate. Coastal folklore tells that Cornish waters have stored the battle cries of soldiers from Arthurian times, which can still be heard beneath the waves. Into this space comes the foghorn, with all the power of industry in its lungs. When it enters, language, sound and the sea coalesce, and begin to form urban legend and unsubstantiated anecdote. Other stories started to reach me, and I began to build my own private collection of modern coastal folklore.

It started small, with a local history blog reporting how there was once a football pitch on the flat-topped cliffs of Souter Point, right next to the foghorn. It claimed that, if the home side were losing, someone would be deputised to switch the foghorn on, blast the visiting team off their feet long enough for the home side to score a goal.

Then a friend's mum in Yorkshire who had been involved in the rave scene said she remembered reading an article about a sound system crew that had acquired a decommissioned foghorn from the navy to add to their speaker stacks. This story was sticky and appealing, because it represented something about the way the volume and power of the foghorn could be co-opted, removed from its place on the coast where it was intended to aid and control the movement of ships, and instead brought in as part of the all-consuming vibratory bass of a Jamaican sound system, where it controlled the movement of dancers. It was a sound emancipated from its windy clifftop to live out its days at carnival. I loved its happy ending, and asked a lot of people about this story. I asked ex-Cabaret Voltaire industrial musician turned David Attenborough's field recordist Chris Watson. I asked journalists writing books on Sheffield music, on sound system culture. I asked members of sound system crews. I never found out what happened.[3] I did, however, hear a story of a rave sound system that installed an aircraft engine that they would start up at the peak of the rave and boost everyone's rush into the stratosphere. It didn't help that I had no date, no definite place to work from. In the meantime, more stories continued to find me, and I continued to chase them. One took me all the way to Jersey.

***

Jersey is a British island closer to France than the mainland, best known as a tax haven. The Channel Islands were the only British territory to be occupied during the Second World War. To fortify the coast as a portion of Hitler's Atlantic Wall, Jersey's natural landscape was defensively augmented with visible and hidden fortifications. All over the island are towers, bunkers, gun batteries and emplacements – great concrete extrusions built by POWs shipped over from the Eastern Front – and underground structures, tunnel networks with great arched ceilings big enough for tanks. These concrete works along the five-mile beach at St Ouen's Bay have moved the sand dunes back, but have also halted coastal erosion.

Occupation was deeply painful for the islanders, and even the occupying forces suffered as supplies stopped coming in. Some of the island's Jewish population were sent to concentration camps (among them schoolmaster Harold Osmand, the only British person to survive Belsen). People were made political prisoners, imprisoned for stealing food and trying to survive – the prison's numbers at one point included the surrealist photographer and sculptor Claude Cahun. Eventually the prisons reached capacity, so you had to be put on a waiting list to serve your sentence.

When the Germans occupied Jersey one of the first things they did was march through the town square. This was not just a visual display of power, but a sonic one as well. Sound is power and power is sound.[4] The message: the population was going to be expected to march to a different rhythm, the rhythm of German jackboots. Radios were banned, but people hid them in cisterns and secret recesses to listen surreptitiously to the BBC. Control of resources was a large part of occupation, and this included access to sound as information.[5]

I had heard from a certified local history guide that when the Channel Islands were liberated, on 9 May 1945, the foghorn sounded all day and all night, in an almighty display of territorial reclamation in sound. The keepers, no longer under Nazi control, would have been the first to see the liberation flotilla come into harbour. They would have started up the foghorn as a welcoming signal, and after this, it would have made sense to leave it sounding, to celebrate Jersey being back in the hands of the islanders.

Notably, liberation was also the first time the outside world heard the island again, as the British ship that arrived to conduct the exchange also carried an embedded BBC reporter, who documented the entire process and reported on the meeting between Allied and occupying forces happening in the background. Listening to scratchy BBC recordings from the day in the archives, I realised there was something missing. If the foghorn had sounded when the ships arrived at harbour, as I had been told, and continued sounding all day throughout liberation, then why wasn't it part of the BBC recordings? It was not remarked upon, which didn't mean it didn't happen. But neither was it audible at any point. I realised, with a sinking feeling, that there were moments when I really ought to have heard it.

I looked up oral histories, listened to recordings, read accounts of the day, but nowhere was there mention of the foghorn. The local history guide couldn't tell me where she'd found it. I concluded it was a guess at what might have happened, which over the years had been gradually absorbed into the retelling of the story.

Her story wasn't a dud, though. She had told me something about how the foghorn served a purpose in marking a reclamation of territory. Jersey's foghorn was so deeply embedded in the identity of the place that if it had sounded for liberation as the guide had said, it represented the people on Jersey getting their voices back, their ability to speak, shout clearly and freely again. The point of the story was that people could make noise again. It was just a story, but it was also impossible to her, as a person born and bred in Jersey and deeply attached to its history and identity, that the sound of the foghorn was *not* sounding for liberation.

Like the language of the complaints – the bulls, the beasts and the myths – these are not just anecdotes, but stories about people, territory and control. Both the story from Jersey and the story of the Jamaican sound system are stories about power. The story from Jersey is about making sound part of the reclamation of territory, in the same way that the sound of German jackboots had claimed the town square years earlier. The story of the sound system was so compelling because it was a story of the power of this sound being taken back from the maritime industry, an industry which, historically, had been part of transporting people against their will into slavery and servitude. The idea of a sound like the foghorn, which is so much part of the infrastructure of this industry, being taken back by a sound system to sound for a rave or carnival, carries meaning as an urban myth. It is modern folklore about sound's role in the control of space and territory.

When police bark at individuals they are apprehending, the shouting is designed to exert control over the individual, to disorientate them so they can be controlled. When people complain about teenagers playing music at the back of the bus, it is because this is felt to invade their personal space – playing music, or demanding it be turned off is about control of the top deck. One of the ways slaves were controlled by colonisers was through bans on what languages were spoken, what songs were sung, and what sort of worship was allowed. Occupying space – whether physical or social – is also about occupying soundscape.

If sound is as much a part of territory as walls and fences, what does it mean for a sound like the foghorn, managed from the metropolitan centre but sounding on the very edges of an island's land border, to be reaching out to sea? And what does it mean for the sound to be placed in stories, in urban myths, about occupation and space?

Jonathan Raban, while he was in a boat full of his books circumnavigating the UK as war broke out with the Falklands, heard in the horns the hostility of the historical moment, heard a country asserting its place in the world through the voices on its coasts: 'When the fog comes down (and it's never long before the fog does come down) the diaphones in all the lighthouses along the shore begin to moo, making a noise so bottomless and sinister that you'd think it could only be heard in a nightmare. England's message to every ship that gets near to her coast could hardly be clearer: DANGER – KEEP OUT.'[6]

A foghorn extends a territory beyond the reach of its landward boundary, into its surrounding waters, and so the foghorn becomes a constituent part of the powers that flexed their muscles across the oceans. It secures safe passage for goods and people in the face of natural forces, not just in the liquid coastal spaces between national and international waters, but it also made safe the passage of ships serving colonial powers, on their way to or from territories already taken. It's possible to hear it as offering both safety from harm and an exacerbation of it.

These contradictions were at the heart of what made it so compelling, and what presented many faces and many readings of the foghorn's sound. Finding a sound was one thing, but tracing its meaning was a tangled path. While the foghorn's interjections into false memory and urban myth made its power obvious and understandable, its machinery linked it to bigger, national interests. However, these great horns didn't just combat the landscape and weather, they also made their presence felt when they flexed their muscles around those who counted a foghorn a part of their local community. I was also just about to find out that this power worked on other, more intimate, levels too.

II

Sound control

Despite being a June day after a week of temperatures in the mid twenties, it seems like there is more rain pouring onto the M4 than there is air between the droplets. I'm on my way to Nash Point, which has a legendary restored foghorn.

Nash Point lighthouse is in South Wales along the Bristol Channel, between Newport and Swansea. It is reached down a single-track road, which narrows and keeps on narrowing until it hits private land, high hedgerows and sheep staring from grassy banks. There are men working on the electricity grid by the café at the top of the road, closed on a Monday morning. A freshly shorn sheep baas its objections at me when I stop to take a picture of it with a mouth full of grass.

With my window down to clear the claggy motorway air from the car with mizzle and wind, I hear a buoy, its bell ringing out a sombre percussion. The water is choppy and brown, striped with thick foam. The waterline is edged with yellow spume on the rocks below the cliffs.

The lighthouse here was originally built as a response to the wreck of the *Frolic* in 1831, a paddle steamer that ran into trouble at the end of its regular journey. All eighty passengers and crew were lost and, in response to the tragedy, Trinity

House built two lighthouse towers the following year. The Nash Point fog signal was added in 1903. It is a siren, but has a grunt like a diaphone, for reasons I cannot discern. It is the core of the overpowering sound that punctuates the spiralling madness of the two keepers – played by Robert Pattinson and Willem Dafoe – in Robert Eggers's film *The Lighthouse*. The foghorn sounds the alarm, is the film's sonic motif for psychological danger and rising instability.

The foghorn house stands apart from the main tower, a low-slung square building with a bright green stripe and small windows, which looks like it might bend under the weight of the two enormous trumpets in braced black metal on its roof, with black and gaping oval mouths that are completely out of proportion with the building. It is like a gorilla riding a Shetland pony. For years it sounded for tourists, but at the time of writing it is silent – I turn out to have been one of the last to hear it.

I have come to meet Chris, the retained keeper, caretaker, tour guide and an ex-engineer. In front of the lighthouse, the noise of the sea and the wind is reflected off the walls of the building so it sounds like the lighthouse is a giant speaker system, throwing out static and watery roar. Inside the lighthouse there is constant background noise from the wind whistling through the windows, battering against the glass like it's trying to push its way in through sheer force.

Chris invites me into the lighthouse and makes me a cup of tea. He is kindly and easy-going, with thick glasses and hair in a crop cut. When he turns to pour the tea he looks twenty years younger than his sixty-something age – broad-backed and stocky. He is up for sounding the horn just for me and two others, who are thinking about getting married here. He shows them the mini-fridge where they can keep some champagne for after the ceremony. We finish our tea in the damp circular kitchen of the lighthouse, and drive 50 metres across the compound to the foghorn building to avoid the weather.

Inside there are two enormous engines. Their brass is shiny, parts are oiled, and their bodies are thick with green gloss paint. At one end stand two 15-foot-high air tanks, painted an ochre yellow with black gloss numbers and a pressure dial. Chris says that inside the engines are 103 decibels, but outside the foghorn is 100 decibels. Most deafness in lighthouse keepers resulted from having to stand next to the engines for extended periods of time, he explains, not the foghorns. Today, we have ear protection.

When the engines start up, all else is drowned out. My recorder hits the red, and industrial noise protectors plug our ears. We stand for a few minutes, the rattle trembling our bones, as the machines judder in their foundations like pit bulls on a leash. Outside, the two black trumpets are pointed in opposite directions, so there's a slight dissonance. We step outside the door onto the yellowing scrub grass and Chris tries to shout something that never reaches us before he is interrupted by a horn.

The first honk is a growling, guttural sound. It becomes smoother after a few soundings – Chris describes it as the mechanism having to 'clear its throat'. Tonally it's like the industrial trumpeting of a bull elephant, a boisterous metallic howl that bellows, like 'argh-OOOOOOOOh' – Chris can imitate its sound. Even he thought it was a diaphone until someone came and had a look under the hood.

As the sound fades and we take our fingers from our ears,

the couple and I burst out laughing with glee. Nash Point hosts weddings in one of the tiny circular rooms in the lighthouse tower, and when the guests gather for a photo near the foghorn building, Chris has been known to set it off. It makes for a great photo when everyone jumps, he says.

My recording is going to be gravelly and distorted – the sound is overpowering and rough, not like the soothing moo of the Sumburgh siren at all, but has an insistent, distracting timbre. What I was getting to experience was special and fairly rare, because hardly anyone ever got to stand right underneath the foghorn like this, unless they were the one sounding it. I love these vibratory, revelatory experiences underneath horns, but they are only part of the story of the foghorn.

For keepers operating horns, these could be brash and unfiltered sounds that barged in on their everyday lives. Horns were sometimes so close to living quarters that they imposed a comedic social control. The sound was not just literally powerful, but also infringed in more intimate and everyday ways in the workings of the lighthouse. One ex-keeper told me how, at some stations, your favourite TV soap programme would be ruined if the foghorn sounded in the evening, as you'd miss a few seconds of dialogue every minute or so. Lighthouse memoirs (whose snappy titles usually include some sort of maritime pun) by ex-keepers such as Gordon Medlicott (*An Illuminating Experience*) or A.J. Lane (*It Was Fun While It Lasted*) deal in the minutiae and anecdotes of the working lives of people who loved their jobs, and the foghorn features frequently, often describing disrupted conversations.

When it was switched on, conversation at the lighthouse

happened around the patterns of the blast – each keeper has a turn to speak, before the foghorn blasts a signal for the relay baton of conversation to be passed on to the next person. A Scottish keeper called Norman Muir described how he would wake when the foghorn started, then would drift off to sleep, only to wake again when it stopped. He found these routines of watch duty and foghorns sounding hard to shake after he left the service: 'To be honest with you, how brainwashed they got me, was after I retired, I'd be dreaming or something, and I'd say, "Oh, what watch am I on, is the light all right?!"'

Peter Hill, who worked as a keeper for a short period in the seventies, describes in his memoir *Stargazing* how he had to get used to this rhythm of conversation, and recounts an instance where the keepers tell a gruesome anecdote about an injured quarry foreman on the island and some bush surgery he was subjected to. It's like a short play delivered in fifteen acts, with a foghorn marking the end of each one. The story is never quite finished, except to say that the other quarrymen sewed him up with needle and twine after knocking him out with a bottle of Bell's and a punch to the head, before the foghorn sets off again.

At Sumburgh Head lighthouse, when Brian had come to switch the foghorn on, we had stood next to the lighthouse tower talking, but every ninety seconds the foghorn interrupted. During one blast I had tried to talk over the top of it, but it was futile. The conversation was disrupted, the foghorn was in control, and my transcript was unusable.

An urban myth from Canada tells how on one island the foghorn sounded so often that the residents paused in their speech to let the blast pass, whether it was switched on or not.[1] Other people told me they'd heard of keepers who, once on shore leave, could not slip out of the rhythm of the foghorn. It embedded itself not just in people's memories but in their speech patterns too.

From under the foghorn at Nash Point I feel its power most sharply. This is the moment when the sound of the foghorn is closest, but also when it means the least, because it is before its sound waves have made it out to sea; before it has travelled across a landscape; before it has been altered and changed by the cliffs or coast. This is the way the keepers heard it, with a proximity and power that was mirrored in their experiences of the extremes of water and weather. Those that heard it closest and most directly were the crew of light vessels.

A foghorn on a lightship is a very different prospect to one on a lighthouse. A lighthouse and its accommodations are made of stone, and the stone will go some way to absorbing the sound. A foghorn at a lighthouse could be a few hundred metres away from where keepers lived and worked; it might even be on the other side of an island, if they were lucky. Light vessels, on the other hands, were more like being actually inside a foghorn.

Light vessels (or lightships) are ships with lighthouses mounted on top. They are striking to look at – often bright red (sometimes black) with their names in block capitals painted in white across the hull. They have deep hulls (often metal) and large rudders, but many had no engines, and were dragged out to sea to the positions they were to light, held in place by 1.5-ton anchors and left to mark dangerous offshore sandbanks where lighthouses couldn't be built and where buoys would not be sufficient. A posting on a light-ship was much worse than one at a lighthouse.

To be on a lightship meant being at sea, with nowhere to go, and sometimes no way to move the ship. You were intentionally stranded. It was cold, wet and dangerous – if the sea got up or a storm rolled in there was nothing to do but sit it out. You were more often than not in a busy shipping lane, and in heavy weather were at real risk of being taken out by oncoming ships. Add a foghorn to this, and life aboard a light vessel becomes not just dangerous, but deafening too. To be tossed about by relentless forces of nature that pound at the hull and roll the metal can that keeps you from the depths is an unenviable posting. The stone towers of a lighthouse might have rumbled and swayed, but they had often stood tall and proud in the face of battering storms for a century. A lighthouse keeper has a long line of predecessors kept safe by the structure he keeps. The crew of a light vessel might not have such a lineage. To be in a lightship is to be exposed on a battleground between humans and nature without defences or armour.

Those on board light vessels courted death. In the 1960s the *Varne* light vessel was dragged off its position in a gale. It was at risk of foundering on nearby shoals, so the crew were evacuated in the huge swells. The day after, they returned to the lightship, to the station that had nearly killed them. A few years earlier, in 1954, a hurricane that had caused what a local newspaper described as 'boiling seas, surging over and up through the Chesil Beach', also tore the *No. 90* light vessel from its mooring onto the Goodwin Sands. All seven crew were lost, and the wreck can still be seen at low tide.

While the foghorn on a lightship would have kept you awake there was little else that would alert an oncoming vessel to your presence in fog, and no way to get out of the way if a bigger ship was off course. The lightship *Nantucket* was sunk 'so quickly that anyone below decks had little chance of surviving' after a confusion with the horn signalling meant that it was hit by the RMS *Olympic*. Those aboard the *Olympic* reportedly saw the inevitable collision happen as the lightship appeared dead ahead, looming in the fog. While only four of the eleven light vessel crew members survived, the *Olympic*, having suffered little damage, carried on to New York.

Foghorns had a particularly prominent role in ruining the sanity of those aboard a light vessel. Their metal hulls are essentially resonating chambers – like being stuck inside a bass bin, or the body of a steel guitar, but instead of dub or strings what you are hearing is a colossal horn. I imagine it was a little like sleeping in the body of Bo Diddley's guitar, with the rock and roll of the ship and waves.

On a lightship, there was no sleeping through the foghorn. The disturbance was so detrimental, a stipend was given to keepers on light vessels to mitigate against them being trapped in a metal box with a horn loud enough to rattle the whole ship. 'Fog money' was paid according to the total hours of foghorn sounding that each light vessel logged. The system had a flaw, though, as the introduction of this stipend was apparently followed by a few suspiciously and uncharacteristically foggy years, until the lighthouse boards designed devices that logged the hours – these remained susceptible to tampering, and the stipend was eventually cancelled.[2]

When the foghorn sounded aboard a lightship, the

vibrations of the sound were cartoonish in their juddering, ear-ringing exclamations. The *Nantucket* was said to have had the loudest foghorn ever made. It can barely be said to have a honk, and some recordings of its sloppy parp makes it sound more akin to a Godzilla-like fart. It was recorded by the American composer Alvin Curran in the 1980s for a large-scale radio project called *Maritime Rites*, for which he travelled around the eastern seaboard of the United States recording foghorns, later asking eminent jazz and avant-garde musicians to compose or perform with the recordings. Early on in my obsession, I had video-called him, and he peered into the screen, seeming unfazed by a random Englishwoman contacting him out of the blue to talk about horns.

Curran said the *Nantucket* had one of the most powerful diaphones ever made, but also that there were two *Nantuckets*, which were identical, with two crews, each of which would be out for three or four months at a time. He told me how the crew took him out to sound it: 'Their horns sounded once every sixty seconds, and when they did – if they were eating or sleeping – the entire ship quaked, an incredible vibration.' The horn was, as he described it to me, like 'hearing voices from another planet or from some imaginary world before the presence of human life. It was like some protean force, some archaic signal from the beginning of time.' I listen, and hear a startlingly graceless, blubbering low-end *paaaarp* that is what one imagines the brown note to sound like.[3]

In the sleeve notes to *Maritime Rites*, Curran writes that 'as nature is spontaneous and unpredictable, so is the music of man'. The recordings are striking – in the opening track,

'World Music', the American trumpeter and composer Wadada Leo Smith plays trumpet and seal horn with what is listed as: 'boats passing through Wood's Hole, Massachusetts; the foghorns at Portland Head, Maine, and Point Judith, Rhode Island; the ship's horns of an American Container Line vessel in Port Elizabeth, New Jersey, and a McAllister tugboat in New York Harbor.' In the piece, the horn barges in, a rippling blast, to be answered by the echoing pips of Smith's trumpet. What follows is a dance, between human and machine, where each listens and moves closer. By the end, Smith can barely be parsed from the horns.

John Cage and the trombonist George Lewis were both paired with recordings of the *Nantucket*. In Lewis's *Improvisation*, a parping horn is paired with an extract from an interview. There is the slop and lap of water on hull; words spoken by composer and reeds player Anthony Braxton are isolated like sound poetry with the pained craw-craw of seabirds. There is something gothic in its austere shapes, as the hulking heee-haw of the lightship horn heightens the grace of Lewis's trombone.

In Cage's piece the horn is far away, and he reads a word list – ice, dew, good, crew, ape – close to the mic, bouncing his voice left and then right. The distant horn suggests he is a shipwrecked mariner in an Arctic wasteland, amid the dew of melting ice, without crew or food, listening to an unreachable and useless saviour. The repetitions of the horns hold his loops (and perhaps his sanity) together. It is eerie and lonely, one man and a microphone versus the ghostly foghorn, which is useless for the trapped narrator, neither able to communicate with it nor silence the sound.

What Curran does in *Maritime Rites* is bring together not

just environmental sounds and music, but places and spaces. His publication of the same name contains a series of prose scores for massive outdoor concerts using the acoustics of salt and freshwater spaces. *The Lake* proposes fifty to a hundred singers gathered in boats on a small body of water; *The Docks* uses ships' horns, and other pieces include works for the Brooklyn Bridge, Lake Lugano in Italy and a bombastic Avraamov-worthy amalgamation of all the compositions called *The Waterworks*. *The Fog Bank*, an early version of the recorded version of *Maritime Rites*, is 'conceived for live broadcast radio and employs between ten and thirty fog horns transmitted from one or more accessible locations by fixed microphones, telephone lines or other means to a professional broadcasting console.'

When I spoke to Curran, he said he still used foghorn sounds in his improvisatory performances: 'I use them with a certain amount of reserve but they do turn up, and they're simply part of my musical vocabulary right now,' he says. He says that for him, the lightship *Nantucket* was a sort of holy grail, a sound now silent that he had managed to capture. He was also one the few people who had experienced it up close. There are recordings online, naturally, but at this point I knew from experience that no digital recording could replicate the physical vibrations that were such an integral part of a sound like that.

The *Nantucket* loomed in my imagination, a parpy, protean beast of a different kind than I had ever heard before. Others crept in alongside it, horns that became holy grails to my research for their location, size or legendary status. Curran says his recordings of the *Nantucket*, captured from out in a skiff a hundred yards from the lightship, are 'some of the best prized recordings I've ever made. I really felt like I was recording history, and I actually was, really.'

Curran is almost right. We can no longer hear the *Nantucket*, but foghorns have not passed completely into the past. There remains one place where foghorns still reign supreme, embedded and adopted as markers of the city's identity, still very much in the present. I'd read about the way the fog pours into San Francisco Bay, about the significance of the horns for the city, and by now I knew that there was no substitute for hearing a foghorn in the flesh. Unlike the *Nantucket*'s, San Francisco's horns were not yet relegated to history, and were very much within reach.

Part Three

SUSTAIN

Collection – meaning – memory

12

The bridge

Gertrude Atherton was a Californian writer who eloped with a man who was courting her mother, to go and live on his estate (which became Atherton, California) until he died at sea.[1] She was anti-communist and a white supremacist and a suffragette, writing feminist sci-fi that was sometimes published under the pseudonyms Frank Lin and Asmodeus.[2] One of her final books was a collection of short stories which contained a horror called 'The Foghorn', where a woman recounts a disastrous failed elopement with a married man, where they row out of San Francisco Bay together in a fog at night:

And then the foghorns began their warnings. The low, menacing roar from Point Bonito. The wailing siren on Alcatraz. Sausalito's throaty bass. The deep-toned bell on Angel Island. She knew them all, but they seemed to come from new directions. A second . . . a moment . . . an hour . . . later . . . a foreign but unmistakable note. Ships – two of them . . . Blast and counterblast . . .

The ships are upon them, and her lover is decapitated in

the collision. She lets out a curdling scream, but then wakes to find that her hands are not the smooth hands of a girl, but the wrinkled skin of an elderly woman, and she is on her death bed, having been institutionalised since the accident.

Atherton had mixed feelings about the city's foghorns. They were, for her, one of San Francisco's identifying features, along with steep hills, cable cars, white fogs and dust clouds, and wooden houses with bow windows. Later she came to despise the place, the fog and the foghorns counting out the time she felt she had wasted in the boredom of marriage: 'The foghorn in the bay tolled like a passing bell. I doubted if anywhere on earth one could feel so isolated, so "blue", so stranded, as in San Francisco.'[3]

My first morning in San Francisco I wake up jet-lagged and too early. From my bed, I watch the sun come up in silvery dawn light, illuminating the fog in the Bay, which has settled liquid-like around the red tips of the Golden Gate Bridge. If I make no sound, hold my breath, I can hear the foghorns even with the windows shut, an alarm clock for the whole city. My half-awake mind wheels back to a line by the painter and poet Etel Adnan: 'The fog's lightness surprises the senses, until the foghorn blows its complaint. The heart beats evenly.'[4]

The fog briefly levels out the city's precipitous topography, but it burns off by nine, taking my jet lag with it, gone without a trace, so that I wonder whether I even heard the foghorns at all. I wonder what sort of boats are still passing through the Bay. In this unfamiliar city, who are the horns sounding for? There are cruise ships, tankers and cargo ships here like in Scotland and the north-east of England, but the connection to the foghorns, to what they evoke, is something else. The feeling here is not so industrial, but is to do with the city's identity. Much of the traffic is ferries that transport commuters from Oakland, Alameda and Harbour Bay to the shiny skyscrapers of downtown, or baseball fans to Giants games at Oracle Park.

The city library in San Francisco is in the Tenderloin, a part of the city in which a housing crisis, addiction problems and lack of welfare are painfully evident. The building's ground floor atrium is required to be a social centre as well as a library. A few floors up, past the police and security, behind glass doors, is the historical reading room. It is like stepping into a vitrine, where everything is pristine. I am here because it holds the newspaper archives and collections relating to the history of San Francisco.

It still has an index card system, where subjects and names are catalogued in a long, deep chest of drawers. One reference card just lists two sounds that define the city's identity – cable car bells and foghorns. I had noticed on my way in that the electric streetcars have an electric imitation of the bell sounds made by the rickety old trams that still labour up Kearny Street. I pull out another card, which just has 'foghorns' typed on it. I have no idea what will be in it. The librarian puts a call through to the back room. 'This is going to make you laugh,' he says. 'I have a lady here researching foghorns.'

It turns out to be a folder of loose cuttings, all of them about the foghorns in the Bay. They were so numerous here – one 1970s article reports ninety-one different sound signals – that the horns are talked of as 'the city's music'. A 2009 article on the website SFGate said that: 'In addition to the traditional foghorns on the bridge, there are twenty-two electronic fog signals around the Bay that are controlled by the Coast Guard. Their sound is an unromantic ping or beep. Only a foghorn on the Golden Gate Bridge sounds like a foghorn.'

One cutting mentions a 1954 piece by a composer called William S. Hart. In three parts for piano and horn, it is called 'The Song of the Foghorns' but it no longer seems to exist. Another three-part article in the 1950s went so far as to notate the sound of two of the horns, diaphones on the *San Francisco* lightship and the Mile Rock lighthouse. I send a photo to my friend Laura Cannell, a violin and recorder player, and ask her to record them; she plays them on the lowest instrument she has – a bass recorder. She sends me back what she plays, ghosts she has resurrected, but says they sound flat played inside her cottage. 'You need the acoustics of an entire landscape to give them back their echoes and shape; to really bring them to life,' she says.

In 1981, Bill Fontana's *Landscape Sculpture with Foghorns* captured the way the sound of the horns are shaped by the landscape in San Francisco. He placed microphones at eight sites around San Francisco – Lincoln Park, China Beach, Point Lobos, Fort Point, the Yacht Harbor, Point Stuart and Point Blunt on Angel Island, and on Treasure Island – which picked up the sounds of the horns and played them at speakers on Pier 2. The distances between the sites meant that the sounds overlapped, were broadcast at different times, with varying delays created by the pace at which sound travels. Fontana said the intention was for people to 'hear the whole landscape'.

Online, the San Francisco newspaper archives are teeming

with bellowing men nicknamed as 'foghorns', in a way I didn't find in the UK – a 'Foghorn Miller' and a 'Foghorn Reed', a Bert Vincent was called 'the man with the foghorn voice', and there was once a 'Foghorn Murphy' who rode a horse down Market Street, hollering details of the day's baseball game down a huge megaphone with his name painted on the side.

In San Francisco the foghorns are as deeply embedded in the city's identity as the fog that they sound for, so much so that it is often the fogs themselves that are said to be singing when the foghorns start their chorus. One 1930s book on the city writes:

> The fogs of San Francisco have many voices. They hoot and they howl and they blow sirens. They play strange tricks with distance. It is not unusual to wake up and find a steamer blowing on your roof. You are sure then, as you lie in your bed, that some doggone boat has lost its way and has climbed the hill and is sitting on top of the house, yelling like nightmare.[5]

These voices featured in various parts of the city's culture too. In *Dark Passage* with Humphrey Bogart and Lauren Bacall, the foghorn sounds as a harbinger of death, a motif for the doomed. The music and the foghorns met every time the radio station KFOG played its foghorn jingle, and when the station shut down, its final sounds were an assemblage of field recordings from around the Bay.

There used to be a phone number for San Franciscans away from home, a live audio feed for those feeling home-sick for the sound of the horns, a sort of sonic webcam.

It was still in operation when I started this book. I called over Skype, too excited to check the time difference or the weather, putting money on my account especially for the call. I typed in: +1 415 202–3809. It rang. A click, and a male voice chirruped: 'You are calling the Golden Gate Bridge's south tower. On a foggy day, listen for foghorn sounds!'

The feed then hiccupped, clicked through a split second of music, like catching a pirate radio station, and latched on to a feed that was mainly static. The distorted sound is like human gasping. I held my breath, strained my ears over the digital connection, and realised that what I was hearing was not the shush and crackle of a bad line, but the sound of waves hitting the base of the tower in low bit rate, but in real time. I heard no horns, and as my credit ticked down, I hung up. The next time I called, the number was dead.

The bridge and the fog and the foghorns are the landmarks, sound marks and weather marks of the city. But the bridge and its horns – and the fog that surrounds it – also carry sounds of grief and pain and loss. The bridge is a hot spot for suicides, and there are crisis phones dotted along its entire span. Policemen patrol regularly on push bikes. There are chain-link fences, and building work to build a net and another fence on one side. Way back when it was built in the 1930s, there was an $82,000 net installed underneath to catch construction workers when they fell off.

The bridge and its horns are both objects of the city's pride and its mascots, but also the place where people go when other options seem exhausted. When the foghorn sounds, it is not just for those in the area, but also with grief for those who have jumped. It is comfort and catharsis, a

SUSTAIN

sound that represents San Francisco for good and for bad, a deeply mournful sound, but a familiar one. Here, the sound of the foghorns is both a welcome and a farewell, a requiem for the city's suicides every time the fog rolls in.

San Francisco as home of hippy culture feels like a thing of the past. The city feels hollowed out, and all that is left are fragments of what its energies generated in the 1960s. Maybe it's just the city finally on a comedown, experiencing the hardness of a long morning after, but it feels brittle – especially downtown, where the punitive American culture of the 'self-made man' shows its cruel heart as two cities' worth of people are laid on top of one another: one the metropolitans, buying artisan coffee and expensive homewares; the other a city of poverty and addiction laid right on top. It feels like two cities in the same physical space.

It is around downtown that these stark contrasts are most evident, and are also where Robert Louis Stevenson felt the hard end of American society in the late 1870s. While his relatives were working on foghorn installations for the Northern Lighthouse Board, Stevenson was in California. He sat around writing, miserably waiting for Fanny, the woman he loved, to get divorced. He lost his teeth, contracted TB, lived a monotonous life he hated, where days were punctuated only with regular meals of 'coffee and rolls' (which may have contributed to the tooth decay).[6]

Like Stevenson, I needed to get out of the city. A musician I met named Theresa had told me to head over the bridge to the Marin headlands, where fewer people live and where I would hear owls and coyotes. The best way to get there was to cross the Golden Gate Bridge. I decide to do it on foot.

The bridge still has foghorns – three clustered under the

mid-span and two sat forty feet above the waterline on the south tower pier – and I'd read that they had never been automated like sound signals in the UK, so I stop off to see them along the way. The bridge's central foghorn still has a booming sound, made with vibrating diaphragms, and I wanted to know who switched it on. I email the Golden Gate Bridge's press address, and Paolo rings me back. He says – with a touch of amusement – he doesn't get many inquiries from foghorn enthusiasts, and that he can arrange for me to get into the foghorn control room and talk to one of the people who switches it on.

I meet Paolo outside in the parking lot next to the toll booth as six lanes of traffic rumble on and off the bridge in plumes of exhaust fumes. He is smartly dressed and cheery, shiny in fact, with reflective glasses, Bluetooth headphones and a blindingly immaculate white shirt. His job is public relations for the Golden Gate Bridge – public relations for a national icon like this must be a dream job, I think. I suppose you don't have to sell it to anyone.

The operational headquarters of the bridge are a collection of magnolia buildings and Portakabins, which include offices and workshops for painters, electricians, metal workers and trash collectors. Paolo tells me there are painters painting constantly, but that they're not, as the myth goes, working eternally from one end and back again, and instead touch up key areas all the time.[7]

We walk through the generator room, where there are two huge green machines that power everything on the bridge, including the foghorns. A grey box on the wall about as big as a box file looks after the electronic signal that switches on the foghorns. Past this, there's a metalworking shop, and a jumble of rooms. We reach what appears to be a break room, with a tidy but shabby kitchen, where there's a table to eat at, a few loose-looking fitted kitchen units and a sink. The walls are plain and the lighting is fluorescent, and there are no windows. He introduces me to Phil, one of the bridge electricians, who is wearing black overalls and T-shirt, and is a little nervous because of my recorder.

Phil shows me to the back of the room, where there is a small desk with three standard Dell computer screens, with a wireless mouse for each screen. One is hooked up to email, another has a grid of rectangles in red and green. The top screen has a basic graphic of buttons, made to look like an old nineties keyboard on a plain background. I wonder what I'm being shown, until Phil points to the pixel-rendered button, which reads in bold, basic font:

FOG HORNS

I'd said that I wanted to see how the horns were switched on, and this is what Paolo is showing me. They both apologise that it isn't more exciting. I admit that it isn't quite what I expected, and suggest they at least get a throne in here from which to operate the computer.

Whoever does operate the horns – and there is no special training to click a mouse, no appointed individuals – gets a message through the walkie-talkie Phil has strapped to his overalls. There are always people working on the bridge, and they are all watching for fog, Phil says. It's sunny now, but it doesn't take long for this to change.

What can happen – what I want very badly to happen

– is that one of Phil's colleagues will radio in when a fog front is heading towards the bridge, maybe at upwards of thirty miles per hour, which means it'll go from a sunny day to one swallowed in pale fog in the time it takes to smoke a cigarette. When that radio call comes in – which is a few times a day when it's not a freak bout of sunshine in mid February – someone will come into this break room, someone like Phil, and click that mouse button as if he's opening an email or liking a post on Facebook.

This computer, in this room with no windows, is the beating heart of the Golden Gate Bridge's foghorns. This is it, I realise, the button I most want to press; the place I have wanted to experience. This is the spot where this city's most iconic sound is switched on, a sound that means home, which floods from the bridge across the water, over the park and through the trees, riding up the steep streets of San Francisco and curling around the hills of the Bay.

But it's just a PC in a break room.

For a moment, I wonder what on earth I am doing here – a young woman in the prime of her life travelling across entire oceans to stand in an engineer's break room and ask breathlessly about a mouse click on an out-of-date PC. These people must think I'm mad. I wonder if I am mad. But all I want to do is click that mouse, to send that signal along the cables and hear that big horn sing. In reality, what's crazy is not me travelling across oceans to see this, but why nobody else wants to wield this power. Where is everybody? Who doesn't want to sound an icon? I bet if there was a chance at switching on the torch in the Statue of Liberty, there'd be queues around the block.

Outside it is still sunny, so we stand a heart-wrenching

metre from the computer, chatting awkwardly. There is no way in hell I am going to be allowed to click that mouse button. As my dreams shatter in the strip lighting, I stare at the screen and stall for time, saying small frantic prayers that Phil's walkie-talkie will crackle into life with a fog-based emergency. I have no such luck.

The beautiful weather persists.

I thank them and leave, heading over to the gift shop, dragging my feet in the hope it will bring fog. The gift shop only taunts me. There are playing cards depicting San Francisco fog. There are photos, postcards, magnets, key rings shaped like the bridge that look like they double up as knuckle-dusters. I stump for foggy playing cards, printed on acetate in psychedelic waves of plastic print, so they're particularly difficult to read. There's a snow globe, only it's not a snow globe, it's a fog globe. When you shake it, the bridge is completely engulfed in glittery grey swirls, until it settles in liquid drifts. It is $30. I want it.

I head off on foot across the bridge, keeping my eyes on the horizon in case a fog bank rolls in. It is, so far, a crisp line, bright blue against the aquamarine waters of the Bay.

Crossing the Golden Gate Bridge is a pretty ugly affair on foot, even on a day like this. The bridge thunders with traffic under my feet, the noise is deafening, the pollution heavy and the air has a choking feel of gasoline and dust. Despite this, the bridge's footpaths are full of life. People are coming to and from the city, tourists are admiring the view, and there are runners sweating in vests. I can see dolphin pods down in the water, gulls swooping low over the surface, a huge seal twirling its fat body like a brown ballerina.

At the midpoint of the bridge, I stop.

At this point, with the sun bearing down, I estimate that I'm standing just above the most iconic fog signals in the world. Nobody seems to pay attention to this spot as they stream past in shorts on hired bikes, in spaghetti straps and sunglasses, not least because, with these clear skies, it is not sounding. If this bridge were mired in fog, there would be no missing this beastly chorus. Underneath me there is not one but three foghorns, one facing east and the other two west. Together, they sound as two blasts: a one second blast, followed by a two second pause, then another one second blast. After a 36 second pause the pattern repeats. Some reports say that it'll blow you out of your car seat if you manage to time your passage over it when it sounds. I will have to trust this is true, because the horizon is still horribly perfect.

Over in Marin County, I make it to the headland and hike along the roads and footpaths that snake around the hills, passing a disused Nike missile silo and cyclists streaming down the winding asphalt roads. Most people are here to walk, cycle or drive to a viewpoint and look back at the city. Further along, to the other side of the highway on this side of the Bay is Sausalito, where the hippies moved when the city started to turn, and where Fleetwood Mac went to record *Rumours*. It is a surprise to find landscape like this so close to the city – the rolling, desert-like scrub, wild and open and under-populated. Once I get off the road and onto the hiking path, the sun gets hotter, and I make a hat from my map. I can't remember the origami, so I end up with a sort of paper wimple for my pilgrimage.

At Rodeo Beach I paddle in the icy Pacific until my feet go numb. The sand is coarse and muddy, a strip of brown across the mouth of a reedy lake. The wading birds creech over the sound of Pacific breakers, which are almost big enough to surf. Behind the waves I hear a pair, or a triplet, of bell buoys – I cannot parse them – but they jangle in dissonant carillon.

But still, there is no fog.

It's rare to have so many fogless days. During the foggiest summer months the horns often sound for over five hours a day, and can be on for days.

I lean against a bleached log, run my fingers through the sand. I think I am finding seashells, but when I open my eyes they turn out to be discarded pistachio shells. What I thought might be coral turns out to be sand-coated chewing gum. Feeling the creeping sense of failure, I begrudgingly settle for the clanging of the bell buoys like a child settling for fruit instead of an ice cream.

Then I notice a white band on the horizon between the sky and the sea, as if a zip has opened to reveal creamy flesh. A paleness is spreading out without edges. It sits behind the line of buoys, a band where the bright golden light of the late afternoon sun is swallowed. The bells ring in a session.

The fog is coming.

From the beach I follow a trail up around the headland. The haze seeps in, tendril-like and curling as if searching out the land. It lacks the bulk of a proper San Francisco fog, but I track the mist, follow the road around to Point Bonita lighthouse where Maloney fired his gun relentlessly into the fog over a century ago. The lighthouse is inaccessible – it can only be reached two days a week, when a door in a tunnel in the rock is opened – but from the thin band of rock that leads from the path to a rocky point I can see the sunset and the incoming fog on one side, the Bay and the bridge on the other, as the light turns from gold to pink.

From here, I hear the small *peep*. It is similar to Southend's pier siren, and is barely noticeable. It's not the bridge's horn, but it's something – a thin beep for a thin mist. It's not much, but it'll do. I stay and listen until the sun falls behind the horizon.

It is from Point Diablo, a small signal that sounds all the time. Over here, where Point Bonita and the steep hillsides reflect the sound back into the waters of the Bay, there are few houses, and so there is nobody to disturb.

Once the light fails I head back to my hostel, past the missile silo, now an eerie military–industrial memorial, and hear a coyote call echoing off the surrounding hills. It could be coming from anywhere on these low-slung ranges. From the scrub in the low light a vulture circles. I sprint the winding driveway as the last light leaves the landscape.

On my final day in the city a proper fog rolls in. It is exactly how I'd read it described – like a 'floating island'. It is con-toured and defined, and I watch it as it courses into the Bay like liquid nitrogen. I get up, throw clothes on and book a cab to take me all the way to the Golden Gate Bridge. I cannot hear a horn from the flat when I leave, but I put my faith in Tyndall's mystical phenomena – just because I can't hear it from here, that doesn't mean it isn't sounding.

When I get there the fog is hanging stubbornly high over the bridge, barely brushing its tips. I take a photo but it just looks like I have a grey thumb over the top half of the lens. I sit shivering in the park beneath, clutching a watery coffee and begging this high cloud to become low fog, watching for movement that will signal the need for the horns. By closing time it still sits too high.

As I pack, I retreat into music, and decide to spend my last evening doing the next most San Francisco thing, and listen to the Grateful Dead, my ears on a hair trigger for something, anything, that sounds even remotely like a horn, because, I realise, the soundtrack to the Dead's days here was the foghorns. Janis Joplin, The Grateful Dead, Sly and the Family Stone, some of The Beats – all would have experienced the everyday sound of the San Francisco foghorns. I wonder what it was to hit a show, hear Jerry Garcia jam at the Fillmore East, on legendary engineer and chemist Owsley Stanley's acid, and stagger out, tripping, into a foggy dawn to hear a foghorn fanning out into the valley of Haight Street from the Golden Gate.

Mike Jay, in his history of mescaline, writes that Allen Ginsberg, tripping on peyote, looked out of the window of the Nob Hill apartment he was staying in, 'into a city of mist and fog' which conjured a monstrous vision that became the idol Moloch in the second book of *Howl*.[8] If so, were the foghorns sounding when Moloch was conjured from the fog?

It's reductive to say that music always carries with it the places where it was made. Sometimes it is intentional – the Stooges and Detroit techno crews were actively trying to bring the sound of that city's car factories into their music, in repeated beaten metal and hard-forged rhythms. At other times musicians become pigeon-holed by stereotypes of the places they come from – sunshiney music comes from sunshiney places, it often goes. But it makes a sort of sense that the foghorn, as a surreal technological hallucination of the Industrial Revolution, should have as its permanent home this city where so much acid was consumed.

Considered like this, perhaps my hypnogogic hearing of the foghorns on that first morning I awoke jet-lagged in the city was more appropriate than being able to stand on top of it, or hear them from the headland. It was a sound that sat around the city, that seeped into bedrooms in early mornings, stuck to fuzzy hearings that come and go between states of sleeping and waking, sobriety and intoxication. This threshold between conscious states is the way Rebecca Solnit experiences it too: 'A bed is a ship of sorts,' she writes, 'but a foghorn can't prevent the collisions that may take place there, awake or asleep'; the sound of the foghorn lets her know what is there, 'beyond the reach of our senses'.[9]

Getting up close was something only lighthouse keepers and their families ever really did. Most heard it like I did in that San Francisco bedroom – half awake, half asleep, half cut. The faraway sound of a foghorn seeps into the silence of these transitional states before the waking day brings radios, coffee machines, housemates and children. Early morning hearings bleed into subconscious states, these centuries-old sounds coming briefly inland; that have been present and connected in the history of science and shipping, but remain in a blind spot, hidden by hills and headlands, acoustic clouds and mystical echoes.

There are fewer horns in San Francisco now than ever, according to the founder of the US Lighthouse Society, Wayne Wheeler. In terms of horns with a booming presence, he says there is just the horns on the Golden Gate Bridge and a small air horn at the Berkeley marina, as well as beeps like at Point Diablo.

Just because the foghorn is loved here doesn't mean it's any less obsolete than anywhere else – they might still have a function, but few of the vessels on the water are actually using them. I headed home to find out just how little the foghorn is needed now, and to work that out, I was going to need to get aboard a boat.

13
Pelagic

When I get home from San Francisco, I head up to the port of Peterhead in Aberdeenshire, the largest fishing port in the UK. In 2018, 170 thousand tonnes of fish were landed here. It is a town built around and populated by those involved in the fishing industry. I am staying in a cheap lodging room, usually occupied by the men who come on and off the boats in between stints at sea away from family and friends. It is an in-between place and the walls sweat with the psychic leftovers of loneliness and impermanence.

The room is big but feels empty, the cheap divan bed rolls around on a vast expanse of laminate floor – any quick movement sends it sliding as if to replicate the rolling of a ship. I wonder if this is intentional. The magnolia and dusty pink floral wallpaper is faded, the furniture chipped; a small off-brand TV on the wall feels miles away, and down the hall, through fire doors that are sticky with decades of cream gloss paint there is a shared bathroom that has the aftershave-y odour of generic men's toiletries. It's clean, but also completely soulless, so I leave in the low light to find dinner.

It is grim weather – an unrelenting oppressive mizzle

winnowing into creases in my clothes, around my cuffs and waistband. A warm golden light shines from the fish and chip shop on the high street like light from heaven. I queue up with men who are all of a certain age, with similar haircuts and similar practical-casual clothes – blue jeans and proper outdoor jackets and T-shirts with brand names printed across the front. They have the same hands and necks, skin ruddy and hard. I ask one if I can borrow a lighter as we stand outside, and he warns me to watch my eyebrows as the bright plastic leaps alive with a pointed blue flame, specially designed to withstand high winds. I go to the nearest newsagents and buy one immediately.

I order chips doused in salt and vinegar, wrapped, tuck the warm paper package under my arm and walk through the suburban semis to the shore. I sit with my back against the sea wall where I can shelter in its curve. The weather is too heavy to see the sun go down, and as day turns to night the horizon and the sky fades to a grey-blue gloaming. A mist hangs over the distant sea, yellow streetlights illuminate the industrial debris on the beach below where a large cable spindle washes against the rocks. The breakers are big and chalk-white, driving in on huge swells.

I inhale salty chips that steam with vinegar, the cold wind on my face as a fog rolls in, heading straight for me and my chips. It comes in imperceptibly, stealing detail on the swells as they course into land. Then the fog signal starts up, a thin beep emanating from the electric glow of the port just round the curve of the coast. Three seconds, every thirty seconds.

Against the wall I am unseen and unseeable to all but the fog, which rolls in off the sea. Invisible and alone, I am far from home and feel I have escaped, although I'm not sure what from. I don't have to be back for anyone; I have no work, no errands to run, nobody to call or email, and there is nothing waiting for me apart from my depressing temporary lodgings. I watch, and listen, sit with the foghorn and the fog and wait to be swallowed whole, until my fingers freeze, my nose begins to run, and the chips are finished. I head to the pub. There is one major benefit to places with transient, mostly male populations: the beer is well kept.

I walk in with something to read and a thirst on from the chill of the wind and the salt and grease of dinner, and the freedom of being separated from my normal routine – of emails, deadlines, and regular mealtimes. The other men in the pub (it is only men) stare at me while talking with pals, or look from the corner of their eye at me while not reading the paper, trying to work out who I am and why I am here, alone, in a Scottish fishing port in winter, drinking on my own on a weeknight. I do not want them to ask me, and try to prepare an answer so vague or boring it prompts no further questions.

Explaining that I am on the trail of the foghorn, and how I am fascinated by its magic and meaning, often only prompts further questions from strangers, mostly a long series of whys. I love the sound, am drawn to it, but I still can't understand why, and explaining the knots of power, safety, music and nostalgia I am trying to understand sometimes doesn't make sense to those who have spent their lives at sea using it as a functional warning sound.

Those who heard foghorns day in, day out have often been bewildered by my obsession – when you actually use a sound its familiarity can mute its absurd power. It is no longer special, rendered an ordinary and unremarkable background sound. I have fresh ears to hear it with, for better or worse, and my distance from it is what generates my fascination – I grew up in a landlocked county and heard no foghorns as a child, and so when I did hear it as an adult, its strangeness was amplified by my lack of familiarity with the sound. And now, somehow, I am here. This ought to be a sad state of affairs – the miserable room, the oppressive weather, the lonely pint. But in moments like these I am giddily happy. I have escaped the grind of a nine to five. I am watching, listening, writing; learning things about wind-proof lighters and what this coastline is like. I'm on my own time, my own buck, my own two feet – and it's brilliant.

It is hard to find magic in something you know well, in something you hear day in, day out. The foghorn to those at sea might be as inconspicuous as a kettle whistling, or a microwave ping. In moments like this in the pub, I want to remain inconspicuous too. Sometimes I feel daft for imbuing the horn with so much meaning; for spending so much time thinking about it, reading about it, searching for it. The previous week I had sent Brian what I had written about the foghorn at Sumburgh, the horn and its engines he maintained and sounded, and which he was fighting to be able to keep switched on. Even he was surprised – he said he'd never really thought about the sound of the foghorn being moving, or people becoming attached to it, and joked that 'familiarity breeds contempt, as they say'.

Alone in the dank streets of Peterhead after dark, the fog signal still beeping, it is clear what role the sound of the foghorn has to play for a place like this – it is a sonic link between those on their way in and those on their way out, those fishing near the coast and the people left at home listening.

Foghorns fix places for people otherwise on the move. At Cape Race, the foghorn eventually installed was the first sound of land that transatlantic ships would hear. But there are vast differences in how a modern trawler and a Victorian ship hear a foghorn. When the foghorn arrived in the late nineteenth century, steam ships were becoming dominant, but by the time foghorns were switched off, containerisation was growing at an exponential rate. As foghorns became familiar sounds, huge changes were happening in the construction of vessels big and small. Now, the sounds of the eternal worlds of sea and wind, of historic sound signals, are muted.

The following day I visit the wheelhouse of a brand new pelagic fishing vessel that can hoover up twenty tonnes of mackerel per minute through a suction pipe attached to the ends of its nets. It is like being on the deck of a spaceship. It is warm, hermetically sealed, ergonomically designed. It is spotless.

The skipper sits at a control desk in a huge chair, surrounded by screens that make no sound but show coloured blobs, maps, charts. Each piece of equipment has sound alerts, but all the tech is made by different companies, and those companies do not take into consideration the fact that their device will be one of many used. He intimates that all the manufacturers think theirs is the most important piece of equipment, so while the screens are all switched on, if he had all of the sounds on too, it would be a useless cacophony.

We can still see out of the window, but not hear the outside world. It is silenced by the heavy glass, and sounds are present mostly as translations. The deep-sea fishing industry has become visual, the fish under the waves turned into sound waves, the alarms switched off and the lights on screen flashing. Similarly, in Second World War films, the submarine is 'seen' when it sounds an echo – the terror of the ping heard inside the sub is the terror of being seen by the enemy. This vessel spots fish using echoes: I watch the red streak on the silent computer screen, a shoal of fish, detected by sound, silenced upon their return to the boat. This tech was an accidental by-product of advancements in taking depth measurements – also called soundings.

The topography of the sea comes to us in sound waves and the topography of the land comes through light and sight. This land–sea binary works in a sensory yin and yang of seeing and hearing, earth and water, and the foghorn becomes a theatrical, industrial counterpart to these inversions, where sound replaces sight in the fog.

Our language for sound is full of watery words – we hear sound *waves*, that travel along ear *canals*. These rippling linguistic textures turn ideas of the visible waves of the sea into invisible waves of sound. At sea, senses become transmuted and confused.

Before she wrote the groundbreaking *Silent Spring*, Rachel Carson wrote three luminous books on the sea, and when she describes the discovery of echo-sounding, her language reflects these sensory inversions: 'operators of the new instruments soon discovered that sound waves, directed downward from the ship like a beam of light, were reflected back from any solid object they met. Answering echoes were returned from intermediate depths, presumably from schools of fish, whales or submarines; then a second echo was received from the bottom.'

Echo-sounding sparked a mystery, comically known as the 'phantom bottom'. This was what looked like a solid sea floor, something the echoes bounced back, but was nowhere near the bottom. It was thought to be an inanimate object of some sort, and prompted some Atlantis-like claims that sunken islands had been discovered. It was found to move towards the surface at night and sank during the day, apparently repelled by light. The echoes were later found all the way from Pearl Harbor to the Arctic. It turned out to be mesopelagic fish – tiny creatures that rise and fall at different depths to feed on plankton.

The knowledge that once guided ships has been passed down through generations (and improved upon with scientific and technological advances), but the unpredictability of the sea remains, whether you navigate by stars or by screen. A vessel like this, built for the open sea, is often out of reach of the foghorn. The writer Jonathan Raban, who I quoted earlier, described being out at sea as being in a true wilderness: 'I cannot imagine a solitude more absolute than that of being in a small boat on a rough sea out of sight of land – or even in sight of it for that matter. You are genuinely alone in nature, a creature of the weather and tides, thrown back on fundamental skills like navigation and seamanship.'

Sealed in the cosy wheelhouse surrounded by flashing screens, though, there is not much wilderness at hand. The foghorn too is inaudible and obsolete, superseded by the satellite and GPS technologies that can give a better read on position than the foghorn or lighthouse ever could.

The sound I'd heard sitting on the seafront with my chips was almost meaningless to this fishing vessel, a feeble remainder of a maritime past, perhaps a sound that meant home and safe harbour, but little more. For this vessel, with its sensors and data reads, safety has improved, and is found in the accuracy of the technology, not in shaky attempts to gauge location by eye or ear from lighthouses and foghorns. I wondered how it had changed for other ships. A foghorn would not be used to aid navigation unless everything else failed, and then only to make the last crawl into harbour. The fog signal I had listened to the previous night was probably barely noticed by most crew. I wondered if everyone even knew it was there.

14
Even small boats carry radar

Mike Nicholson went to sea at seventeen. Over the next fifteen years he worked his way up the ranks to captain, before 'swallowing the anchor' and becoming a harbour master in the north-east of England.[1] When he first went to sea there were thirty-five crew members aboard, but when he left there were just ten. 'I've used most lighthouses around the UK,' he tells me over the phone, but says he doesn't remember much navigation using fog signals. For him they were 'a last resort', mainly used by smaller boats. When you're travelling round the coasts you don't need much because you can usually see bits of land, he explains, but deep-sea sailing is a different matter.

He recalls trying to find the mouth of the Amazon, pre-satellite navigation – he had been in fog and cloud for ten days and had no reliable position. The river has a huge bar, a sandbank twenty-five miles offshore with only one gap big enough for his ship to get through. 'We waited for twelve to eighteen hours for sights, to try and locate ourselves,' he says. 'Then a ship came out the other way and seemed to know where it was going, so I just slipped in after.'

While he didn't use foghorns, he does remember being haunted by their sound. The one he most remembers was in the treacherous waters of the Pentland Firth: 'It was not a nice call,' he says. 'It was a very discordant "waking the dead" sort of call – like something from beyond the grave, or I suppose, something to keep you out of it.

'When it's foggy, it's usually still and calm, so it's eerie and your senses are attuned,' he explained. 'So when you heard something like that, it would make you double check your radar because it would sound closer than it was.'

I ask Mike if he remembers how sounds and navigational techniques changed from his first ship compared to his last, but he says it's like your kids growing up – you're there all the time, so you don't notice the incremental shifts in technology until it's happened. 'It creeps up on you,' he says. 'But then, when you look outside, the view around you mightn't have changed for millions of years.'

For those who live and work at sea, the experience has changed dramatically in ways that have come to render the foghorn obsolete. The horns I have heard close up – Souter Point, Nash Point and Sumburgh Head – are no longer sounded for mariners marooned in fog but are sounded for tourists and enthusiasts like me. Air travel too has distracted us and distanced us from the sea. Now, not many of us travel by water, and most of us that go to the coast are unlikely to be as aware of its dangers as those in the nineteenth century, despite the fact that journeys remain as risky as ever to those without the luxury of technology or well-maintained boats.

In *Fish Story*, his photography monograph on containerisation, the artist Allan Sekula writes about how these changes mean that ports are now often also relocated outside cities, and so are invisible to those who depend on them (which is almost everyone) – 'the metropolitan gaze no longer falls upon the waterfront, and a cognitive blankness follows', he writes. The maritime industry calls this 'sea blindness' – referring to a disconnect between how reliant we are on the sea for trade and supply, and people's awareness of it. In the UK, for example, the chair you sit on, the cushion, the cushion cover, the tablecloth, the computer and the TV, the books and the pens, the tea in your mug and perhaps even the mug, may have arrived by boat.

We still need ships, but these ships have changed, and increasingly do not need navigational aids such as light-houses and foghorns. Some of the biggest container ships in the world come down the Thames, and when they do they dwarf the landscape, gliding like space stations down towards the port. The wheelhouse towers above the landscape, the pier's fog signal like a mouse trying to grab the attention of the moon.

The installation of silent coastal navigation aids such as radar and radar beacons, and on-board positioning equip-ment such as GPS and satellite, mean that ships like this don't use the pier's foghorn, and probably don't even hear it. The only vessels that now need them are some small pleasure craft and kayaks, but these days, even the tiniest craft usually have access to GPS in one form or another.

GPS and satellite positioning can map on screen a vessel's exact position much better than the human ear can map a position upon hearing a foghorn sounding from the cliffs. In the *Marine Quarterly* I find an article from 2012 by a mariner called Annie Hill, who writes how GPS can make fog transparent, if you can navigate only using electronic instruments. It is a blessing in fog, she says, because it means that you can get back to land safely when completely blinded by the weather. Without this, you might have had to anchor in place till it lifted, which could have been several days.

However, ships and navigational aids are tied more tightly than just in terms of usage and obsolescence. The lighthouse boards are funded by what are called 'light dues', which are taxes paid at port, depending on cargo or tonnage; taxes that pay for the maintenance and running of the navigational aids in that coastal region. Containerisation means that foghorns are obsolete for the larger ships, and it's the larger ships that pay the highest light dues to keep them running. They see no reason why they would need to pay fees to a lighthouse board for something that almost none of them are using any more.

I called up Captain Phillip Day, the director of operations for the Northern Lighthouse Board, to ask about how the way ships use sound signals has changed in his lifetime. Day started his career on petrol tankers built in the late fifties and early sixties, and by the time he came ashore to work for the lighthouse board, he was working on a brand-new shuttle tanker.

The difference between the experience of working aboard the ships he began on and the one he ended on were enormous, he says. While the ships built in the 1950s didn't technically have open bridges, they remained open to the elements, and he explains how the wheelhouses were always cold and draughty. 'You always had the downwind bridge door open,' he explains, 'you always had a listening watch.' A listening watch was a shift spent listening for sound signals from foghorns, bells or the horns of other ships. The new shuttle tanker, on the other hand, had a comfortable closed bridge with electronic charts, digital radars, GPS and other positioning technology. In the former, the foghorn can be heard, and there is someone listening out for it. In the later ship, the wheelhouse crew are largely sealed off from the outside world.

I was beginning to understand just how dramatically the vessels that sail the world's seas and oceans have changed since the foghorn arrived. It's a bit like comparing a horse-drawn carriage to a Tesla, if you consider that when the foghorn arrived clipper ships with masts and sails were still around, just about, and I had recently stood in a wheelhouse that felt like it was built for space travel, not fishing. A ship's crew is now differently exposed to sound, and their world may be one of white-noise engine rooms or the bleeps of digital screens, but is unlikely to include the sound of foghorns.

Day explains that regulations still require ships to have an audible watch, and for this there is a standard workaround to having someone stand outside – the addition of a microphone and speaker. The microphone is mounted onto the outside of the ship, and it plays through to the cosy wheelhouse. The bluster from the mic means that unless the vessel is in fog, low visibility or in busy waters, the speaker is switched off, closing off even a bad feed of the soundscape outside. 'The only time it tends to get switched on is when you are navigating in fog, and then all you can hear is your own fog signal,' says Day. Anyone who's tried to record sound in even a light breeze will tell you that this is more like listening to a detuned radio than it is a useful connection to the sound of your surroundings. 'The rules allow this speaker,' says Day, 'but the reality is it just gets drowned out by noise from wind. It's like if you're standing talking on your phone in a windy place, it's exactly that, and it's hopeless.'

The foghorn arrived with a transatlantic maritime boom in the second half of the nineteenth century, but this industry took a swift one-two in the post-war period. The jab was from containerisation, and the hook was commercial flights. British shipping and maritime industries declined enormously, although the City of London remained one of the world centres for ship broking.[2] The stats track a tumbling graph for Britain's maritime status whichever way you look at it. For example, in 1913 Britain had 61 per cent of the world's merchant shipbuilding market (one sixth of which 'thundered down the slipways of the Clyde shipyards' according to historian Ian Friel) but by 1997 the proportion was down to 0.7 per cent, with Japan and South Korea receiving 80 per cent of new ship orders.[3] The numbers of workers employed on docks in London was 32,000 in 1955, but only 3000 in 1985 despite more weight coming through ports.

When container ships arrived in the 1950s, their size and capacity grew exponentially, as did the tech they used, and they now represent around a quarter of the world's total shipping. We're now in the era of the mega-ship, with the biggest vessels sailing between Asia and Europe, as well as huge tankers, bulk carriers and, more recently, mega-cruise ships.[4] Britain's maritime boom is now well and truly over, and it has become forgetful about its status as a small island. Still drunk on its own nineteenth-century excesses, the post-European hangover is now waiting in the wings.

As coastal trade changed, it meant that maritime navigational needs changed too, leading to some foghorns being
switched off around the UK, many around the time lighthouses were automated. Automation was a massive project,
which looked to cut the high costs of manned stations by
transferring lights to automatic control from a central headquarters. This long-winded process of transferring lights and
foghorns to automatic operation happened over decades.[5]
While some stations could be controlled automatically much
earlier, it really began in earnest in the 1970s, coinciding
with the deepest decline of the maritime industry in Britain.
The lighthouse boards were not blind to this. An internal
memo from the 1970s at the Northern Lighthouse Board
states that the lighthouse redundancies that were coming
because of automation needed to be handled with care, due
to the 'national mood of depression and unemployment'.

Initially, foghorns proved more difficult to automate than
the lighthouses, and actually slowed the project down. The
reasons are easy to understand even for the most technologically illiterate of us – how does one automate two engines
like the ones Brian had started for me on Sumburgh? How
to put the little cap of petrol in, adjust for rattles? And
then there was the problem of sensing for fog. This had
always been done by a keeper, who watched a particular
checkpoint at that site – at Sumburgh it was when Horse
Island, its halo of spray and the yellow scrub across its back,
was covered in fog.[6] One ex-keeper told me a story about
an attempt to automate foghorns with a sensor trigger, the
idea being that when fog was detected, the foghorn came
on. But the triggers were initially too sensitive, would get set

off by rain – or once, a swarm of moths – and locals would complain about foghorns being set off needlessly.

However, over twenty years after the main body of the automation project got underway, the last lighthouse keepers waved goodbye to their stations for the final time. The last lighthouse keeper in Scotland left Fair Isle South lighthouse on 31 March 1998, and the last Trinity House keepers left from the North Foreland in November of the same year, at a station a few miles round from where Tyndall did his testing sessions. The last keepers in Ireland had left the year before, from the Baily lighthouse on Howth Head. When they left, it brought an end to a 200-year history of lighthouse keeping. When the flag was lowered at Baily in Ireland, the *Irish Times* reported that one of the former lighthouse board employees was heard whispering that the lifeboats brought to take them off station were their hearses.

Lots of the keepers loved their jobs – it was well paid, and if you could get into the rhythm you had a few weeks of work on the lighthouse then a few weeks of absolute freedom. The pensions were good and some of the keepers say they still wear parts of their uniforms, which were high quality and hard wearing. In Scotland, the last keeper was the late Angus Hutchinson, who saw his redundancy coming. 'When the Russians and Americans put satellites up in space, that was the beginning of the end,' he told reporters at the time. The last keeper at the North Foreland, Dermot Cronin, told the BBC: 'A lighthouse was meant to be lived in . . . ships passing, day or night, knew there was somebody there, looking at them.'

Ian Duff, a keeper for the Northern Lighthouse Board who was stationed at Skerryvore and Duncansby Head, among other places, remembers the beginning of automation. He recalls it beginning with a five-year effort to automate Barra Head in the late 1970s, when he thought that if it was taking five years per lighthouse, his job would be safe, but then soon enough there were more and more lighthouses being automated each year. 'The writing was on the wall,' he said, 'and maybe what Angus [Hutchison, the last lighthouse keeper at Fair Isle] said was right, the day they put satellites in space was when the days were numbered.'

Progress is not a one-sided coin. The flip side is often obsolescence, for someone or something. Many of the people still around who remember foghorns, like Ian Duff, are also those who watched industries fail or careers wither.

All Trinity House lighthouses and fog signals are now controlled in Harwich in Essex, from a grey, blocky building next to a vast warehouse that houses buoys and other navigational equipment. They also take over the monitoring of Irish and Scottish lights at night. I have sent multiple emails to ask if I can have a look, and a nearby ex-keeper has been in to physically make my request for me. It has taken months of requests to be granted access to what may seem a fairly underwhelming room, but to me is a missing piece of my puzzle.

In the foyer at Harwich I am greeted by an information officer for Trinity House, who wears a flimsy veneer of politeness. I can feel his annoyance radiating in my direction, but perhaps he is just disdainful of researchers demanding his time. I am sure entertaining foghorn enthusiasts is not part of his job description. After explaining to me what a foghorn is, he asks me what exactly it is I want to know. I explain that what I want to know is, if all lighthouses and foghorns are centrally controlled from Harwich, what on earth is that control room like? More importantly, what does it sound like?

Yet again, it is an anticlimax.

He ushers me into a room that is like many other ordinary offices, and is all but silent. There are five or six people working, mostly in cubicles on the other side of the room. The furniture is beech-effect laminate and there is a powder-blue industrial carpet. Near the door there is a high reception desk with one man sitting behind it, and on the wall are eight screens, which they set to show various maps, alerts, and live news. At the time, a storm had been through the UK, and one of the people who worked here set up what they tagged 'Windy TV' – an on-screen live map of the nation blotted out by fluorescent pink and white clouds obliterating the UK during the storm.

For a foghorn to sound, a signal is triggered on site by a fog detector, which shows in a green box on a panel here, on the screen that lists the various navigational aids. I ask if there are any sounds made in the room. There is an alarm system, the chap behind the desk says, for when something isn't working properly. On screen there is a list of faults in red, most of which are not really faults, but doors being opened to let in engineers, or some such. New ones pop up in a box on the right of the screen. The alarm beeps from a small metal box in the corner, but they have it switched off – 'It would go off all the time, so we turned it off,' he says.

My host points out to me that the network of navigational aids around the UK is still essential. There is a chance

of human error and failure in electronically powered positioning technologies, so the network of lights and sounds
around the UK acts as a backup.[7]

I ask him few more questions, but I feel unwelcome, like
he is offering to help mostly in order to get me out as soon
as possible. Nobody in the room is looking at me, and I
hit a wall of apathy and give up. I thank him and leave,
climbing back in my car and driving off less than half an
hour after I had parked.

While there are no lighthouse keepers living at lighthouses
any more, it's not quite true to say there are no more keepers.
There are (mainly dotted around difficult-to-access Scottish
islands) retained keepers such as Brian who sounded the
horn for me on Sumburgh. None of these live on site, and
they don't work weeks or months on before taking time off.
They're people who do engineering and maintenance, fixing
broken optics and polishing the brass, or clearing up after a
bird strike.[8] They are still there, and, like Brian, they'll often
switch the foghorn on for you, if you ask nicely.

In reading about the decline of foghorns in the UK,
the link to automation of the lighthouses and winding
down of lighthouse keeping, as well as to industries such as
ship-building, I realised that the *Foghorn Requiem* was not
about the death of the foghorn so much as the death of
industry. The foghorn was associated with that working life,
that landscape, that industry. When it was switched off, it
became an industrial monument to a dead sound. It is at once
the sound of an industry and its death knell, a link between
present-day absence and past prowess. As Mike the harbour
master had said, it was a sound from beyond the grave but one

that kept you out of it. We become shaped by what we live, work and pass through, and our lives absorb the soundtracks to our experiences, becoming deeply entwined with our biographies.

15

Harbour symphonies

Sound and music can transport us; can act upon us like Proustian time machines. Every hearing person has sounds that trigger memories, that are associated with certain places. The sound of the Drifters' 'Saturday Night at the Movies' calls back not just my mum's old Ford Escort, but its smell, its damp, the time the broken sunroof tipped rainwater on the piano teacher we did not like. Summer at my parents' home is the sound of a fat wood pigeon in the garden, drifting through the window in my hot attic bedroom. There is an early noughties pop song I can no longer identify but sometimes still hear, which is the defining sound of a summer romance abroad aged sixteen. 'Peg' by Steely Dan means my thirtieth birthday in Tokyo, in a karaoke booth where we couldn't work out how to change the tune so sang it six times in a row. An obscure remix of a 1980s Lebanese group titled 'Tanki Tanki' is directly associated with dance floors lifting off for extended freak-outs with friends who have since become extended family.

Sounds associated with places we know might not be ones we're explicitly conscious of, or which we can easily recall, but hearing these sounds again, particularly unexpectedly, triggers a response. Not all sounds register in the same way – the sound of a fridge, or a fan, might be constants in our day-to-day lives, but these are ones we often tune out, ones we do not 'hear' until they are switched off. Like Liz who said that the wind on Shetland was a sound bed she tuned out and didn't notice until it was gone, our relationships to the sounds of places are ones that can be triggered by finding them elsewhere, or losing them.

In Sweden the pedestrian crossings have two-speed clicks, and at quiet junctions at night, the clicks pulse distinctively in an accidental minimalist composition. When my partner and I lived apart, this was the sound of early rising on cold mornings to get the pre-dawn bus to the airport – it was the sound of goodbyes, an ugly emotional gear shift from a life together to life alone again. When I cycle along the coast to my office, I pass the amusement arcades, where for a long time the rows of claw machines played a phased rendition of Jean-Michel Jarre's 'Oxygène'. Hearing it again now takes me back to damp mornings on empty seafronts (of me getting up late, again). The music has since changed to rushy trance music, and the seafront sounds out of joint.

The sound of the foghorn is a sound with an emotional power and resonance, the rhythmic soundtrack to fog and heavy weather. It has filtered into the collective cultural con-sciousness, canonised in culture after a century of honking in local places for the local people. It has been borrowed, co-opted, for its power to evoke the lonely coastlines on which it stood. In the early twentieth century the foghorn started getting regular cameos in literature, film and music. It has a bit part in the work of Virginia Woolf, and in

that of the previously mentioned Gertrude Atherton, Ray
Bradbury and Nigel Kneale. Iranian artist and poet Etel
Adnan writes beautifully of fog and the foghorn; and in a
poem about the film *Red Desert*, Anne Carson writes that
'A foghorn sounding through the fog makes the fog seem
to be everything.'[1] In Ingmar Bergman's *Persona*, fog and
the foghorn appear in a scene where Elisabeth appears in
Anna's room, sounding danger at the moment where Anna
and the viewer's grasp on reality begins to loosen. It even
sounds a long, loud warning in the psychedelic sci-fi of Jeff
VanderMeer's Southern Reach trilogy.

Once you start looking for something you see it everywhere – it cropped up in a William Gibson short story,
in books on the history of industrial music. I wondered
why I was finding so many foghorn cameos. They appear
in Dire Straits's 'Down to the Waterline'; the Band's 'Whispering Pines'; in Van Morrison's 'Into The Mystic' (as well
as 'Song of Home', 'So Quiet in Here', and 'In Tiburon',
which mentions the San Francisco horn – Van Morrison loves
foghorns). In James Taylor's 'Another Grey Morning' the foghorn's repetition and a baby crying grate on the song's deeply
depressed protagonist. Moondog once spent a foggy day
jamming with the horns on the Hudson River. Elsewhere,
'Pirate Jenny' from the *The Threepenny Opera* – sung best by
Nina Simone and Judy Collins – tells a story of a woman
working in a flophouse scrubbing floors. The foghorn is the
harbinger of a black freighter with a skull on its masthead,
which sails into town and takes murderous vengeance on
the townspeople for their mistreatment of Jenny, who sails
off with the pirates.

Is it any surprise big horns come with heavy baggage?

Trumpets and horns are a summoning, a harbinger. In Judaism, there is the *shofar*, a large ram's horn trumpet. In the Bible, the apocalypse is signalled by seven angels playing seven trumpets. The Tibetan *dungchen* – the Buddhist horn – is said to sound like the singing of elephants. Played with a rising tone like a diaphone foghorn, their purpose is to suppress demons. The foghorn is in one sense just a navigational aid, but in another it is in a family of huge horns with social and cultural connotations.

As a member of this family of sounds, the foghorn becomes a trope, a sort of shorthand for a mood and a feeling: it denotes confusion, disorientation; it signals something is coming, or something has changed. It also calls people home, and its fixed sound can come to represent a place. With all its associations – not just of trumpets and menace, but coastal folklore, bulls and beasts, I wanted to know what happened when foghorns were switched off – did anyone object? In the UK, the coasts used to be mapped in sound, but now few of these markers were left. What does it mean to lose a sound that had come to identify a place so distinctly?

The foghorn was never *just* about aiding navigation. It might only have existed to guide those at sea, but just like the unbounded spread of sound itself, the foghorn reached beyond its function and came to define the soundscape of a place. In the time between their installation in the closing decades of the nineteenth century and through to the 1980s at least, foghorns on coastlines had become, for those who lived there, a sound that represented an entire place.

Turning off a sound that is obsolete is one thing, but for those that lived within earshot, their foghorn had become part of the places they lived, whether in San Francisco or Jersey. They were not just a link to the past, but a part of the present, a reminder of the industries that had formed these places, of the people that had come before. This meant that when automation of the lighthouse service silenced many foghorns, it stirred up feelings lots of people didn't expect. People who had not thought an awful lot about their foghorn would suddenly realise their attachment to it. Lots of people didn't want to say goodbye to the sounds they had grown up with.

When the automation of lighthouses was in full swing in the 1980s, the Northern Lighthouse Board conducted user consultations, where they asked various organisations and businesses whether foghorns were still useful. Even in 1987, very few vessels were still using foghorns to fix their positions, except in dire circumstances. Smaller craft like fishing vessels and pleasure craft, particularly those using harbour horns, often stated that they did still use the horns, although larger vessels and ferry companies often expressed indifference.[2]

Of those that ran larger ships, ferry operators in Corsewall on the west coast of Scotland said they would like to see the use of foghorns continued so that their ferries did not have to help smaller vessels in distress so much. But it was those that sailed smaller vessels who often asked for the horns to be retained. It's acknowledged as 'a thing of the past' for anything other than smaller vessels – the Scottish arm of the Royal Yachting Association expressed 'grave concern', writing that 'from the point of view of the inshore navigator one cannot contemplate the discontinuance of any of these fog signals with other than considerable disquiet'.

When a foghorn was removed there were frequently

objections. La Corbière lighthouse on Jersey had an electric fog signal from the 1970s, but one with a particularly deep and pleasant sound. In people's memories it is remembered fondly – while I was on Jersey multiple people told me that falling asleep to the old diaphone at La Corbière was one of their earliest childhood memories, a sound on the edge of sleep and memory.

When it came time for the foghorn to be switched off in 2015, the harbour consulted with those that would be hearing and using the horn, and with the general public, about how they felt about it being silenced. Many of those consulted admitted that the foghorn was functionally no longer essential to safety at sea, but that it nonetheless would mean a dramatic loss to the soundscape. One respondent said that: 'Corbières would not be the same on a foggy night without the mournful sound of the foghorn', although another noted that 'time has moved on and the foghorn is a relic of times when navigation was an instinctive manual art.' In one letter, the St Aubin's Boat Owners' Association wrote: 'We consider the fog horn to be a unique part of our island heritage and tradition which would be missed by many boat owners.'

The passing of time seemed to have rehabilitated the foghorn while technological developments made it obsolete. What I found looking into these consultations, letters typed on headed paper and bound into volumes or uploaded as massive PDFs, is that it wasn't until the foghorn was due to be switched off that people realised just how much it had formed part of their connection to a place. This has something to do with the way we listen to our environments, what we tune out and what we take for granted.

Light dues have been falling, so maintaining a foghorn and all its machinery, fulfilling health and safety require-ments and paying the staff to maintain it is no longer a priority. In some ways the foghorn's presence is completely in opposition to its actual function. Why should big ships pay to maintain nostalgic attachments to sound?

Alongside protestations against change, foghorns were turned off, but as they began to be lost, switched off, demolished, others were looking to preserve, collect and record their sound.

The World Soundscape Project was a group set up in the 1970s by composer, academic and environmentalist R. Murray Schafer, at Simon Fraser University in Vancouver. Schafer wanted to research and record how people related to sound in their environment, how it was changing, and what it meant to lose sounds as others were gained. The project started locally, in Vancouver, and Vancouver in the 1970s was alive with the sound of foghorns.

The group's influence grew, and now Schafer and the WSP are parents to a whole academic discipline known as acoustic ecology. What they proposed was that since the Industrial Revolution, man-made machines had spread, become noisier, and that the sound world we all live in had deteriorated as a result, becoming more 'lo-fi', where there's lots of ambient sound that means we struggle to pick out detail, as opposed to a 'hi-fi' sound environment which has low ambient sound and in which we can hear more detail and nuance.

Schafer enjoyed the musicality of the world around him – he quotes Norse descriptions of the sea as sounding like boulders being smashed together, and elsewhere describes the 'throb' of water at Ostend in Belgium, or water with a 'recital' and an 'ostinato'.

The book that resulted from the WSP's research, *The Tuning of the World* (later republished as *Soundscape*), remains, for all its faults, a foundational text for those studying how sound features in the soundscape. It helps that it's accessibly written and doesn't fall into the teeth-pulling language of much academic writing. However, it has an axe to grind, and scholars since have enjoyed criticising Schafer's tendency to aestheticise sounds according to his tastes, as a jumping-off point for their own work (myself included).

Crucially though, the WSP described sounds such as foghorns as 'soundmarks' to identify a sonic version of a landmark – a sound that defines a place. There are obvious ones, like Big Ben's bongs, but a soundmark might also be a call to prayer, the songs of street sellers, or the particular jingles of a metro system. It might be the sound of trams in Istanbul, or the dinky fruit trucks that pootle around the streets of Naples blasting prices through crackly loud-speakers.

Foghorns are an easy soundmark to identify – their sounds flow through streets, bleeding from the coasts into towns, villages and hamlets, and are known by those who live, work, or holiday there. They have distinctive character and differ from place to place, and people are attached to them. Vancouver at the time had the Point Atkinson foghorn, and there was also another, particularly unique soundmark in the O Canada horn, a heritage horn that sounds the first four notes of the Canadian national anthem every day at noon.

On a recording the group made called 'Entrance to the

Harbour' there is the sound of the Point Atkinson foghorn, the light sloshing of water on the concrete structure, a small plane passing overhead, a buoy bell ringing out in the bay. Coastal birds tweep-tweep and craw, there are gulls, maybe a wader. A put-putting engine passes by, people come over with strong Canadian accents – 'Hi Neil!' The Point Atkinson diaphone is a one-two – an initial stab of sound that drops for a second, lower gut-punch blast.

Hildegard Westerkamp was a core member of the World Soundscape Project. Arriving to work with Schafer in Vancouver as a young researcher in the 1970s, she developed a practice that now includes composition, radio art, teaching and sound ecology. Her compositional material is the sounds around her, which have been used in Gus Van Sant's *Elephant* and *Last Days*. One of her earliest compositions, *Fantasie for Horns*, is a piece constructed using sound recordings of various horns, stretched and manipulated using analogue studio techniques. I email to ask if she'd have time to talk about it, and she writes back: 'I'd be pleased to talk to you about foghorns, train horns, boat horns etc., even bells if you wish!'

Hildegard tells me that *Fantasie for Horns* was the second composition she ever made, after a piece called 'Whisper Study' which she had recorded to use in a teaching exercise in a class: 'Essentially, I was playing around at that time [in the studio],' she tells me over video from her home in Vancouver. 'But it came out of this incredible fascination for listening to the environment and researching sound.'

She soon found that she loved studio work: 'That type of listening and also the privacy of it,' she explained, 'that you're *with* the sounds and you're getting immediate feedback. You can make a relationship immediately, between what you're hearing and what you want to compose.

'I decided I'd like to work with horns, because they are very musical sounds, very beautiful sounds. The horns here also made me feel very connected to Vancouver. That sense of the harbour and shipping and also the train horns of course – they're symbolic for the hugeness of Canada. They have this very evocative, beautiful sound.'

It was the interplay between the physiological and the psychological ways we hear and listen that she found compelling: 'The thing that interested me the most was the edge between the original horn sound, and then what our own imagination does when we're listening. We're listening to the sound, and we're recognising its beauty, or we're recognising its inner pitch qualities or rhythms. So the processing in the studio symbolised that – it's what we do anyway when we listen – we process, we interpret.'

She also noticed that working closely and intimately with the horn sounds in a studio generated a feeling of belonging. She had been in Vancouver around five years, and says the thing she noticed, 'was that it kind of gave me a more settled sense of home. I felt so much more grounded in Vancouver through this experience. And, you know, maybe I didn't articulate it that way, then in hindsight, that's what happened.'

Fantasie for Horns eventually became two pieces – one solely using studio techniques (*Fantasie for Horns I*) and a second version which also included a French horn (*Fantasie for Horns II*). The second composition is the only one readily available, the first only ever released on cassette. It has what sounds like foghorns, train whistles, ship's horn, the tugboat's air horn. Horns arrive in call and answer, a train careens through a landscape, and their long decays move across a sonic field into atmospheric washes of echoes and resonances without source; there are glugs and bubblings, and a horn sound with its attack spliced out so it is transformed into a solid drone; a high-low honking is followed by the terrifying hee-HAW of the Point Atkinson diaphone.

I notice when listening closely that Westerkamp's compositions are not just about taking sound from the outside world and arranging and manipulating it, but about the context for sound, and what this means for the way we experience our environments. 'We have our relationships to places and it's very meaningful,' she says. 'And so when you're trying to find the deeper sonic qualities of a sound, then you're also discovering the sonic expression of the sounds. In a horn sound, for example, you will hear an echo – you hear the landscape. You may hear some reverberation, you will hear the environment around it – you're not just hearing the sound of the horn. And so immediately it's about these relationships.

'My compositions are all trying to somehow speak about the relationship between us and the environment. And that is emotional.'

Horns came up again for her when she was asked to make a work for the opening of the Canada Place pier and building in Vancouver Harbour, commissioned by the Canada Pavilion for Expo 86. On 2 May 1986, one hundred and fifty ships gathered in Vancouver harbour to perform a piece she had conceived called *Harbour Symphony*. Prince Charles and Diana were meant to be in attendance, but had bailed early because the weather was so foul.

It was played via a simple seven-minute score. The boats were all tuned to the same radio channel over which the seconds were counted and they would play according to the blocks indicated on their score. It was, of course, almost impossible to rehearse. The closest Westerkamp got was to gather the skippers in a room with glass bottles filled with water to blow into, to try to approximate what it might sound like.

She says the chaotic nature of the piece meant she really wasn't sure how well they all followed it. There were over a hundred ships, a train horn, and the O Canada horn also came in at one point. 'It all worked,' she says, 'but I can tell you, when I was standing on the deck of Canada Place, listening, I just laughed, because it's so absolutely the opposite of *Fantasie for Horns*.'

A newspaper at the time wrote that it 'sounded like a herd of happy elephants caught in a traffic jam', a review Hildegard says she thought was an accurate description.

She had seafaring people in her own family, so knew about the relationships of ships and horns and the ocean. 'I was very excited to do [*Harbour Symphony*] because I had never really met any seafaring people in Vancouver,' she says. 'And suddenly I was among so many people who had a strong relationship to the sea. They were all familiar with the foghorns and all those things that I had learned through the World Soundscape Project. So I got a very strong sense of that community and how meaningful this relationship to the sea is.'

Her relationship with the sea was particularly personal, as her brother had died young as a cadet sailor on a ship called the *Pamir* when it went down in a hurricane in the mid Atlantic on 21 September 1957. She dedicated *Harbour Symphony* to him. 'It was a huge event in my family,' she says. 'I was only eleven when it happened.'

It was a chance encounter that led to her dedication. 'I didn't know at that time that the *Pamir* had travelled between New Zealand and Vancouver,' she says. 'I found that people knew the ship, knew it here in Vancouver. Suddenly I discovered all these people who had this really strong relationship to the *Pamir*. One even had some parts of it – a shackle I think. It put a personal note in between some of the people who knew the *Pamir* and myself. It was very, very powerful. I hadn't thought of dedicating the piece to my brother until that happened.'

There have been other, different 'harbour symphonies'. A biennial Sound Symposium in St John's, Newfoundland, invites musicians to compose one, with the idea to fuse the New Year horn sounding with some 'light touch' composition, whereby on each day of the festival the piece is performed from noon by any boat that happens to be in the harbour that day. The architect whose idea it was, Joe Carter, described how in one year 'a low fog had rolled in, the harbour went out of sight and the sound came up like spears through a roaring white blanket'.

Other ship's horn 'concerts' happen fairly regularly. In March 2020 a 'big ship orchestra' of all the ships' horns in the harbour, sounded to commemorate the 150th anniversary of the lighting of Scurdie Ness lighthouse in Scotland. Cruise ships and other vessels in port are known to often honk together to bring in the New Year, including in Vancouver. Sound artist Felix Blume's *Fog Horns* uses as its source material a chorus of boat horns in Athens, Greece.

Cruise ship horn battles are easy to find online, the most graceless perhaps being those between Disney cruise ships, which involves flatulent versions of 'When You Wish Upon a Star'.

In these giant theatres of sound, performances have been dramatically scaled up to fit the landscape, or to fit the power of the foghorn, and in them there is an articulation of place, people and community, whether land-bound or seafaring. In these instances, the foghorn leaves its function behind and is elevated, singing of deeply personal and emotional connections between maritime working lives, histories, lost people and remembered places. In these ship's horn battles, and the honking in of New Year, there is both cathartic release and recognition – for both an industry and its landscape.

The World Soundscape Project is often criticised for being too black and white in its categorisation of natural sound as 'good' and human-made urban or industrial sounds as 'bad'. I had been one of these people, frustrated and rolling my eyes about the apparent lack of consideration for the breadth and complexity of people's feelings on sound and music. Talking to Hildegard, I saw things in a different light. At the time the group was working there were no conversations like this happening in formal ways, and Schafer 'had a tendency to rant, and he had an activist in himself,' she says. He railed against the influx of these sounds in a passionate, brash way, with language that now does not always stand up to scrutiny. His book, *The Tuning of the World*, 'came out of a specific time, the seventies,' says Hildegard, 'when we were all ranting, we were against authority, we were going to change the world, and I loved it, because Schafer had the courage to be a bit loud about all this, and it allowed me – when I was young and much more timid – to lean into this. But really, our main concern was the quality of the acoustic environment. Listening to it was at the base of all our work as a way to viscerally understand and address the ecological balances and imbalances in our soundscapes.'

Meanings, perceptions and experiences of sound depend so much on context. Sound, historically and culturally speaking, is a multi-track happening – sounds from one place make it to another, from the coasts they make it into composition, and sometimes the compositions can occur on a coastline. Listening to the foghorn doesn't just tell you about a history of sound, it also tells you something about a landscape with a past, present and future. It still carries the grief of Foulis, the deaths it was sent to prevent, and the industries it watched waste away.

In identifying soundmarks – these important sonic markers of place – Schafer and the World Soundscape Project had drawn attention to the way we live with sound, the way it affects us, for good and bad, but also how it is connected to the identity of places. Hildegard, in explaining how she had used the recording of the horns as compositional material, seemed to me to have been reaching out for a sound which she associated with this new city that she had only relatively recently begun to call home. The stretching of these sounds was a way to tease out and to try and find a sense of permanence.

This transition, from horns once loathed to ones which people became attached to as they became attached to the places where they were sited – from a navigational aid to a soundmark – was one that changed the way the foghorn itself was heard. However, at the same time, composers and artists like Hildegard, like Alvin Curran and Bill Fontana, found themselves in these places, the foghorn presented a powerful piece of sonic material that could be used in new, avant-garde forms of composition, that could carry the vastness and complexity of a landscape, and the cultural resonances of both trumpets and fog. As these creative projects began to happen, the foghorns carried on being switched off, and as they were discarded, others started to memorialise them in different ways, salvaging, collecting and restoring them to their former glory.

16
The collectors

The most inland lighthouse in the world is on top of Bidston Hill near Birkenhead, lived in and looked after by Mandy and Stephen Pickles. Mandy is a witch, the good sort, Stephen assures me, and in the cottages attached to the lighthouse (parts of which they are converting into self-catering accommodation) they also house the archive of the Association of Lighthouse Keepers. Previously it was kept in the bedroom of Gerry Douglas-Sherwood, the most legendary of all living ex-keepers in the UK.

Gerry has written a glossary of lighthouse terminology and is a vintage motorcycle enthusiast. After leaving the service, his love for his former job remained, and he became a repository for all that had not been taken from lighthouses by professional bodies. He collected what he could, kept what he was allowed to, and as the years turned to decades, people increasingly sent him objects, photo albums, optics, that other museums or Trinity House considered were too small, too inconsequential, or too expensive to store.

Stephen and Mandy are members of the Association of Lighthouse Keepers, and Mandy took over as official protector of Gerry's trove of stuff a couple of years ago.

Stephen has just finished building a prototype digital archive of Gerry's meticulously kept logbooks of his archive. He has given me the first non-admin access to the archive database, and has asked me to pick my favourite lighthouse to set as my temporary password. Apparently Gerry's spare room was stacked to the ceiling with the stuff they have now – visitor books from decommissioned lighthouses, slides, metal canisters of film on a top shelf (nobody knows what's on them yet, and there is no equipment on which to play them, let alone any idea if they're still playable). This stash is almost completely off-grid, institutionally speaking – the equivalent of an outsider art project that has little or no connection to institutions or establishment. That doesn't mean it isn't well organised, though, and Stephen's database means it's now searchable.

There are things here I could never find elsewhere, like a photo album of lighthouses from all over the world. Another contains postcards of almost every lighthouse in the UK. There are albums of photos keepers took of daily life – thumbs leaving a half shot of grinning keepers on sunny boat landings, slightly blurred in navy Trinity House-issued jumpers. There are also shelves of old books; leaflets kept in plastic; rare nineteenth-century volumes on lighthouses whose dust covers are crumbling; self-published pamphlets on local maritime history.

In the middle of the room where I'll be staying is a single bed, surrounded by all this stuff. I imagine absorbing all the memories in the room as I sleep, the photos whirring into life like films, slipping off the shelves into my unconscious mind. The Pickles have set up a little lighthouse lens as a bedside light, mostly as a joke, because despite its tiny size, it is blindingly bright when we switch it on, and flashes in sequence.

I have only arranged to come for a night, and there is both too much here, and too little – I do not know where to start and I do not know where it ends. I am not sure what I wanted from this place, its contents are so different from the other archives. Here, more than anywhere else, is the day-to-day life of a twentieth-century lighthouse keeper, its awe and tedium, the cramped bunks and the luxury of a guaranteed sea view at work. But I am looking for their rogue descriptions of sounds and feelings, accidental anecdotes. I pull photo albums off the shelves randomly and flick through them. Am I here for these lives, or am I here for the foghorn? Are the two things even different?

Every year the number of keepers attending the Association of Lighthouse Keepers AGM diminishes. Gerry is now frail, and one of the well-loved founders passed away a few years ago. In these photo albums are scores of keepers no longer with us. The people and the sounds – the life and the work. The foghorn becomes momentarily invisible to me, obscured by this cache of memories, by a workforce lost and forgotten.

Stephen brings in a small silver stereo for me to plug in on the pasting table set up for me to pore over everything, and shows me a CD-R he found that I would definitely be interested in. It has about ninety tracks, each one a horn recording. The provenance of these recordings is uncertain. Most of them are ghosts, horns that have long been silenced, including twelve different recordings of the siren at Lizard that so disturbed Thomas Hart. I sit on the end of the bed and crane my neck towards the tinny speakers, listening for more than what is there, listening for answers, listening for meaning.

Over dinner Stephen and Mandy put on another CD rip of an obscure recording by an Italian sound artist called Davide Mosconi, a collection of horns and some landscape sounds. It's awkward music to have on over dinner, but suits us fine, although there are swathes of quiet atmosphere of sea and birds, punctuated at intervals with the sounds of foghorns. It's a bit like playing at being lighthouse keepers, complete with foghorn interruptions to our conversation.

The original Mosconi album was on LP, in a plain sleeve with black text running along the bottom edge. It is titled *La Musica Dell'Anno Zero,* the music of year zero, which lends it a post-apocalyptic feel, and it comes with an insert that is a photocopy of a map with the locations of sirens and diaphone horns marked in biro. Mosconi was a composer and photographer, and in the 1970s founded an improvisatory collective called N.A.D.M.A. (Natural Arkestra Da Maya Alt). The recordings on *La Musica Dell'Anno Zero* were made off the coast of Scotland, near Loch Hope and Loch Eriboll where even the nearest road is miles away, never mind a town. It's a collage of sorts, but not manipulated in any way. It is rather a piece of sound art, or a false document, depending on which way you look at it. These field recordings are augmented and exalted, spliced and collaged but not processed with any effects. Like the horns on this record, many of the foghorns I hear on the CD – along with those on film soundtracks and sound effects recordings alike – are now silent. There are stashes of recordings like this made by enthusiasts and collectors, scattered all over the world.

It seems that it is only when faced with things in decline, or at risk of being lost, do people pick up and want to preserve what is already there. We see initiatives to protect parks and buildings and monuments, but with sounds, it is only fairly recently that access to cheap recording equipment has enabled non-professionals to make their own recordings. The foghorn's beginnings predate recording history entirely. Now, if you have a smartphone, you have a really good microphone on hand all the time, but twenty years ago, the same recording quality would have meant equipment the size of carry-on luggage.

I make sound recordings like other people take pictures. It means I don't have to stand still (which I am terrible at) and I don't like pointing my phone at people without their permission. They're not good recordings, but they're my way of capturing what I experience. I have recordings of myself whistling alone in the atrium of the archaeological museum in Naples; the tannoy announcement on the ferry across to Staten Island in New York; the Viking marches of Up Helly Aa in Shetland; a piledriver in Amsterdam; noises from broken speakers on public transport; air conditioners in pub gardens; the thump-thump heartbeat of club toilets as the doors rattle in time with the beat; and the sound of an England World Cup goal broadcast to a side street at Bristol carnival, where dancehall mixed with football chants in a perfect soundclash. I tried to record the Siberian geese that migrate to Essex for winter and provide a constant surround-sound gobbling along from Southend to Leigh, but the mic didn't hear the space like my ears had. I had the time of my life recording the drop-and-roll of the National Bagpipe Band of Oman at the Glasgow International Bagpipe Festival, where the traditional Scottish Highland pipes are augmented with Omani percussion – kasir and rahmani drums – and there's no readily available recordings of that group so they're all I have.

Recordings like this are my notes on place, my snapshots in sound, because listening gives me a way of remembering and understanding the world around me, and of fixing my memories. A sentence transcribed can omit the feeling with which it was delivered; a fault in an engine is heard before it is seen when rattles indicate a problem. Sound is a way of knowing things.

In the early 1990s, years before recording technology became easily portable, a lecturer called Alan Renton started noticing that foghorns in the UK were being switched off. So he applied for support for a project, partly from the British Library sound archive, to record foghorns around the country onto quarter-inch tape with a directional microphone. Trinity House were supportive of his project and he was able to secure funding. From there he just had to call up a keeper the day before and ask if they'd be able to switch the horn on for him.

There was an urgency to Alan's project at the time, as many of the older horns were being phased out and those left were on the cusp of complete obsolescence. 'That was the angle I played on to get the funding,' he tells me over the phone. 'Trinity House knew what the automation programme meant, they knew that within three years or so, maybe five years, of my project, my proposal, the whole service would be wound down.'

He made a note at the time, which listed Trinity House's

fog signals: four sirens, one diaphone, three SuperTyfons, four triple horns, one bell, and about twenty electric horns. Alan didn't bother with all the electric horns, as they were so uniform, he says, but he managed to record the rest.

Alan, like Hildegard, wasn't interested in just the sound of the horns, but in the way the horns picked up the shape of the landscape: 'Us landlubbers usually hear them from the land,' he explains. 'If you hear them out at sea you'd probably hear them a bit more clearly. From the land you're getting all sorts of reverberations and reflections off cliffs and buildings and whatever else. With some of the recordings I would try and point the microphone in the other direction because I was interested in those other sounds – I didn't just want the clearest signal sound, I wanted the ambience. In a lot of them you hear the bird sounds, you hear the water, and you get a [fog signal's] strange note – even if it's just an electric horn, like the one at Falmouth, it's quite an evocative sound. The actual air signals are just terrific, but that 12-inch siren at Pendeen, that was astonishing. If you were anywhere near it when it went off, it was terrifying!'

Alan figured out pretty quickly that there was nowhere where all this information was recorded, particularly the foghorn's technical history, save in the memories and minds of the last generation of lighthouse keepers. Documents would suggest a certain piece of equipment was installed, but the peculiarities of a site meant that plans had changed when it came to installation. He asked keepers, scoured archives, and pieced together an accurate idea of exactly what sound-making machinery was in each place.

Alan only just caught them in time. Five years after his recording project, the last keeper left his station, and just a few years after that he published his book, *Lost Sounds*, which is the definitive work on fog-signalling equipment used around British coastlines.

When I speak to him, it's over twenty years since he closed the project, but he has strong memories of it, of the lighthouses' smells and sounds. 'They always smelled great,' he remembers. 'They've got that greasy smell – the smell of diesel and Brasso, and that sort of strange electrical smell coming from the battery chargers. They were sort of buzzing and alive, you would get this sound wherever you went – a purring noise, before you switch anything on and get it going.'

A month after we chat he emails to say that talking about that time had reminded him of how much he loved it, and he's started to think about putting together a gazetteer of foghorns in the UK. At night, from the top of the hill near his house in Redruth, Cornwall he can see lighthouses, plural, including Falmouth and Trevose Head. He can see St Ives, and on a really clear day, when the lamp was more powerful, he could also see Eddystone from the top of the hill.

Now Alan's recordings are stored in the vast depths of the British Library and can be pulled up on any computer in a reading room, as part of the sound archive. I start writing notes on all of them, on what the fog signals sound like and the spaces in which he recorded them. Some recordings are better than others, sometimes the horn is almost drowned out by the weather:

- Portland Bill lighthouse: fog signal giving one blast every thirty seconds
  Hard and heavy blast that coughs at the end. Militaristic

and combative in tone, it drops like lead, with a rattle
and a splutter at the end that drops the pitch to an
unexpected, belly-rumbling, quivering sound.

- Beachy Head lighthouse: fog signal recorded from main entrance to the lighthouse
The shore, with some movement in the immediate vicinity.
It is much further now, the sound not just quieter, but
somehow muffled, sadder. Why is it that sounds that travel
over open spaces feel more melancholic? Gulls can be heard.

- Longships lighthouse: fog signal recorded from cliffs between Sennen Cove and Land's End
Quiet, coming in at four o'clock in the sundial of my hearing.
Its timbre is piercing, even at this distance, cuts through.

- Lundy South lighthouse: two-tone SuperTyfon fog signal recorded 1500 m away on high cliffs near Shutter Rocks
Very faint, but terrific sound, multiple tones sound at once
like an American train horn. One blast, faltering in the
middle like a train coming in over a mountain pass.

- Pendeen lighthouse: close perspective recording of the twin trumpets and then machinery within the fog signal building
A desperate, short single parp that falls in pitch at the
end, bending downwards as if drooping. It is grizzled,
as if muzzled, or rusty, a slight rattle to the sound.

There is something magical about listening to field recordings. They are as truthful as a photograph, which is to say, imperfect and partial, a sort of time travel through someone else's ears. A recording is a snapshot of a time now past that will never be repeated, and Alan's recordings are nearly all ghosts. They record partial details in a way that forces one to hear what you wouldn't notice if you were there, and excludes things you would be able to see but not hear, like the weather and the light. There may be similar moments, even twenty-five years later when the horn is switched back on after a restoration, but what's captured will never be exactly the same again.

What Alan reminded me of was that the sound of the foghorn, especially for those who lived and worked in its proximity, came with smells and other sounds – the chug of engines, the buzz of the battery chargers – that were not part of most people's experiences of the horns. These sounds were about the intimacy of working with those machines, and they were things that I can never really know, as parts of the keepers' working lives that are now properly of the past.

However, Alan had not worked as a keeper, and like Hildegard and myself, hadn't grown up with foghorns either: 'I'm from the Midlands, so I never saw lighthouses or anything like it for most of my life, apart from when we used to go on holiday to near Berwick-upon-Tweed where my dad was from, where there was a lighthouse on the end of the breakwater. That's about the only thing I can remember of what my first exposure to a lighthouse would have been,' he says. Later, as a film student, he visited South Stack at Anglesey and made a film, and then in the early eighties got a job teaching at the art school in Falmouth, where the horn at St Anthony's Head could be heard all over town. He made a recording, and started digging around, and found that there wasn't a whole lot of documentation of these sounds from around the coast.

At the time he began travelling around recording the foghorns, the lighthouse service was being wound down and automated, and so most of the keepers he met were the last ones to ever work at the lighthouses they were stationed at before everyone was made redundant. 'Of course you'd hear them say things like how the way someone would tap their pen or the way they whistle would just drive you up the wall,' he says. 'But I don't think I met anyone who had ever regretted being a lighthouse keeper.'

The youngest people Alan spoke to were in their forties, because Trinity House hadn't been recruiting for a while. 'They all knew it was happening,' he says.

Alan was one of the last civilians to be able to hear the foghorns and see them operated *in situ* by the people who lived closest to them. He says the only regret he has is that he didn't conduct a proper oral history with the keepers he was meeting, alongside the historical and recording work on the foghorns. It must have made an impression, though, as after he finished the project, he ended up running the lighthouse museum in Penzance.

It strikes me that the people who really got snagged on foghorns, those whose curiosity turned into something more serious, were all people who didn't grow up with the sound of the foghorn, but who were dropped as adults into places where they meant a huge deal – myself, Hildegard, Alan, we'd all had landlocked childhoods, and found ourselves in the presence of these sounds. All of us had enjoyed the introspection of these sounds too, in one way or another. Alan and I had travelled mostly alone on our journeys; Hildegard had loved the isolation of the sounds in the studio. All of us had found meaning in working with these sounds. Perhaps it took people like us, those for whom the foghorn was unfamiliar, to get really preoccupied with the sound, to notice both how ridiculous and evocative it could be, and to start asking what it meant.

As word travelled of my obsession, other people emerged with odd infatuations, who collected not just foghorns, but horns from gargantuan ships, trains, and one holy grail sourced from NASA.

17
Sky trumpets

On YouTube there is a user called BIGMIKESOCAL (all caps). He is huge. One massive flexed bicep fills most of his profile picture and looks big enough to have its own set of abs. Mike's interests include competitive bodybuilding, muscle cars and horns. Big ones, naturally. He has all kinds of horns, from ships, trains and lighthouses. He has the foghorn from Slip Point lighthouse in Washington State; a horn from a freighter that travelled the Great Lakes in the 1950s; a horn from a mega-yacht; 1930s diaphones and Second World War air raid sirens, and something called a Nathan Airchime from a locomotive.

Mike drives a boxy silver car, on which he mounts his collection, hooking them up to compressed air in the boot, and sounding them in the vast echoing landscape or long empty tunnels near where he lives in southern California, blasting a trail of deafening honks to ricochet in bouncing echoes behind him.

A video of the foghorn he saved from Slip Point lighthouse in Clallam Bay, Washington, includes slides of the rusting corpse of the rescued foghorn, with stats on its 71-inch aluminium trumpet, and captions explaining the subsequent life-saving transplants of its bronze diaphragms, over an instrumental of 'Con te partirò' (Andrea Bocelli's 'Time to Say Goodbye'). Mike, clad in bright-red ear protection, sets up the horn in his garage and records it from 500 feet away – the horn's low juddering blast belches a small cloud of dust out over his driveway.

If you sit through the slideshow of red text scrolling over images of the Doran Cunningham 6-B ship horn (usually found on Second World War US Navy destroyers, and apparently considered the best ship's horn ever made) to the sound of Queen's 'We Will Rock You', the video cuts to a shot of Mike's car from across a sandy parking lot, in the silvery blue light of a summer evening turning to night, the hills in the background like a Hiroshige woodcut. Nothing moves, Mike is out of shot, and then the horn honks and the landscape replies.

The echoes come in two rounds, one after the other, a five-second one that bounces into a second, which flexes to another three or four seconds of sound. The honk bounces upwards into the bowl of the landscape, spreading in a long, drawn-out reverb like a cat stretching in the sun. Apparently it can be heard ten miles away, even at the relatively low air pressure Mike is testing. In another video of this horn, he records a 'drive-through' – where he zooms through a tunnel with the horn sounding as the echo ricochets out like a pinball.

There are enthusiasts like Mike hiding everywhere. Just like any niche interest group online, within the horn collectors' community (and there is one) there is etiquette and convention in the way collections are documented. The train horn people are the most numerous, but there are also more adventurous makers and collectors like BighornHunter, HornyRob, hornsEurohorns – the latter of whom has a *Viz*-magazine eye for scenery that includes a PVC-clad babe idly flicking through a book in every shot. None of the 'horny' double entendres are accidental.

These people are interested in both engineering and sound, but the engineering usually comes first, in a section at the start where information scrolls through in an uncool font, or we're introduced to the horn's operational stats, with perhaps some grainy photos of the parts or images pulled from a search engine. Because a horn honk lasts just a few seconds, there's a sort of extended build-up I usually skip through, where a wobbly hand-held camera tours the horn, or someone points to different valves. There may be adjustments with a wrench or a walk-through of an air line hook-up. The run-up sometimes has music, something rousing like 'Eye of the Tiger' is ideal.

When the horn finally sounds, it's either a wild and beautiful echo that activates the shape of the surroundings, or an explosive honk that looks set to blow the roof off the garage. The landscape, the space, isn't in shot, but when the horn sounds, whatever is off-camera is manifest in the way it feeds back sound.

Mike is by far and away my favourite of these collectors. It's not the breadth of his interest that's different, but the details, and the scale and acoustics of the places he films from – the dusty orange landscapes in the wide-open spaces of California, and somewhere he calls Echo Point which I cannot find on a map.[1] I find the size of his car endearing – it is counter to the typical gargantuan American auto, a car of a type you might expect a local florist to use, not a muscle-bound bodybuilder transporting his gargantuan horns along wide US highways.

Big Mike's real name is Miguel Muniz. He hasn't posted for the last five years, and his last videos were more to do with muscle cars and his recovery from an injury than his tens of videos about horns. I was worried. Was he even still around? I managed to track down a very old email address, and shoot off a greeting, not expecting a reply.

Two days later my inbox pings.

Mike tells me that his horn obsession started by accident. He was run off the road so badly that his car was totalled and he was seriously injured: 'I was driving my 1962 Chevrolet Nova down a two-lane road. A gravel truck decided to change lanes into the lane that I was already occupying. I honked my horn, but the truck did not hear.'

He doesn't tell me how bad his injuries were, but when he had recovered, he bought another car, and this time he installed a horn from a big-rig truck – an American HGV – to give his car a bark bigger than its body. 'Every time I honked the horn, it put a smile on people's faces,' he says. 'So I looked for something louder.'

He says it then turned into a bit of a joke: 'I ended up sourcing an actual locomotive horn, installing it on my vehicle, and my friends got a kick out of it. After that, I started appreciating the difference in sound between the different horn manufacturers, and started craving – obsessing – for a fuller sound.'

While most of us would have hit eBay and hoped for the best, Mike began searching much wider. 'I bought my first large ship horn from a marine collector in the Midwestern United States,' he tells me. 'I honked it for the first time and was instantly hooked.'

From there his obsession grew, until he was known in various places as someone who would buy horns. He went deep, trying to find all the different ships' horns and foghorns he could get his hands on. 'It wasn't easy,' he points out – there is no such thing as a shop that sells the stuff that was the size he was looking for, but in time he became known, and people would contact him. 'Word spread to other collectors in the marine field. Emails started pouring in, letting me know who or where to find certain horns.'

He ended up going to Alang, in India, the world's largest ship graveyard, followed by Chittagong ship-breaking yard in Bangladesh, and Gadani in Pakistan, where he would buy ships' horns direct from the individuals who were breaking them up. He bought a total of thirty-six horns.

Often what he was buying were damaged or completely corroded horns, their mechanisms neglected or rusted. He fixed them up, sometimes manufacturing his own replacement parts, since most of the manufacturers are no longer in business. I was so taken with Mike's collection because he was so clearly, deeply in love with the sound. He thinks people who haven't heard a foghorn 'in full song' as he so beautifully puts it, have missed out on a part of history, although he says those within range of his house on a New Year's Eve are guaranteed to get an earful.

Nowadays the horns are somewhat in the past for him, and he's slowly moved his focus: 'Once I obtained the holy grail of horns (Doran Cunningham 6-B, NASA reverberant chamber horn, Leslie Tyfon AE-425-87MB, and the Leslie Tyfon 425 Foghorn),' he writes, 'I've slowly moved my focus to my original love . . . Building race cars.'

The reverberant chamber NASA horn is Mike's most

impressive video. This horn was originally used for testing how aerospace components handle high sound pressure. It has a fifteen-second decay that drifts off into the mountains as Big Mike stands in a navy fleece. The NASA horn is bigger than a foghorn, his boxy car dwarfed by the square mouth of this obscene metal beast. I had no idea something like this even existed. The foghorn momentarily slips into second place in my heart as the decorous NASA reverberations make me swoon, even over YouTube.

I plough through his videos, reading the comments, and come across another foghorn-related piece of modern folklore. Some years ago a video started circulating online, documenting a phenomenon known as 'sky trumpets'. It began with a strange home-made video from Kiev in 2011, where wobbly footage shot outside a nondescript apartment block appeared to record great metallic moaning sounds coming from the sky – the sound of colossal girders moving, scraping, heaving against one another, or the sound of one of Mike's horns.

Since then, there have been more than 150 logged instances of 'trumpets in the sky', according to one website, and many of them are described in the same terms: 'a metallic-type groaning sound coming from the sky as if someone just put the key in the ignition of a large, invisible vehicle and started it up.'

I recognised this description – it sounded like a diaphone.

These low trumpet sounds appear to come from the sky itself, and are credited variously with being harbingers of biblical events, the sound of secret government operations, or the arrival of extraterrestrial life. They are ripe fodder for various conspiracy theories. Sometimes it's thought to be the horns described in the Bible's Book of Revelation that arrive to signal the end of the world; elsewhere secret military aircraft testing is fingered as the culprit. Often the target is the US Air Force's HAARP (High-frequency Active Auroral Research Program), a project that explored the ionosphere, operating a high-powered radio frequency transmitter from Alaska, but about which there was much tin-hat conspiratorial analysis.[2]

Many are hoaxes – faked copycat videos made with basic editing software. Tales are told, repeated and slightly adjusted, a blockchain of authorship where there are edits, reposts, fragmentations and duplicates. Perhaps theories about the military–industrial complex's hidden activities are a type of post-industrial folklore, as beliefs passed on not by word of mouth, but on message boards, forums and in the depths of comments sections. Videos like these could be viewed as a digital upgrade to the nineteenth century's photographic 'proofs' of ectoplasmic seances and faeries. However, not all the videos are hoaxes, and there are other, similar, unexplained sonic phenomena such as 'the hum', likely caused by various after-effects of industrialisation.[3]

While chasing clues in Mike's profile, I find a comment he's left on someone else's video, stating confidently that one instance of trumpets in the sky in Germany was the result of another horn collector just like Mike, joyfully honking a free concert to an unsuspecting audience. In the same way the atmosphere and landscape conspired to mute, reflect and throw sound when Tyndall was testing horns on the South Foreland, I wonder how many suburban horn collectors are the cause of these apparent sky-borne harbingers of the apocalypse.

There is another more elusive American character, who

operated in the decades previous to Big Mike and who I have never been able to pin down. His name is the Fogmaster and he is, or was, a collector of horns. Best described as a guerrilla sound artist, he would take his horns to a public place and fire them up in a glorious and brutal unannounced cacophony, until someone came to shut him down. Reading about these mischievous performances, I saw how radical they were, like 1960s Fluxus happenings on a deafening scale. They rejected expectations – no stage, no lights, no tickets. They were defiantly outside of convention, and challenged the need for institutional endorsement. They also included the Fogmaster in a ridiculous costume – full body armour made from noise-dampening foam. (He also had one for his dog.)

There was a brief time when I managed to get hold of him via Facebook, but he has since disappeared. Security in public places went into overdrive in the aftermath of 9/11, and he said he could no longer play for long enough to make it worth it. He used to be able to get a good half an hour of honking out before he was shut down, but it was reduced to just a few minutes, and eventually he grew tired of the hassle, put his horns in the garage and went into hiding, somewhere in the Midwest, or so I heard.

You can buy one of his foghorn sounds as a ringtone online, which I did, but I soon had to change it, because there's no fog on the top deck of buses, and every time it went off it would cause a busload of people to stare in my direction. By this point I was getting funny looks explaining that my main job was researching foghorns to my extended family, and didn't fancy the same from a whole busload of strangers. The ringtone had to go.

While I was trying to track down the Fogmaster again, an artist called Nick Sales got in touch about how he had acquired an F-type diaphone, which he and some collaborators used to overwhelming effect in performances in Birmingham and Whitstable – and would I be interested in hearing about it?

'An F-type?' I think. This must be an error. An F-type is truly enormous, not the sort of thing you could chuck in the back of a car. He must have it wrong, I think. An F-type is meant to compete with the oceans, surely too big a sound for an art performance, never mind too big for a typical sound artist's budget. It *must* be something else.

Nick replies with a batch of photos of the horn, and my jaw drops, because it really is an F-type. It's a beauty, and it is also a beast. He attaches a video of one of the performances he did with the diaphone in Birmingham in 2007. 'Blast' was described as 'an aural explosion in celebration of the City's steam-driven past', performed by a group that included Nick, the living members of the Bow Gamelan Ensemble (the sculptor Richard Wilson and artist Anne Bean), along with experimental musician Ansuman Biswas and artists Mark Anderson, Helen Ingham and Kirsten Reynolds.

Nick had got hold of the horn from a scrapyard in Portsmouth, after it was removed from one of the Trinity House light vessels. It was in a terrible state, he says, so with a group of others, he stripped it down and separated the sound-producing piston part from the actual horn, and decided to see if it was still working: 'They need a huge amount of air-flow to make them sing, but even running it off a puny shop air-line with just the motor valve running

*Artists Richard Wilson and Kirsten Reynolds with The Mighty
Diaphone – 'Blast' performance, Birmingham, September 2007.*

the piston, and no "speaking air" it made the upstairs floors move,' he writes. 'The first time we fired it up properly was on site in Birmingham for 'Blast'. We didn't have any of the switching gear or pilot valves for it, so operated it by hand with two hoofing great ¼ turn ball valves – one for the motor and the other for the "speaking air". These were – in retrospect – stupidly close to the actual horn . . .

'The crew were hardened veterans of the industrial music/ outdoor performance scene and stood arms-crossed a few meters away with "Go On, Then" expressions on their faces. I was wearing earplugs under ear defenders so my ears were saved when I turned on "The Taps Of Doom", but my eyeballs and internal organs were actually vibrating.

'I gave it a few experimental honks until I'd had more than enough punishment, and turned round to see the ashen-faced crew, now standing at Some Considerable Distance. We ended up making a baffle [for sound protection] out of wood and mattresses to give the Intrepid Horn-ist some sort of protection as they honk'ed.'

He described the volume of the horn as 'somewhere on the spectrum between Sunn O))) and a Vulcan Bomber'. Just a short video of the performance makes me realise Souter Point was positively restrained. It was an industrial foghorn performance in the vein of Rammstein. It had fireworks, fires, arrays of train whistles hooting with hot steam, as well as a 'Large Hot Pipe Organ' plus 'Pyrotechnic Whistles', 'Flying Rockets', 'Pyrophones' and 'Balls of Fire'. It was the conflagrant nightmare of a health and safety officer, and it was brilliant. Apparently, the performance's final foghorn blasts could be heard in Coventry.

After the show, the horn couldn't easily be housed

anywhere because of its size, so it was sold to someone in Cornwall who has one of the largest collections of steam whistles in the world, on the grounds that it could be borrowed again should a performance arise in which an F-type was needed.

Richard Wilson, the sculptor and part of the team for 'Blast', has often featured horns and sirens in his performances. His *1513: A Ship's Opera*, composed with experimental musician Ansuman Biswas (who also worked on 'Blast'), marked the 500th anniversary of a petition made to King Henry VIII for safe pilotage (to get vessels in and out of London safely). It consisted of a forty-mile voyage down the Thames from the mouth of the estuary to Tower Bridge. The finale was a riotous eruption of horns in front of the bridge, conducted by Biswas from the top of *Trinity* lightship in what resembled a London update to Avraamov's *Symphony of Sirens*. The *Financial Times* reviewer however – one of eight spectators that heard the whole fourteen-hour-long piece from a renovated tugboat where all passengers were required to shovel coal to keep the vessel in motion – was not impressed by this Russolian embrace of industry in music, expressed disappointment that it was such a loose take on what opera should be, and was quickly bored by the 'interminable honking'.

In certain quarters, Russolo's dream of futurist music made with noise and machines has become real. When it comes to foghorns there are Curran's *Maritime Rites*, Fontana's *Landscape Sculpture with Foghorns,* Westerkamp's *Fantasie for Horns* pieces, and recordings of her *Harbour Symphony*. In more contemporary experimental music they can be found in the work of Howlround (aka Robin the

Fog), Felix Blume and others. In Ingram Marshall's *Fog Tropes* (which appears in the Scorsese film *Shutter Island*) the rhythmic calls of various horns, the shushing of outside space conjures ghosts that gather in mournful chorus, while brass smoothens and breaks the tension. It is an anxious piece of music, with presence and drama.

The sound of the foghorn has now been adopted as compositional material, as an instrument, appearing sombre in some instances, and boisterous in others. Distance from their early soundings has softened the rudeness of their interruptions. At the same time as their voices are immortalised, they have become functionally obsolete, and their bodies lie as industrial debris along the coast. The sound of foghorns can still be found in bombastic one-off performances like 'Blast', and the objects themselves are being collected by people like Mike and the elusive Fogmaster. However, while the horns and their mechanisms are being saved and restored in some quarters, the architecture that housed them has often been abandoned. The sound has been absorbed, but the structures have been ignored.

18

In ruins

How do you hold on to something you cannot touch? When buildings and objects decay, it is often visible on surfaces and materials, and restoration can be done. But how do you preserve a sound? A recording on shellac is an object, and can be digitised, restored, protected, but what happens when the technology to access a sound recording has become inaccessible or obsolete? This is an easy discussion to have when thinking about the music formats we listen to – vinyl, tapes, MP3s – but what about when the sound emanates from a lumbering piece of technology like a foghorn? How do you show something is historically important if what's valuable about it is invisible?

There is a huge divide, culturally speaking, between the way we think about sound heritage, compared with objects and architectural heritage. At the time foghorns were switched off, their buildings and machinery were not considered unique or historically important, so they were ditched, sold, scrapped. Foghorns were often decapitated or demolished because they were not old enough to be considered of value, and they had been superseded by more efficient fog signals. Heritage is not about that which is immediately behind us, but that which is far enough in the rear-view mirror for its defects to be out of focus.

Lighthouse boards such as Trinity House have only become heritage organisations by owning some really old buildings, on sites that tourists visit on clifftop walks and coastal holidays. These buildings are protected by law, meaning the lighthouse boards are obliged to maintain them. However, there's no law or guidance protecting a sound like the foghorn, and there's often nobody thinking about how the more transient aspects of historical lighthouses are being taken care of. Community attachment to a sound is no shield against demolitions, removals or a silencing.

The people I met who were involved in restorations and preservation were often most interested in the engines that drove the foghorn. Few people had come to it primarily as a sound. This isn't to say they weren't in love with or attached to the blast, but those that kept the machines working were largely engineers, and to them, the sound was great, but so was the smell of petrol and the fine-tuning of mechanical movements. When it came down to detail we diverged – I was interested in memory and identity, whereas the experts I was talking to were obsessed with valves and materials. Brass or steel? Piston or siren? What pressure per inch should the air be in the tanks? I cared only in as much as I needed to understand the sound that came out of the horn's gaping mouth.

Buchan Ness lighthouse stands on a pimple of land on the east coast of Aberdeenshire. It bulges out from the mainland, separated by a short spit that is underwater at high tide. As usual, I am here in the off-season, this time on a trip with the Association of Lighthouse Keepers. The weather is unfriendly, and I pull my hood over hair already sodden from the jostling wind and persistent drizzle.

The lighthouse has one broad red stripe around its middle, with mustard-yellow ironwork on the lantern. The foghorn here used to be in front of the lighthouse, accessed by a rough concrete path running around the perimeter wall, which bridged the rocky ground and grassy dips in the land. Its horn faced out to sea, partially shielded from the village of Boddam by the lighthouse buildings.

Earlier that day Roy – a formidable ALK member who seems to be able to get access to the most unlikely lighthouse sites – had brought me a piece of the foghorn building he'd collected on a morning recce for the afternoon's tour: 'Jennifer, I've got something for you!' he said, handing me a fist-sized chunk of concrete, whitewashed on one side. When I looked bemused, he explained: 'It's a piece of foghorn!'

The penny drops, and I am so thrilled I have to hide my glee, put a lid on my bubbling joy. It looks like nothing, but it is really something, to me at least. There is barely a trace of the foghorn here now, unless you really go looking for it. Roy had gone looking, had picked up a chunk of the old buildings he spotted in the grass.

When Buchan Ness was decommissioned and the equipment had been removed, the foghorn building was packed with explosives and demolished. It sounds like fun, the last ugly boom of a beautiful machine, all crash and no symphony. Perhaps the keepers were glad to see the back of it, or perhaps they just took an opportunity to play at exploding things. It must have been cathartic to watch part of your workplace blow up if you were being made redundant.

The part of the archives containing evidence of the demolition is still closed, so I don't know how or why it was razed
to the ground. Now it takes a trained eye, or someone who
knows, like Roy, to see that there was a proud horn and its
chugging engines here at all.

The little shard he's gifted is not useless debris, but a
fragment of something bigger – one of the few remainders
of the sound that rumbled through this concrete, a shard
of a building dampened by fog and dried by the sun, then
obliterated by explosives. This chunk of broken concrete
is as close as I'll get to holding a dead foghorn. Its history
vibrates in my hand, a worthless piece of concrete that is of
no interest and no use to anyone except me, but which tells
me how little this sonic history was valued.

As I pick my way across the rocks I spot other fragments
of the building: huge concrete slabs split in half, cogs and
nails longer than a finger that are rusting red in the stiff
grass, industrial oddments left behind when the machinery
was removed, all now becoming fused into the landscape.

Roy assures me this is not the only place where this happened, although tracing the other exploded foghorns – still
locked in closed documents or in ones just not saved – is
almost impossible, so information comes by word of mouth.

Some weeks later, Roy writes to say that the Northern
Lighthouse Board had on occasion demolished anything
no longer required at lighthouses – fog signal buildings,
outhouses and dwellings. Alan Renton says he found this
in England and Wales too. Sometimes this was because they
would have been expensive to maintain even silent, but some
were also teetering on eroding coastlines, their concrete and

stone foundations at risk of tumbling down cliffs, or slipping quietly into the sea.[1] Demolition was not necessarily a bad idea when compared to the risks of collapsing structures. In the immediate aftermath of automation, the horns were not valued as heritage machinery, but dead weight, obsolete technology that had been superseded.

When the old diaphone was switched off at La Corbière on Jersey, most of the equipment – the engines, the air tanks and the pipe work – was left on site, but the horns themselves were given a brutal decapitation. The narrow necks are still *in situ*, but reduced to stumps, someone having been sent to slice off the trumpets and take them away for scrap.

However, some foghorn buildings survived if they were older and considered historic. In places such as Lizard and Sumburgh Head they exist as museum buildings, with original Victorian tiling and painted friezes on the creamy walls, so that tourists can see what it was like inside, even if nothing is running. In some places the engine rooms have been cleared out and co-opted as space for displays about the lighthouse. At Portland Bill the old compressor engines and air tanks for the foghorn have recently been removed to make way for the lens to be displayed.

In the UK, lighthouse towers, as well as being protected by statutory heritage listings, are still operational structures providing aids to navigation, where 150-year-old lenses might still be in use. This means that in one lamp room there might be over a century of history, an essential maritime navigational aid and a tourist attraction all clustered together. Newer lights are compact, but it's sometimes not practical to dismantle the heavy prisms of the nineteenth-century optics and remove them, so there might also be two lights sharing the same space.

There is no right or wrong way sound should be preserved, particularly if the sound has a specific function. Heritage laws mainly protect what is physical, tangible and material.[2] Sounds from the past are not protected, particularly not the sounds of machines, and they come and go as technology changes, as industry moves and as populations shift. Heritage work related to the foghorn often happens around its heavy physical presence as a piece of technology you can see, touch and understand, but rarely around the massive undertaking that is the resurrection of its sound. The trumpet for the Duncansby Head foghorn, for example, has been rescued and is being materially restored, but will not sound; ten years ago, a 19-foot-long horn with a 9-foot diameter was made by a blacksmith for an arts festival in the Black Country, based on real designs from the archive of the Chance Brothers' glassworks and manufacturing company, but it was a physical installation, not a sonic one.

Commemorating or quantifying the value of a sound from the past is a nebulous business: whatever is immediately behind us often loses out. Keeping a foghorn running, functionally or as a tourist attraction, is about the machinery and the expertise required to operate it. Questions about how its sound fits into a soundscape, or how other dying sounds of the recent industrial past can be preserved are – practically speaking – incidental.

However, these coastal locations are not just boundaries between land and sea, but zones where the so-called 'natural' and the industrial coexist, where past and future conflate, and collapse. A foghorn on a coastline, for all its animalistic noise, is not a species in a natural habitat, but remains an industrial intruder. Greater understanding of sound and ecology in recent decades has meant that organisations like the RSPB worry that re-sounding foghorns might disturb reproductive cycles, as some lighthouse sites where old horns have been restored are also crucial for nesting seabirds. When considerations like this come into play, a question hangs over the wisdom of reinstating a sound. Do our fond remembrances really trump these ecological worries?

In the UK most horns were switched off without fanfare – the last sad blast of Sumburgh was played to nobody except a keeper who hated its sound, like a washed-up crooner playing seafront shows to more bar staff than audience. San Francisco's foghorns were championed as part of the city's identity, but only once most of them had been turned off. It took until the coastguard was about to silence the last horn on the Bay for there to be a public outcry about their loss.

Their switch-off was treated as a loss to the city's character. 'We want them for historic reasons and nostalgia,' Wayne Wheeler told the *San Francisco Examiner* in 1992. 'It's so much of San Francisco's background. You've heard of national historic landmarks. Well, this is a national historic soundmark.' Wheeler, the president of the US Lighthouse Society, said at the time that his phone rang off the hook with people wanting to save the horns, and he was fond of referencing John Huston's *The Maltese Falcon* to the newspapers, invoking Sam Spade chasing a crook down Kearny Street, and how it wouldn't be the same scene if it wasn't soundtracked by foghorns.

The campaign to keep the foghorns sounding was taken on board by two politicians who competed to lead on the issue, both trying to claim success in preventing the switch-off – one used the threat to the foghorns as a banner under which they could trumpet the fact they were a San Francisco native, born and bred, whereas the other was not. The fight to save the foghorns became one overshadowed by a political fight for authentic San Franciscan-hood; they were fodder for arguments about identity, not heritage or safety.

However, the campaign worked, and the coastguard agreed to hand over some of the horns to any local groups who wanted to operate them (although there is little evidence of this having happened). The crew on the Golden Gate Bridge during this time seemed to be operating at one remove from the debate, and said their horns would still sound no matter what. Many were switched off anyway, or swapped for mewing electric signals. The *San Francisco Chronicle* reported that the last of those that warned local mariners off the rocky cliffs of Alcatraz was removed 'unceremoniously' and replaced with a small beeping horn. The soundscape was changed, in some areas for the first time in a century.

There is a story about the renovation of Souter Point that was told to me by different parties on trips with the Association of Lighthouse Keepers. Souter Point is now looked after by the National Trust, who crowdfunded the renovation of the foghorn. Once the restoration was complete, a few of those who had been part of the project travelled from all over the country to huddle on the cliffs at Souter Point. One of them was Gerry Douglas-Sherwood. When the momentous switching-on of the horn happened, this small but specialist audience knew something was wrong. 'It didn't sound right,' said Gerry. Souter Point's diaphone should have had a gorgeously rough, forty-a-day grunt at the end, and while the reanimated horn had sounded well, it wasn't the sound that Gerry and others remembered.

The Souter Point horn had lost its grunt.

I emailed him to ask what happened.

'You can imagine the disappointment amongst the handful of ex-keepers when the blast was plain enough – but without the all-important diaphone "grunt" that differentiates a diaphone from, say, a nautophone or SuperTyfon,' he wrote.

Everything was in order – the air pressure, the engineering, the valves had all been restored accurately to their former settings. But Gerry and some of the others had known the voice of this horn as well as they knew the voices of their own children. The cause took a long while to find, but eventually the culprit was identified as a tiny piece of rubber that had perished in part of the mechanism, which had knocked the grunt flat out of the horn.

Luckily, someone knew someone who had dead stock of these rubber valves, and one was sent for. When the part was replaced, its full throaty grunt returned, and a phone call came through to the lighthouse from a stranger miles away, who rang just to congratulate them on getting it sounding right again.

The thing that struck me about this story was how powerful the memory of the sound was in the minds of those who had known it well. Decades after it had been silenced, the exact character of Souter Point was still fixed enough for those listening to know immediately that something was wrong. While the machinery of the foghorn provided a physical link to a way of life that was in the past, the memory of sound still had enormous power.

When I had first spoken to Chris Williams at Nash Point, he had a particular reverence for his restored horn and its machinery: 'It's very much a great privilege to be able to operate something like that, you know,' he had said, in hushed voice, 'let alone get to listen to it.'

I'd visited Nash Point a second time, when the foghorn was switched off for repairs, and Chris said that some of the brides and grooms who had been denied their wedding day foghorn had been reduced to tears. I asked if he had noticed local people welcoming back the sound of the foghorn when they'd first switched it on again. 'We're much more aware of local people coming up and saying, "Oh, it's lovely to hear it again",' he had said. The neighbouring farmer thought it was wonderful: 'He's probably the closest living one that gets it full force, and he thinks it's brilliant.'

Caroline Woodward, the Canadian keeper mentioned earlier, has a moment in her memoir where she writes:

At 3:15 a.m., getting out to do my first weather report, when I hear the Chatham Point foghorn baritone *oooo-aaahhh* alternating with a cruise ship's booming bass horn as it heads from Discovery Passage into Johnstone's Strait, and a fishing boat's assertive tenor toot coming in from Nodales Channel, all three of which converge below the station cliffs I am thrilled. And then melancholy, thinking to myself: Remember this, memorize the pitch and the rise and fall of those sounds, because you will not hear them once you are far away from this life.

There is a 500-page tome by French historian Alain Corbin, which documents the role of bells in nineteenth-century French villages. At first it seems too esoteric to be real, but Corbin digs into their significance through excavating in painstaking detail all the ways in which bells were protected, salvaged and fought over during the French Revolution. Bells had practical and religious roles – they defined village boundaries, working hours, sang for deaths, weddings and saints' days. When the revolution happened a conflict arose between the secular and the religious, and the material demands of war. Bells were threatened with being melted down for cannon, and when this happened, villagers sometimes conspired to save them. There were night-time protests where a community formed a human shield; switcheroos where a fake was swapped for the bell and sent off to the foundry, or was buried to hide it from the authorities. People were deeply attached to their bells, not just because of their sound and purpose, but because of their power to represent them as a community. In these stories I heard an echo of what had happened when foghorns were switched off: people were surprised by their strength of feeling about a foghorn they had lived with, but only when it was threatened with removal.

The feeling when switch-off came around was that the sound – not so much the building – *belonged* to the local people. A foghorn, for the communities that lived near it and slept through it, was a daily part of their lives, and when it was switched off something in that community was lost. There is a feeling of ownership towards these sounds of bells and foghorns, as sounds fundamental to a place – as soundmarks, as the WSP had described them. We know them, whether we live there or are just passing through. The horn at Partridge Island, the site of Robert Foulis's first foghorn, was switched off without any consultation in 1998, and was dismantled almost immediately afterwards. One local wrote an essay lamenting the loss, referring to it as 'our horn'. These sounds can become as important to our identities as the music we listen to.

Renovating foghorns is no small task. The parts have to be sourced, often through the same underground network of engineer enthusiasts that have delivered some of the research and stories for this book. These sites are all looked after by heritage societies, caretakers and enthusiasts, or, as with Sumburgh, retained keepers like Brian.

At the DeTour Reef Light, offshore at the top of Lake Huron near the US–Canadian border where freighters pass through the mouth of the St Mary's River, there is a lighthouse that has been restored and is now, in the summer months, staffed by a handful of volunteer keepers over the weekends. They clean, polish and maintain all equipment, and act as tour guides. They also get to sound the foghorn.[3]

Other restored horns include Low Head in Tasmania and the East Brother lighthouse in Richmond, California. I hear from Wayne Wheeler that a lighthouse museum in Ohio has a signal they roll out on a cart for special occasions, and that a group in Duluth, Minneapolis took over an old diaphone signal for a while.

People like Chris and Brian tend to be ex-keepers, former engineers or mariners, whose role is both to run visitor centres and maintain the mechanisms. Brian worries about who will be able to run the horn when he leaves, as there is nobody to pass his knowledge on to: how to tinker and tweak these machines so they sing; how to listen out for tune-ups and problems. The barriers to these restorations happening is not so much finding the energy, time or enthusiasm of people to do it, but modern health and safety regulations coming into conflict with the operations of old machinery, and lack of funds from lighthouse boards whose light dues are not supposed to fund passion projects. More than one lighthouse undergoing renovations to make the best of opportunities for tourism has hit a wall when health and safety officers discover that the entire nineteenth-century optic in the lamp room is turning on a one and a half ton bath of extremely toxic mercury.

When I heard stories like this, saw the older generation of enthusiasts leave or be removed from the machines they cared for, the foghorn's demise seemed near at hand.

But then I meet Aodhan.

Aodhan is an anomaly, by virtue of being younger than any other enthusiast I've met by a good three decades or more. He has a huge designer watch, an occasional stutter and also plays the pipe organ – he tells me about one he played that had a diaphone stop like a foghorn.

I had met him at an Association of Lighthouse Keepers meeting in a caravan park in Wales, and while the other members were excited to have someone young in their midst, I was already plotting to swipe him away from the lighthouse chat about optics and lamps, and ask him how the hell a twenty-five-year-old from Belfast had found himself maintaining a pair of nineteenth-century foghorn engines. Perhaps we could even form a splinter group, I thought – a foghorn subdivision of the lighthouse association.

Over a prawn cocktail Aodhan told me about how he had come to foghorns by way of an ex-keeper called Henry Henvy at a lighthouse in Northern Ireland, who took him under his wing at a difficult time. He found an unexpected escape and a friendship, and learned how to restore and maintain the engines at the lighthouse, falling in love with the machinery and the sounds, the smells and the routines. When Henvy died, he carried on looking after the engines, as a way of remembering and memorialising his friend, mostly out of his own pocket.

The engines he takes care of are particularly beautiful, and much older than those I've seen at other stations – by a half a century or so. They are from the late nineteenth century, and have huge shining flywheels. He polishes and oils them, sometimes turns them over by hand. He has two trumpets he can hook their air supply to.

Aodhan has wanted to be a keeper since the age of four, he tells me, when he first visited a lighthouse. He now lives with his parents, and talks non-stop about lighthouses and foghorns. 'Don't you ever talk about anything else?' they say, to which he replies, 'What else is there to talk about?'

However, he has a problem. The lighthouse board in Ireland has stopped insuring the building holding the engines, so he's no longer allowed to run them at all. Just like a car, if they aren't given a regular spin, the engines will clog or seize. They need attention to be kept alive, so he occasionally checks things over to stop the mechanisms deteriorating beyond repair, keeping them as smooth and gleaming as he can, in the hope that he'll be allowed in again sometime soon. He's worried that the lighthouse board will throw a fit if they find out he's been looking after the engines, despite the fact he's saving a piece of history from ruin and decay. Perhaps his fears are warranted – Chris Williams had his foghorn shut down and left Nash Point after the engines were found to be leaking oil, and there were worries being voiced by the RSPB that the horn should no longer be sounded in summer at Sumburgh Head.

However, we lose sounds all the time, and maybe that's OK when it comes to technology. Do you wish your mobile phone still made the same sounds it did twenty years ago? If we never lost anything the world would be an unbearable cacophony, with infinite and indistinguishable layers of sound from the past all coalesced in the present. On the other hand, if we never save anything, we lose knowledge of how things were, are left to piece together or guess at the sensory experiences of those that came before us.

Aodhan is not old enough to remember the sound of the foghorn *in situ*, and yet yearns for it, chases it, like me. The sound of honking old engine-driven beasts has a timbre our ears can recognise without us realising – they sing as hot metal and machine parts, and trigger nostalgia for this mechanical sound in a digital world, and that nostalgia is rooted in its many meanings and associations.

The foghorn remains a sound connected to the past, and it evokes the times it came from. Whether that's a memory from the 1970s or before, it's a sound that is about the maritime industry, of time at sea, on boats where there was no escape from the weather. Save for a handful of renovations, the foghorns of the power and scale that disturbed residents in Dunoon, which were recorded by composers and historians like Alan, are now mostly silent. The sound that has taken the place of the older horns is very different from their rattling blasts, and is often more like a mewing beep. Wayne Wheeler had said these were installed just to wean people off the big old beasts. They no longer offer salvation, and are often too quiet to console. Now, operational fog signals are a last-gasp failsafe, for when small boats get into big trouble.

Part Four

RELEASE

Returning – remains – reminders

19

Boom to beep

I hear the fog signal in Southend on my way home late one night. The yellow-orange of the streetlights reflects off the wet pavement, the fog hangs in dense pockets, washing out the yellow and brown tiles of the dirty underpass. Up the steps past the Unitarian chapel I think I hear something, a high-pitched beep that could be any sort of machine, but it's faint, and I assume it's some roadworks down on the front. In the narrow alleyway by the house that is surrounded by bluebells in spring, I hear it again. It's regular, not like machinery being used. I realise it is the fog signal, just about audible from two miles away – it is travelling further inland than usual, finding me on the breeze. I stop, turn towards the coast, and wait.

I strain to listen past the sound of cars on the main road, of tyres searing over damp tarmac. I hear it louder, and stop to count the beeps from all the way at the end of the pier: one two-second blast, followed by a six-second silence and another two-second blast. It's quiet for twenty seconds, and I wonder if I imagined it, but then it repeats.

The next day I take a walk down the pier, set off to find the foghorn I have heard but never located. A local in the pub tells me that it is manually operated, and it is not a Trinity House horn, but looked after by the council. I wonder if someone has to traipse to the end of the fog-covered pier to press a big red button, and what the walk from the illuminated amusements out into the nothingness of the pier sunk in mist must be like. Perhaps like drowning, or falling asleep.

The pier is touted as 'the longest pleasure pier in Europe', but the only real pleasure, apart from the little tram that runs up and down on rails, is getting to the end, where there is an uninspiring café and a custom-built modern building that is all turquoise, glass and angles, and is an awkward place to host almost anything. On a summer's afternoon, though, it has the most spectacular view. There are sometimes seals, and on a high tide their heads bob like grey footballs on the water. There's also an RNLI station, with a spiral metal staircase leading to a top deck where there is a bell, and what I think must be the foghorn, although I can't be sure.

I once came here with my friend Tim to watch the Isle of Grain's cooling tower – a massive visual marker on this relatively flat landscape – being demolished, where the middle section burst in a controlled and silent explosion of dust and debris, and ten seconds later the sound reached us. The loud dry crack when the tower was detonated only reached us when it had already disappeared, dropping straight down as if the ground had opened up underneath it. What we had heard was already in the past.

The signal is just a small beep, sometimes accompanied by gigantic container ships sounding their horns in the estuary. The bigger the ship, the bigger the horn, and these days, as container ships reach mega-tonnage, some of them sound louder than any foghorn. From Tim's garden I heard one of these, and his wife, Hayley, had urged me out on my bike to have a look. It was a hot week and the still air had sunk the estuary in a syrup of hot air. Noises were oozing weirdly around the streets and houses, travelling further on the heat-slicked air. I zoomed up to the sea wall in the dark to see two fishing boats with bulbs strung like fairy lights around the decks passing in front of a massive cargo ship. Unable to swerve, the ship had honked urgent warnings as the boats sped out from under its nose, bearing down on them like a black avalanche.

The fog signal is puny compared to those reverberant honks. I can't even find it in the collection of boxes and equipment on the end of the pier. There is no big trumpet facing out to the deep-water channel, no way to tell what it might be among other communication tech and weather devices. Unless it's sounding it's inconspicuous. A beeping electric siren like the one here is very different to the old foghorns I love. They are completely different devices, like comparing electric scooters to a tank.

When foghorns were switched off they were sometimes replaced with new electric emitters like Southend's. A number of factors came together to effect this change. Firstly, there was automation, and the stubborn old horns often could not be operated remotely. By the mid-1980s fog signals were downgraded from navigational aids – things that help mariners find their way – to 'hazard markers' – things that mark a sticky spot or structure.[1] They're no longer in the same family as lighthouses, functionally speaking, and have been demoted. In the time since the foghorn was invented it has gone from a desperately requested navigational aid, to a rarely used beep for tiny craft and kayaks. The difference between navigational aid and hazard marker is subtle but significant – foghorns helped locate ships in difficult waters, whereas now they just yelp at something in the way. It meant that high-powered fog signals, with their juddering engines and massive range, were no longer required, particularly by bigger ships.

The first time electric fog signals were considered was in 1929, at the first International Conference of Lighthouse Authorities, according to Alan Renton, but a variety of electric signals were produced from around the 1950s onwards. Alan writes that these emitters were in use at some stations for over twenty-five years, and were still being installed into the 1980s. They included a 300Hz sound signal, which had a neutral tone a bit like a test tone – pretty characterless as it goes. These are 'pure tone' electric emitters, and don't have the same harmonics as the old horns. Their innocuous boops are likely to be what you've heard around the coasts in recent years, particularly in the UK. They have no throaty warm-up blasts, and sound like the electric devices they are, rather than mythical bulls or prehistoric beasts, although their plaintive note can still haunt a headland in fog.

Dungeness, with its experimental station, was front of the pack in the adoption of modern sound signals, just like it had been in the 1860s. Its new lighthouse, first lit in 1961, is lanky, with no accommodation inside, and so no windows break its spindly black and white tower. Near the top, under the lantern, there are what look like holes punched in the front. These are cast-concrete casings for the speakers inside, a sixty-strong array of triple-frequency emitters, which sound three blasts every sixty seconds.

Triple-frequency emitters sounded three frequencies to better be heard by ships over engine noise, and to give them harmonics. Old horns had natural harmonics because of the mechanics of the beasts, whereas newer electric horns could sound a pure tone much more accurately. Tater Du in Cornwall has a 72-speaker stack array, as does South Stack on Anglesey in Wales. There are now around twenty-three fog signals left in Trinity House's jurisdiction, mostly on light vessels, whereas the Northern Lighthouse Board has none.

There are, however, hundreds of fog signals around the UK, although most of these are offshore where most people will never encounter them. I had emailed the UK Hydrographic Office for a list of still operational fog signals, and was surprised by the reply – I had guessed there were 40 or so, but an email informed me there were in fact 426 fog signals in UK waters.

Many of these signals are on offshore structures like oil rigs and wind farms. So now, the place you're most likely to hear a fog signal is not on the coast but out at sea. On the Kentish Flats, a broad field of turbines visible from the Thames estuary on a clear day, the fog signals measure just 2 metres by 30 centimetres, and their sound will not usually reach the land.

The fog signal has not just been downgraded and stripped of its power, but has also been pushed out to sea, sent out of view of the land and the local communities that might otherwise come to know its call. Horn sounds don't reach into hotels and streets and houses any more. Children will not be rocked to sleep or families reassured of the safety of their loved ones, although as suggested by previous chapters, it might take a while for them to get used to even these smaller sounds.

I finally manage to arrange a meeting over the phone with Simon Millyard, the engineering and operations manager for Trinity House, to ask him about how horn sounds changed after the big beasts became impractical, and lighthouses were no longer manned. He tells me that, generally speaking, new foghorns or changes to foghorn sounds still result in noise complaints today. I am surprised to hear that Trinity House still receive noise complaints, just like in the nineteenth century. There is a link between what Millyard was explaining to me and a letter from 1897 I had found in the archives in Glasgow. In it, David Allen Stevenson had written to say that while people complain at first, they eventually get used to new sounds. He was writing about how they would get used to the new Cloch horn, just like they had got used to the previous boiler whistle signal, but there were others too.

The acting secretary for the Boddam District Community Council in 1978 wrote of Buchan Ness that 'the present fog signal seems to be very sensitive and triggered easily. Residents in the village have complained about the high frequency tone of this signal [and] also the fact that it sounds when the weather is clear.'

As I finished this book there was a dispute in North Wales about plans to remove the Trwyn Du bell. The bell has been *in situ* for over a century because the lighthouse was never given a proper foghorn, but now there are plans for the ringing of a bell to become an electric beep. Those in the local area are not happy. A local café proprietor complained that the new horn 'just sounds like some sort of hideous siren for prison inmates'.

Complaints, from either century, don't seem to be so much about the sounds themselves, but about the way people adjust to changes in the sounds of their everyday environments. When things change, we have to get used to the new sound all over again. Lots of us won't enjoy it at first, purely because it is new, and its newness means we have not yet learned to tune it out when we need to. This was true when I traced some of the other complaints about new foghorns. Hartlepool's 'Bellowing Bull' caused a disturbance while it was sounding differently because of a malfunction in the 1950s. When I looked it up in the *Hartlepool Northern Daily Mail*, the locals were later described as having got used to the sound. One reporter waxed lyrical, perhaps over-egging it by writing that 'it is believed that time has turned the notes of the one time "bellowing bull" into a lullaby. Children and others, I understand, merely smile in their sleep when its call rings out across the bay.'

Perhaps this is a rose-tinted view. One unnamed house-holder punctured the romantic rendering for the journalist (and myself), when they were quoted as saying: 'If you sit on a pin long enough you get used to it.'

What does it mean to get used to a sound? It isn't that you haven't heard it, but more likely that you are so accustomed to it being part of your environment, that you become able to tune it out in favour of the sounds you need or want to hear. In the inverse, paying attention to all the sounds that we tune out can reconnect us with our surroundings – listening like this is a form of meditation that can re-engage us with a world we may have become distant from.[2] Sometimes we can tune things out, sometimes we can't. The foghorn's regular rhythm helps us to adjust to it, and perhaps stop noticing it.

So much of our experience of the world is defined by the attention we pay to the sounds around us. These experiences are often nuanced and depend on us being multifarious individuals with different tastes and preferences, amalgamations of past listening experiences coalescing into our own complex aural biographies.

Listening closely and attentively to our environments can be like cleaning the windows through which we look onto the world. Sitting writing at my desk, I can turn the music off and shift my attentions to the sounds of the space around me, notice things that I had tuned out. I can hear cars on the main road at the top of my street, and children coming home after school, and sometimes sparrows in the back garden or seagulls overhead. However, when I'm focused on something, I'm not actively listening to sounds such as these.

Those who live in cities might have experienced the deathly silence of a night in the countryside – haunted by the quiet, unable to sleep. Those in rural areas can be kept up by the sound of urban environments at night. At one point in my twenties I lived in a mouse- and ant-infested flat on three 24-hour bus routes, where my head was just a few feet from the double deckers straining round a tight bend. I do not remember many sleepless nights.

Some sounds I cannot tune out, and these become a nuisance. My upstairs neighbour's continuing inability to play 'Baker Street' on his saxophone; the ice-cream van in summer, which parks so close to the flat that its tune distorts and the 'Teddy Bears' Picnic' feels more like a demonic invasion than an invitation. There is pleasure and nuisance to be found in what we want to hear and what we do not, and these things are about both hearing, and listening.

We can often (but not always) get used to sounds in our environment when they become familiar. It's when something changes that we notice. Another member of the World Soundscape Project, Barry Truax, described the way our feelings about sound change over time as moving from a 'sound phobia' to a 'sound romance', whereby the latter doesn't just call the past to mind, but idealises it along the way. Attachment grows as the past recedes.

I had started my research looking at the time when the foghorn was a new sound, a nuisance sound. From being a sound that had punctured sleep and disrupted lives, people had got used to it. But as the sound used changed from honks to beeps, the job of getting used to it began again.

There is now a nostalgia for the foghorn. This is perhaps what I feel – a love of a sound that is far away from me. The etymology of nostalgia refers to both an ache and a home-coming, and the warm feelings conjured by the foghorn are about returning to places of safety and security. Its sound, after all, has always meant home for the mariners that relied on it, whether they were on familiar or foreign shores – a foghorn is a sound of civilisation.

Nostalgia was first identified as a disease in 1688 by a young Swiss physician in training called Johannes Hofer, who named what he thought was a life-threatening con-dition – a yearning for home he described as 'the pain a sick person feels because he is not in his native land, or fears never to see it again'. The young Dr Hofer identified a number of case studies of people who were afflicted with anxiety, fatigue, palpitations and fever; lack of appetite, pallor, muscle weakness, general sadness and hopelessness – feelings that had apparently disappeared when the patient returned home. This disease so often resulted in death that Swiss soldiers suffering from this malady were relieved from duty.

However, Hofer had jumped the gun – the disease he had named turned out more often that not to be a misdiagnosis of tuberculosis. The romance of the disease was so compelling – an actual physical ailment caused by separation from one's home soil – that the Swiss took up this new sickness with vigour, and news of its identification spread across Europe, turning it into an epidemic through the enthusiastic diagnoses of doctors compelled to identify a patriotism so deep it had physical symptoms.

The power of nostalgia lies in its partiality, its imperfections. It operates over a period of time elapsed, and the fallibility of memory that creeps into the gaps shields the bad and highlights the good. It gives people like me (and Aodhan) feelings at one remove from experience, for a sound we know but never experienced in our lifetimes. Nostalgia acts upon our memories to clean them up, to cast them in the rose-tinted spectacles of the past, and this partiality is the source of its power. Would I really have come to love the foghorn if it had arrived at the end of my garden as it did in Thomas Hart's?

That which is nostalgic might offer comfort, but it can also have a toxic side – what Doris Lessing called its 'poison itch'. Nostalgia can corrupt us, with selective remembering, or distant facts. We are more likely to remember our fondest dance-floor moments in the warm hues of lights, friends, music and escape, than the chill of the queues and the epic comedown the morning after. When it comes to the foghorn, we are likely to remember its romance and melancholy, not the nights when it woke us early or kept children awake.

It would be nice to think that Thomas Hart, after decades in its sonic shadow, would have complained as much about the removal of the Lizard's horn and its replacement with a beeping siren as he did about its installation, but the realist in me doubts it. Hart would have loved to see the back of the horn that ruined his coastal escape. I might embrace the horn, might have loved the Lizard's 'weird and melancholy' sound had I heard it, but I get to visit, listen and leave. I get to choose when I hear these sounds. Up until now, I had been listening to the foghorn by choice. But at the Lizard, I slept within earshot of a functioning electric fog signal.

I had woken too early in a pre-dawn light, as the pale-grey dimness bled weakly through the curtains, sloped sleepily out from under the duvet, walked barefoot to the window. I poked my head through the curtains wondering what had woken me, to see that the fog had rolled in while I slept. In place of the black rocks and churning pale-blue sea, there was a pale void. As my eyes strained to find depth or detail, I heard the modern fog signal, its high electric beep plaintive and reedy.

The Lizard's elegant horns stand silent in front of the lighthouse, their wailing sound replaced by a signal that is mounted on the side of the lighthouse, only as big as a few wastepaper baskets, and barely noticeable, especially in fog. This leads to a deception between the visible horn and the source of the sound. People visiting assume the foghorn is sounding from the huge black trumpets, but are confused, as it seems to be coming from the lighthouse. I have heard there is sonic subterfuge down here, as the wind throws the sound around and obscures the source. Standing sleepily at the window, I watched the unmoving black swan-like horns a few metres away, silently haunting the headland in the fog, before shuffling back to bed and slipping back into sleep.

When I woke, the mist had gone, the fog signal was silent. It had slipped from my conscious grasp, into a realm marked by fogs real and figurative. I felt isolated and unsure of my feelings. I'd been chasing this sound for years, long enough to become a novelty item in people's pub chats. I could trace a timeline of other people's feelings on the foghorn, could draw the network of links between its history and connections, to Tyndall and the South Foreland; to shipbuilding on the Clyde; and a desktop computer next to the Golden Gate Bridge. But in the dense fog of that early morning I realised I had been submerged in possible readings of the foghorn, lost in a tangle of past, present and future. I knew so much about it, and yet I could still not shake the memory of that first hearing at Souter Point. My mind had become suffused with the foghorn, and I knew I needed to go back to the start, back to where all this began, to find out exactly how I got here. I needed to go back to the *Foghorn Requiem*. I needed to talk to Lise.

20

Something as abstract as sound

12 March 2020

It's almost five years since I saw Lise Autogena and Joshua
Portway's *Foghorn Requiem*, and I want to talk to Lise about
what it meant, and whether it was as I remember it. It was
this performance that started my obsession, and I want to
check whether I've gone too far; whether I have read *too
much* into its sound.

Lise is a Danish artist who lives in a mooring on the
Thames near Wapping, in an ex-cargo vessel that has been
converted for domestic living. It is spacious and light, with a
full kitchen, shelves piled high with books, a hammock chair
hanging next to the kitchen table, and a working engine.
She recently injured her leg, and it is strapped in a grey
foam boot, but she hops around the rolling boat with no
difficulty, lifting the trapdoor to show me the engine under
the deck. I stick my head into the cool dark space and it
smells like metal and grease.

The last time I spoke to her was on the phone, just before
the performance seven years ago, as she was in the middle
of a flurry of press interviews. I was a journalist writing a
feature on the performance, and I had asked what it was

going to be and how it was going to work, at a time when foghorns barely even existed for me. Joshua is on Lise's boat too, although he has his hands full – his young daughter is very busily playing with an inflatable pirate's macaw when she should be going for an afternoon nap. Helicopters fly noisily overhead, punctuating our conversation, preparations for a pandemic that is not yet formally declared.

This boat is on a mooring with a group of others of historical note – they all have silver plaques detailing their provenance, and they all have functioning engines so they can come and go. On this mooring are a group of neighbours, she explains, who fought for many years for the right to be here on the river near Tower Bridge, 'So I'm really involved in maritime culture and history,' she says. 'When you are in a boat, you don't have any borders, and you can do things in water you can't do other places.'

I notice that this is not just about the possibility of moving the vessel, but in terms of the lack of sensory borders here too – the boat is very much in and on the water. It moves, and I notice that I cannot just feel the movement of the river but also hear the water slapping against the hull and the engines of other vessels moving down the Thames. Lise says she knows these rumblings so well she can often identify a type of ship or boat by its engine sound, as if it were birdsong.

Foghorn Requiem was a commission from the National Trust and South Tyneside Council to do something around the lighthouse. 'I think they probably thought they would get a light installation or something like that,' she says, but when she and Joshua went to see the lighthouse and foghorn, it became immediately clear that the sound would be the focus of the work. She spent a year around the Tyne, and around Newcastle and Sunderland, talking to people, scoping things out, and thinking. They commissioned composer Orlando Gough to write the music, as he had worked on other unconventional works on a similar scale and with a similar theme, notably *Transmission*, where two young drummers played the body of HMS *Belfast* for the Thames Festival.

'Initially, people thought that I was mad trying to make a piece of music with fifty ships on the North Sea,' Lise says. 'It took me a while to start conversations, but they soon became about a lot more than that – about the history of vessels and the social and emotional connections to vessels that people had, and how that related to their relationship to that region and maritime history. Every single boat that took part in *Foghorn Requiem* involved really special conversations, and every boat was really important to the piece, however big or small it was.'

On their first recce to the lighthouse, the sound of the foghorn up close came as a shock: 'I had the memory of it as a somehow melodic sound,' she says, 'because you always hear it at a distance. But when you hear it up close, it's incredible, just roaring and aggressively loud, and it really affects you physically.'

Lise didn't have any particular memories of foghorns, whereas Joshua had grown up in Cornwall, and had strong childhood associations. Lise's passion for the project was about how a sound like the foghorn contained history and a sense of belonging. 'All along the Tyne the old wharves were removed for new housing; the traces from the past were eradicated,' she says. 'Living on a boat and having fought very strongly against the removal of a maritime landscape in the middle of London – after all, the boats are what built London – I find it strange how, in cities, these histories are being eradicated.'

They were shown how the foghorn worked – how the engines compressed the air into tanks, which were then fed through pipes down to the foghorn building itself. One of the people who worked in the lighthouse – they were mostly ex-skippers, who Lise says had moved there after losing work or retiring from maritime activities – showed them how they had tuned the foghorn back to its original grunting presence. 'There was one day, one of them took a ship horn from my boat here in London, and we attached it to this enormous tank of compressed air that feeds the lighthouse foghorn. And the most beautiful, beautiful sound came out of it. It almost made us cry. There were quite a lot of people there, and we were all totally, deeply affected by this experience.'

She then went to Sweden to visit a ship's horn factory, where they made and tested horns for large ships, and convinced them to sponsor the project by giving them a collection of ships' horns that could be tuned like instruments. Three thousand people bought tickets to be on the ferry, which was the bass note for the ship orchestra, and so far away from shore those on board wouldn't hear the brass at all, only the foghorn and some surrounding vessels.

For Joshua, who was tasked with much of the tech for the performance, it was one of the most difficult projects he'd ever worked on. Horns with custom hardware were installed on each vessel, in order to make them remotely controllable according to their place in the orchestral positions the composer Gough had mapped. This wasn't just about timing, but about calculating how far each of those vessels was from land; on the speed that sound travels and the gap between horn sounding and the clifftop receiving, plus factors such as temperature and wind direction that might slow down transmission. It strikes me that these issues were as much a consideration for Lise as they were a hindrance for Tyndall – these forces of nature with the power to toy with human-made sounds at sea as much as they did when the testing sessions happened 140 years previous. As harbour master Mike had said, the vessels and the industry might change, but everything outside has been the same for millions of years.

All the way up to performance day, the tech wasn't working, despite modelling in a Newcastle University research lab. They had done testing with harbour tug vessels, everything. 'We were basically trying to get the electronics to work together to test it. But nothing worked.'

They couldn't understand why until very late, when someone realised firstly that the sheer physical power of the horns was having an impact on the hardware, and secondly that there was a corrupted file. 'So many people came to help us,' says Lise, 'Joshua basically didn't sleep for a whole week. It wasn't until we actually did the performance that it actually worked.'

They spent the morning of the performance delivering the devices to the ships, and nearly missed their own performance, having got stuck because of the road closures that had been put in place for the show. Then, finally, everything was in place.

A single trumpet player stepped onto the lighthouse

gallery, and with one plaintive note released like a dove over everyone's heads, the performance began.

Despite knowing what was going to happen, all the hurdles and the fatigue, the fact they didn't know whether it was going to work, when the sound of the brass and ships' horns rippled out across the coastal landscape, Lise says she was utterly overwhelmed.

'It was wild that you could get so many people to come together to make a performance like this around something that is as abstract as a sound,' she says. 'This performance could only happen if the people who lived in the region wanted it to happen. They were the performers, so if they didn't take part, there was no performance.'

It was one thing for me to have heard the foghorn up close, but what Lise represented was someone who understood both proximity and distance, and how that could be represented in the way sound and music were brought together to mean something, to move people, whether they had grown up with the sound or not.

I ask her about the final note of the performance, the wheezing and grunting, coughs and splutters leading to a final gasp, a progression of completely unexpected sounds that had left the audience gobsmacked and frozen, some of them weeping. I had written about this sound, but when I had listened to recordings of the performance afterwards none of them had come close to the drama, the detail, the volume that had come from those square black jaws. I had begun to doubt whether I had remembered something real, or whether I had augmented it with fondness.

'I have the memory of that last thing like you're saying,' she says. 'The recordings don't do it justice. It was just so, so weird and strangely human, or animalistic. It was really haunting . . . It had a sense of loss, of something that had a really deep historical, emotional and physical value to people who have lived with that landscape.'

As she says this we pause, and a quiet descends on the boat. I see on her face the same look I saw on the faces of the crowd at the performance, as if something had passed through, trailing a memory I didn't know I had.

Foghorn Requiem has had a longer tail than expected. Lise has given talks on the performance, and even the video has been known to bring people to tears. I know myself how powerful the story can be, having told it to rooms of people and felt static fizzing in the air as I describe what I heard and felt. Lise says she knows of a man who wrote a children's story about the piece, and another who had written poems about the day, and there are paintings too. She says she'd like to go back and see how people remember it, which would add layers to the story, as the memories and associations accrue and compress like geological strata.

When I talk about foghorns, people invariably come and tell me about a foghorn from their childhood that they remember falling asleep to. Annoyance at the great bulls and beasts from the late nineteenth century is gone, replaced by affection, so that the foghorn has somehow become a part of the landscape. Those who admit it is no longer useful nevertheless feel a loss at its silencing.

I had been wondering about how to remember or retain sounds, about the balance between spending funds on maintaining obsolete sounds versus a practical functional technological reality. However, Lise and Joshua's inclusion of the foghorn in their performance spoke not just to those that knew its sound intimately, but also dramatised it for those that didn't, recasting this outlying machine as a trigger for emotions, reflections, memories. To use the foghorn as an instrument in a formal composition places it in a structure many people recognise. Mass experiences of music can be profoundly moving, and connection with a crowd is a real high, whether it's a pop concert, in a grotty basement, or on a blustery clifftop in the north-east of England.

'It's something that is difficult to explain,' Lise reflects about the sound and its resonances. 'It's a kind of immaterial heritage I suppose, and we don't think about things like that – these things are not so tangible as they don't have a material value as such.'[1]

The combination of Joshua's childhood memories of how foghorns can identify a place and Lise's focus on the preservation of maritime landscapes and societies, were catalysts for the enormous emotional resonance of the piece, the twin points of the work which, if those crying could have articulated it, would perhaps have been what the tears were about. A performance like the *Foghorn Requiem* tells us to listen to what a sound can be, to how grand, how moving. If this sound can do that, others can too.

Ships' horns can evoke similar feelings, sounding for New Year in ports and maritime cities. National anthems are designed to imbue a sense of nationality, pride and belonging. Religion has always known the power of sound – calls to prayer that echo across entire towns; church bells that count out time; organ drones that resonate within epic cathedrals; chants that eliminate the ego.

'Early on we made this kind of initial sketch that looked

like a child's drawing,' Lise says, 'but the piece ended up looking like that, more or less. It was what was driving us, this utopian image of the optimism of people coming together to celebrate a sound, at the same time as we were actually making a requiem. There was a beauty and melancholy in bringing the past into the present. That kind of poetic turn is really important; it is where you can meet everybody in the same place. And when you can meet everybody in the same place, you can make magic happen.'

As I leave her boat, I find a lump in my throat. Talking about this sound, this performance, that had spoken to me so clearly, I realise that what I have been chasing is not a definitive answer to what the sound of the foghorn means, but an understanding of the power of sound itself to communicate; to carry with it human experiences and emotions, to sound on behalf of entire communities, entire landscapes. What I had found in talking to Lise was an answer that was there all along – that music, performance, culture, have the power to memorialise sound in a way that carries all the baggage the foghorn has collected over its 150-year history; that the sounds of a recent industrial past can make way for the new, while being canonised for future generations, so that the foghorn lives on through music and memory, in unexpected ways.

There remains a sense of grief in the sound of the foghorn. In the north-east particularly, a requiem performed on that scale by those players was a way to bear witness. The foghorn was the trigger and the symbol of loss – of work, of industry, of life. The *Requiem* had crowned the foghorn, for life and death, safety and danger, desolation and civilisation, and for its power as a gut-shaking sound made to defy the gods of sea and weather. Horns like Souter Point, those like bellowing bulls and dying beasts, come to life again when they sound, once more articulating a whole landscape and its memories, giving them a booming voice with which to speak again.

Epilogue

The huge old foghorn sound that I heard at Souter Point had blasted me 170 years back into the history of the sea and the shore, life and death, safety and civilisation – into an obsession that started out as personal, but came to join with collectors, enthusiasts and composers. It is now part of an outdoor coastal museum. Souter Point, Sumburgh Head, Nash Point – these horns do not sound for sailors any more, they sound for tourists. Added to this, I never got to hear them sound in fog from the deck of a ship that has sighted no land or stars for days. The experience of the foghorn has changed, as have the lives connected to it, but its sound carries its history forward, in ways that continue to surprise me.

At the time of writing, there is a prevalence in a particular strain of drum and bass music, that stalwart genre of club music, for foghorns. A string of tunes has popped up from labels such as Hospital Productions, which sound like they are actually sampling foghorns. In these contemporary digital productions, foghorn sounds stand out a mile as crude, rippling metallic sounds. Present-day fog signals, for the most part, are no good as samples – their sound lacks the bass rumble to really shake those stacks. Some samples sound like train horns or SuperTyfons, some like synth pads with the levels and settings dragged around to give it a really wet parp, but a few tracks sound like actual foghorns, the timbre and tone sounding richly distorted, out of place against the shimmering quantized backdrop of contemporary drum and bass. Around 2019, this trend got so prevalent after a few tracks went big on dark, sweaty dance floors, that there were entire forum threads suggesting there were in fact, 'too many foghorns' in the genre.

The people who would have used the old horns are now closeted away from their sound, there are no keepers to start the engines, and those tucked up in warm beds on damp nights are no longer sent off to sleep by its low rhythmic pulse. In North America it is different. Foghorns live on as an icon of San Francisco, looked after and operated in a windowless control room, but still honking hellos and goodbyes to people entering and leaving the city, in the city where the fog still sings.

Most horns may be silent, but they remain shorthand in film and TV for the gothic and the ghostly, and it's here where they're still locked to the fog that they sound for. Souter Point is now separated from fog, owned by nostalgia, and kept for preservation. It is for enjoying, not for navigating. Its machinery is now obsolete and its sound is no longer required.

There are still fog signals, sort of, although their sound is more correctly described as beeping, not bellowing. Boats and ships still have horns too, and as the ships get bigger, so do their horns.

Listening to the foghorn had showed me how histories

can split and tangle; that there can be a whole world to discover in just one sound. In the foghorn I found the history of the Industrial Revolution and maritime advances, the home of the Grateful Dead and the new sound of drum 'n' bass. The foghorn has spread beyond its coastal locale, beyond the concrete foundations and engines that powered it, far from its original purpose. It began as a navigational aid, but the mood that fog bestowed upon it transposed meanings onto broader culture, where it could sound again in wordless calls of loneliness and civilisation, life and death. In the years it was most in decline, the foghorn transcended.

Whether it's the Golden Gate Bridge or a remote headland on Shetland, when a horn blasts, we are hearing a sound that is of the past, but is still present in memory and in feeling, as a sense of place, or a sense of melancholy. It's a sound that means home, and a sound that has gathered up the detritus of its cultural echoes. It is a massive piece of sonic ephemera which remains in some ways elusive, no matter how many people I talk to or archives I plough through.

My obsession had started as a personal, esoteric quest, but as it progressed I became more and more sure of its profundity. I often tested this feeling, as it seemed so absurd to have found such great meanings in a remote coastal sound. In moments of doubt I would challenge myself to convince people – in pubs, at parties, gyms and cafés and evening classes – of the profundity of the foghorn. I would describe its scale and the tendrils of its meanings. I laid out the ways in which it looped through Western culture, and people became interested.

I could both see and was blind to the ways the foghorn

was a weird thing to be obsessed with. Perhaps other people's perceptions of it as esoteric or novelty were something to do with sea blindness. The foghorn, at first glance, is an absurd and esoteric piece of sonic history, tumbling off the furthest edges of the land. Maritime preoccupations, whether practical or intellectual, are often out of view, and so a sound from this world is perceived as totally far out.

I knew that looking for the meaning of the foghorn – for one meaning – was never going to bring me to a satisfying conclusion. Just like art, or music, the meaning of these things to me is quite different than it might be to you, and like art and music, they are infinite and eternal. A foghorn to a fisherman is something quite different to a foghorn in suburban Southend, or in avant-garde composition made in a studio in Vancouver, and more of these experiences continue to reveal themselves.

The foghorn has a history that is as intangible and real as the stories we tell; that we kid ourselves are solid and immutable, when they might be as illusory as the great invisible walls that echoed sound back to Tyndall. It can not only physically and emotionally move us, but also amplify edgelands and exchanges that are often neglected. No matter which way you cut it, the foghorn was not an inevitable solution to a problem, and yet it ended up as the dominant sound signal on many coastlines. It guzzled fuel, its engines needed constant attention, and it disturbed those in its vicinity. A lighthouse is needed every single night, the foghorn only for a few hours a day in the foggiest of locations. Added to this, it was known to be unreliable from the very beginning.

I could reread the foghorn I'd started with as a monstrosity, a hooligan of the Industrial Revolution whose job was to enforce the structures and control and power that were essential to the functioning of that period. I could read it as a tool of empire, the manifestations of the colonial past which the home nations have become attached to and revel in as a sign and sound of a better time, when white men were in charge and imperialism had enough hubris to think it could overcome the endless power and force of ocean.

I could also hear it as an error, a great folly by an organisation scrabbling around just to do something in the face of deaths and media outcry, even if that thing did not work – the spin could carry because there was no way to test whether it was saving lives anyway. I could also read it as the voice of places, as a sound that gave a sonic identity to those who work at sea and those who are left behind awaiting their return. It is the ghost and the voice of a place, it is what speaks to the sea on behalf of the land, and what asserts the presence of people, community, safety and civilisation.

Crucially, the silencing of this sound is representative of the disappearance of a human presence on the coast. The lighthouses lost their eyes when the lighthouse keepers left, as there were no more fog watches, and when the foghorns were silenced they lost their voices too. The final blast of the foghorn for the *Foghorn Requiem* at Souter Point was unlike any blast from that horn (or, I suspect, any other horn) heard before or since.

The horns I heard over the course of writing this book are the last massive horns, monuments to an empire and industries such as shipbuilding that are gasping their last in the West, on British coastlines that often feel forgotten, deeply suffering the effects of austerity and poverty. There are retained keepers but nobody lives on site now, and there are few horns, just electric sirens that beep to mark a hazard. They are not in conversation with the landscape any more but stripped of their power and pushed out to sea.

Future predictions for the maritime industry include driverless ships, which will need no visible or audible signals. By the time this book is published, the first is due to be launched in Scandinavia. The *Yara Birkeland*, a zero-emissions, battery-powered container ship designed to carry fertiliser between ports in the fjords of southern Norway, will have no captain, no crew.[1] The benefits are huge, environmentally speaking: when the *Yara Birkeland* becomes fully autonomous, it will cut 40,000 lorry journeys per year. Battery-powered vessels can be recharged in port while being loaded and unloaded, and no crew means no need for air conditioning, lights and water, or superstructures such as the bridge. This both increases cargo space and makes the ship more energy efficient, and if crew do not need to board the ship then it's possible to make it very difficult for pirates to board. However, it also threatens jobs.

The idea of a ship loaded with chemicals and without a driver conjures nothing but a disaster film in the making, exposed to attack or on a collision course when a crucial remote connection drops out. A key challenge is not the technology – most of this exists elsewhere – but the need for completely new navigational rules, which present the need for entirely different types of navigational aids, ones completely separate from human sensory experience. If these new vessels succeed in replacing international shipping, our coasts will sound different again.

Sound is always invisibly in motion, is always transient, and the sounds of our surroundings come with baggage, with associations, with the shapes and memories of a place and its history. The story of the foghorn's infiltration of people's lives is also about something else – it is about listening to our environments, about the way we judge and categorise what we hear, and also how things can change when we're not paying attention. Actively listening to the foghorn can show us a different way of thinking about ourselves and the way we relate to the places we find ourselves. The foghorn's identity is not just about its original purpose, nor is it only about its volume and power, because a sound like the foghorn is not just something we hear, but something we feel.

The old foghorns are not quite dead, but they're not alive either. Catching a sounding is like catching sight of a rare bird – you have to be in the right place at the right time, in the right season – although unlike birdwatching you often have to know someone who has the key to the engine room and can wake the beast.

I wonder how future generations will remember this fearsome, lonely sound. Will it still draw associations with the coast, or will its obsolescence render this huge old sound strange again? What will their maritime landscape sound like? Just like in Ray Bradbury's short story, the old and mighty foghorns I searched out have become the last of their kind. Eventually the coasts will all fall quiet, the foghorns' voices silenced and machinery seized, their dead trumpets pointing out to an empty horizon, where there may be nobody to save except themselves.

Acknowledgements

A book about foghorns would not exist without the support of people who saw something compelling and worthwhile in a wild idea. Thanks: to Cathy Lane for seeing the potential of this project from the start; to Angus Carlyle who faced down my stubbornness and pushed me to write more and better; to my wonderful agent and cheerleader Natalie Galustian, my editor Lee Brackstone for his faith and affirmations, and to the brilliant Ellie Freedman, Sarah Fortune, and the team at White Rabbit.

Thank you to Luke Turner and Ellie Matthews for their feedback, to Davis Moats for being unflappable, to Laura Cannell for pushing me creatively, and to David and Heather for the cupboard. Thankyou also to Erik Davis and Jennifer Dumpert, Mark Pilkington, Alan Renton, Dave Tompkins, Chris Williams, Big Mike, Nick Sales, Hildegard Westerkamp, Paolo at the Golden Gate Bridge, Mike Nicholson, Captain Phillip Day, Simon Millyard, the Fisherman's Chapel in Leigh On Sea, Erin Farley, and all the Allan family. Thanks to all those who sent tips and anecdotes from their corners of the world, to everyone who helped in Jersey, to Dave Tompkins, Deborah Egan, and Sam Binga for the dubstep horns.

Thank you to the Association of Lighthouse Keepers for being such a welcoming group with whom to share my obsessions. I am particularly grateful for the help and hospitality of Mandy and Stephen Pickles, Brian Johnson, Ian Duff, Gerry Douglas Sherwood, John Best, Neil Hargreaves, Roy Thompson and fellow foghorn lover Aodhan Quinn. Big thanks to the archivists whose work makes them the unsung heroes of books like this, particularly Claire Titley at London Metropolitan Archives, and those at National Records Scotland.

The TECHNE AHRC Doctoral Training Partnership funded the PhD that was the foundation of this book, and I am extremely grateful for their support. Thankyou also to The Society of Authors and residencies with ArtHouse Jersey and Sumburgh Head that gave me time to think and write and listen. A particular thanks to Jane at Shetland Amenity Trust, and to Ian Smith for an afternoon eating cake and talking lighthouse-keeping. The final, biggest blast of thanks must go to Lise Autogena and Joshua Portway, who showed me the true reach of this colossal sound.

Illustration credits

18   Celadon Leeds Daboll patent, 1860.

20–21 Robert Hope-Jones Wurlitzer patent, 1902.

69   South Foreland sound map from Professor John Tyndall's 'Fog signals' report, addressed to the Corporation of Trinity House, 1874.

75   Syren horn diagram from Professor John Tyndall's 'Fog signals' report, addressed to the Corporation of Trinity House, 1874.

92   Notice To Mariners, 1908. Courtesy of Northern Lighthouse Board Archives; photograph author's own.

104   Photocopy, made in the 1960s, of a 1901 report to Parliament by The Corporation of Trinity House Fog Signal Committee (CLC/526/MS30083). Courtesy of Trinity House; photograph author's own.

127   Russolo, *Intonarumori*, instruments built for music-piece 'Bruitism', partly operating on electricity. Scan from *The Art of Noises* by Luigi Russolo, 1913.

233   'Blast' Performance, Birmingham, September 2007. Courtesy of Nick Sales.

Notes

1. First blast

1   According to *The Canadian Encyclopedia*.
2   It's said he first came up with the idea in 1853 or 1854, although the horn wasn't installed until 1859.
3   Foulis's foghorn was removed, without fanfare, in the late 1990s, by which time other engine-powered fog signals were also being switched off on coastlines across the globe.
4   The 1860 filing was for a 'Fog Alarm'.

2. Heavy weather

1   Edmund's parents do not share my love of the foghorn, though. Mary complains that 'it won't let you alone. It keeps reminding you, and warning you, and calling you back', whereas the father, Tyrone, complains that it is like 'like having a sick whale in the back yard'. (O'Neill, *Long Day's Journey Into Night*, 1966)
2   The International Association of Marine Aids to Navigation and Lighthouse Authorities (IALA) defines a navigational aid as: 'A device, system or service, external to vessels, designed and operated to enhance safe and efficient navigation of individual vessels and/or vessel traffic'.
3   The smell of rain on dry soil is called 'petrichor'.
4   Also known as *Live at the Kaleidoscope*.
5   There is a serendipitous connection between the fog and the foghorn here – the novel was published in 1886, the same period in which Stevenson's uncles (the lighthouse-building Stevenson dynasty) were advising on the installation of foghorns around the coast of Scotland for the Northern Lighthouse Board.
6   Nothing more was heard of it after one newspaper report. Corman designed it in his lab at Byron Moore's Machine Works on 11th Street. When he weighed 'the little rascal' which promised to revolutionise navigation, it clocked in at a whopping five pounds. A patent

was taken out on a machine to help him grind lenses, but no fog-penetrating lens ever made it to market.

7   Hull describes how tapping his stick produces echoes by which he can navigate.

3. Underwater bells

1   The frequency of firing was increased to one blast every five minutes in the 1890s, when knowledge about hearing damage from loud noise was still in its infancy, and no such thing as hearing protection was seriously considered.

2   A 'lighthouse bagger' collects visits to lighthouses – the lighthouse equivalent of a train spotter.

3   For more on this topic, #ballastwater is a surprisingly active hashtag.

4   As described in Andrew Adams and Richard Woodman's history of Trinity House, *Light Upon The Water* (2013).

5   The doctor, Edward Spry, took up testing the capacity of living things to ingest lead with morbid fascination, force-feeding dogs molten metal and watching them expire.

6   As described by a writer named Arnold Burges Johnson in 1889, in his book *The Modern Lighthouse Service*.

7   As detailed in Bella Bathurst's *The Wreckers* (2005).

4. Shipwrecked

1   Cape Race was also the receiver of the RMS *Titanic*'s distress call, after making contact earlier in the evening so passengers could send messages that were relayed to New York.

2   Many thousands of migrants die at sea each year: 2,560 died in the Mediterranean alone in 2017.

3   A lead line is a simple device for testing depth of water – a piece of string or rope with a lead 'plummet' which can also pick up material samples from the seabed.

4   According to T.C.W. Blanning in *The Nineteenth Century: Europe 1789–1914* (2000).

5   *Open Fields: Science in Cultural Encounter* (1996).

6   Recorded as 'Sweet William' by Shirley Collins in 1958, and also by Peggy Seeger. Also sung by Ewan MacColl as 'My Sailor Boy' and known as 'Willie the Bold Sailor Boy'. In some versions the sailor is a soldier, and in one version, he is a lumberjack.

7 Daboll apparently conceived the idea of 'applying the principle of the clarinet to a large trumpet to serve as a fog signal for mariners'.

8 A report was filed to the House of Commons the following year, collecting the results of these trials and detailing the dangers of navigation in the Gulf of St Lawrence, including the numbers of shipwrecks between 1861 and 1883 and the possibility of a sunken rock around Cape Race.

9 The bovine will reoccur later. This scene is described in Christine Corton's *London Fog* (2015).

10 In John Evelyn's 1661 text *Fumifugium*, he proposed moving polluting industries and planting fragrant gardens around the city to improve air quality.

5. Testing, testing

1 While the archive is properly looked after, the deposits made there are full of holes – frequently I found indexes to minute books, with no corresponding minute books.

2 Commuters moving between the underground and Fenchurch Street station will walk past it.

3 Nigel Kneale's made-for-TV horror film *The Stone Tape* hypothesises that rooms and buildings can store psychic memories of what they have witnessed. Spend a day in a reading room and you might just start to believe it – the walls talk in voices we cannot hear, whispering about focus, concentration and learning.

4 Who later fell out with him for not giving his US foghorn experiments enough credit.

5 Some of his peers moaned at the pressure to, as they said, 'Tyndallize' their language, and make it accessible and engaging. These included the physicist Peter Guthrie Tait (with whom he had a long standing dispute over the movement of glaciers) and mathematician and physicist James Clerk Maxwell.

6 Gillian Beer has suggested that Tyndall's work on waveforms was an influence on *The Waves*.

7 At the time, it was held that fog dampened sound, a claim originally made in a 1708 paper in the *Philosophical Transactions*. Tyndall establishes that fogs 'have no such power to deaden sound as . . . has been universally ascribed to them'. He wrote up his findings in a two-part paper for the *Contemporary Review*, stating that humidity, not

temperature, was the most important factor affecting the transmission of sound. Two years later the idea that fog mutes sound persisted, and years later journals are still making this error.

8 A temperature inversion is a reversal of the usual behaviour of temperature in the troposphere, where temperature normally decreases with height. In an inversion, a layer of cooler air is nearer the earth's surface than warmer air.

9 In the report, the syren is described by Tyndall: 'The principle of the syren is easily understood. A musical sound is produced when the tympanic membrane is struck periodically with sufficient rapidity. The production of these tympanic shocks by puffs of air was first realised by Dr. Robison… In the steam-syren patented by Mr. Brown of New York a fixed disk and a rotating disk are also employed, radial slits being cut in both disks… Just as in the syren already described, when the radian slits of the two disks coincide, a puff of steam escapes. Sound-waves of a great intensity are thus sent through the air; the pitch of the note produced depending on the rapidity with which the puffs succeed each other; in other words, upon the velocity of rotation.'

6. Sound of sirens

1 Records in Trinity House show the fallout – a consultation does decide that, going forward, there should be three, not two, keepers in remote locations, to prevent an incident like this repeating itself. Dates are, however, a little squiffy. A pamphlet came out in 1858 that tells the story and sets the date of the tragedy in 1801, naming the dead keeper Howell, but in Whitchurch parish register there is a death notice for a Joseph Harry in October 1780, who 'died and lay dead on the Smalls two months'.

2 The final intake of keepers, many of them the last to work at certain stations before automation, are now in their seventies, if not older. The Association of Lighthouse Keepers has made the aforementioned film, and the Northern Lighthouse Board conducted oral histories with a number of its still-living ex-keepers along with their wives and children. I heard about the latter when I met a historian called Erin Farley, who had conducted the interviews, and promised me that the foghorn had 'loomed large' in the memories of the keepers.

3 Dorothy Henderson, wife of a keeper called Alistair Henderson, told an interviewer that the first time her husband had been stationed on

a rock lighthouse he rang her frantically asking how on earth one cooked mince.

4 Ailsa Craig is where all curling stones were once quarried.

5 Rats arrived on Ailsa Craig by boat, perhaps as escapees from shipwrecks. The first was spotted when a dog killed one in 1889, the following year a dog killed fifty-nine in a single day. The infestation remained until 1991.

6 On 15 December 1900 all three keepers at the Flannan Isles vanished without a trace. A routine visit ten days after the log book's last entry found the clock stopped, the lamp ready to be lit and everything in order. It was thought that they had gone out in bad weather to secure the mooring, and been taken away by a freak wave, but no cause for their disappearance has ever been proven.

7 All Scottish foghorns were switched off in 2005.

8 The idea of these 'characters' or blast patterns is sometimes attributed to Charles Babbage, but what he suggested was slightly different, attributing a numerical signal to foghorns a bit like Morse code.

7. Revelation in music

1 R. Murray Schafer wrote: 'The sense of hearing cannot be closed off at will. There are no earlids. When we go to sleep, our perception of sound is the last door to close and it is also the first to open when we awaken.'

2 The music writer David Stubbs posed this question in *Fear Of Music* (2009), which asked 'Why People Get Rothko But Don't Get Stockhausen'.

3 While Rayleigh's tests suggest he thought of the foghorn in a more musical way than Tyndall, a letter marked 'private' in the archives of the Northern Lighthouse Board suggests they were more like experimental sound works than experiments with sound. In this letter, Stevenson vented frustration at Rayleigh's failure to implement proper scientific controls, complaining of their sloppiness. Behind the scenes in Rayleigh's tests, there is a comedy of errors. The machinery isn't very reliable. The operator of the Barker's reed horn went AWOL, another silenced a siren when it should be sounding. Rubber perished.

8. The greatest nuisance

1   The full poem was printed in the *Dunoon Herald*, 4 May 1897, the author listed as W. W.

9. Bulls, reoccurring

1   From Ray Bradbury's 'The Foghorn' (1951). The story later became the basis for the film *The Beast from 20,000 Fathoms*, whose final scene involves hazmat-suited scientists carrying a bomb on the Coney Island rollercoaster to be deposited in the despairing creature's gullet. It is the first film Ray Harryhausen – a pal of Bradbury's – ever crafted an animated monster for.

2   This story can be found in a collection of Nigel Kneale short stories called *Tomato Cain and Other Stories* (1950).

3   Her lovers were likely to meet with a gruesome end.

4   The overthrow of the cult found in Crete in 1900 by British archaeologist Arthur Evans has been suggested as the root of the Minotaur myth, when the bull-worshipping Minoans were overthrown by Zeus-worshipping Greeks.

5   There is an alternate version of this story in Buddhism, where the Bodhisattva asks the Jade Emperor if the heavenly ox can help people plough the fields. The Jade Emperor refuses, because when the ox loses its strength the people will kill, eat and tan the beast. The Bodhisattva pledges his own banishment to hell if this should happen. Inevitably it does, and the Bodhisattva is sent to hell.

6   In German studies (in Berlin in particular), findings suggest the bourgeoisie did the most complaining about noise (for more on this see Karin Bijsterveld's *Mechanical Sound* (2008).

7   A later edition of the speech was published with Tyndall's 'Prayer Test', in which he suggested a scientific test for prayer – that in order to test their efficacy and God's apparent omnipotence, everyone in Britain should focus their prayers solely on the sick for several years, to see if it could produce any measurable effect in curing them. His proposition was that it would make no difference.

8   Baku was where oil was first discovered.

9   The Germans annihilated and interned unknown thousands (if not hundreds of thousands) of West Africans at this site, after revolts against colonial rule.

10. New myths, old power

1   As described in a 1967 paper by the mathematician Mandelbrot.
2   From Jennifer Westwood and Sophia Kingshill's *The Fabled Coast* (2015).
3   I also posted on the forum dedicated to the topic, but got kicked off.
4   'The audible occupies ground through its reach, power belongs to whoever has a bell or a siren', wrote the late French philosopher Michel Serres.
5   Lighthouses and foghorns were a crucial part of wartime navigation. Lighthouses were no longer lit at nightfall, and lighthouse keepers were excluded from the draft. Foghorns, on the other hand, often operated normally. When Jersey was occupied, the foghorn and lighthouse fell under the control of the Nazis.
6   Jonathan Raban, *Coasting* (1986).

11. Sound control

1   As documented by artist Hannah Rickards in *Grey Light: Left and Right Back, High Up, Two Small Windows* (2016).
2   According to Gerry Douglas-Sherwood's *A Glossary of Lighthouse Terminology*.
3   The brown note is a mythical frequency which is said to be able to cause people to lose control of their bowels. It is often hypothesised to be in the infrasonic zone, but it probably originated in a satirical article in *New Scientist* published in the 1970s.

12. The bridge

1   Full name Gertrude Franklin Horn Atherton, appropriately enough.
2   She believed America was formed by 'Nordics' and referred to immigrants as a 'flu'. She caused some ruffling of feathers in polite circles with a novel called *Black Oxen* in which women are rejuvenated by X-rays to their genitals while men are left to age and decay. *In the White Morning* is a near-future sci-fi novel in which German women organise to overthrow the government and institute a left-wing regime with a female leader. *Senator North* was an entire novel warning against interracial marriage.
3   As she recalled in *Adventures of a Novelist* (1932).
4   From *Sea and Fog* (2012).
5   This quote is taken from *San Francisco: West Coast Metropolis* by Edwin Rosskam (1939).
6   During a period spent in Monterey down the coast, he also allegedly

set off a forest fire to see if it was in fact the moss that was catching fire (it was, and he did not put it out).

7 The Forth Bridge is also said to need repainting as soon as a repaint has finished, an industrial update to the myth of Sisyphus.

8 Mike Jay, *Mescaline* (2019).

9 From a piece called 'The Foghorn', written for *The California Sunday Magazine* in 2016.

14. Even small boats carry radar

1 To swallow the anchor is to leave seafaring life and return to shore, taking a job or retiring on land.

2 Along with New York City, Singapore and Tokyo.

3 The Clyde, where the Cloch once hollered at the fast flow of traffic, was also home to towering shipyards. On the *Waverley* I had sailed past one, its shadowy bulk sheltering a ship that seemed enormous on dry land. In 1913, the shipyards on the Clyde alone were responsible for one sixth of the world's merchant shipbuilding market.

4 Mega-cruise ships are typically classed by their ability to carry 5000 passengers or more. The largest cruise ship in the world as of 2020 is the *Symphony of the Seas*. It contains an ice rink, theatre, basketball court, a zip line ten decks high and two rock-climbing walls.

5 The Health and Safety Act 1974 also impacted upon the viability of foghorns. Documents in the NLB archive, on white paper that is still crisp, contain letters directing the wearing of newly provided ear defenders to protect against hearing damage caused by a foghorn.

6 Fog signals had a major part to play in the lighthouse keeper redundancies that automation brought – a cutting in the NLB archive from 1987 reported that the lighthousemen's union (which I could find no other trace of before or after) had countered proposals to close ten fog signals in Scotland because it reduced labour requirements at lighthouses.

7 There's also a political safeguarding element to this, as GPS is owned and operated by the US government, so it is not under UK ownership or jurisdiction.

8 A bird strike is when a flock of birds flies directly into the lighthouse's beam.

15. Harbour symphonies
1   The full poem, 'Ode To The Sublime By Monica Vitti', can be found in Anne Carson's collection *Decreation* (2005).
2   These smaller vessels were all too small to be paying light dues and contributing to the running of the foghorns.

17. Sky trumpets
1   It is somewhere along Angeles Crest Highway.
2   Hugo Chavez once said it prompted the 2010 Haiti earthquake.
3   Accounts of hearing it are concentrated in cities across North America and Europe, with some scattered around South America and Australia. The UK has logged a particularly high number of reported hearings since the 1970s, particularly in Bristol. The hum is described as a disturbing low-frequency sound, which has no apparent source, and causes dizziness and insomnia. One of the few scientific papers written on the phenomenon concluded that the most probable explanation was that some people have the capability to 'interpret radio transmissions at certain wavelengths as sound' – that they may be hearing electromagnetic energy.

18. In ruins
1   For example, foghorns at Copinsay and the Butt of Lewis were decommissioned and then demolished in the 1980s.
2   UNESCO has a programme protecting 'intangible heritage', but it is focused on preserving traditional music and folk practices by at-risk ethnic groups. It's not intended to preserve an obsolete machinery that has become embedded in the coastal soundscape, and is aimed at oral and social traditions, not Industrial Revolution era technology.
3   One woman, Susan Ager, worked as a volunteer lighthouse keeper there in 2006, but her account of the time focuses on the lighthouse's spider infestation. The windows were a haunted mess, and she didn't dare open them, and there were so many spiders they had to be hoovered up every day. When she cleared them from the lamp room, it left her covered in cobwebs 'like Indiana Jones'.

19. Boom to beep
1   As referred to by the International Association of Marine Aids to Navigation and Lighthouse Authorities.
2   The musician Pauline Oliveros called this 'sonic meditation', and

developed a wide-reaching and influential meditative practice that grew into a whole school of thinking about sound. Her meditation 'Native' instructs one to: 'Take a walk at night. Walk so silently that the bottoms of your feet become ears.'

20. Something as abstract as sound

1 Boats, Lise pointed out, might be as immaterial as sound as well, in that they are not fixed, and are often on the move.

Epilogue

1 Rolls-Royce has also been successfully testing remote pilotage using existing mobile phone networks. In a press shot of a trial, a pilot sits on shore in a control room with a 360-degree floor-to-ceiling screen, showing his remote view of the outside world.